20 W9-AFY-454

A BRAND-NEW YEAR—
A PROMISING NEW START

Enter Sydney Omarr's star-studded world of accurate day-by-day predictions for every aspect of your life. With expert readings and forecasts, you can chart a course to romance, adventure, good health, or career opportunities while gaining valuable insight into yourself and others. Offering a daily outlook for 18 full months, this fascinating guide shows you:

- The important dates in your life
- What to expect from an astrological reading
- How the stars can help you stay healthy and fit
- Your lucky lottery numbers
  And more!

Let this expert's sound advice guide you through a year of heavenly possibilities—for today and for every day of 2002!

SYDNEY OMARR'S DAY-BY-DAY
ASTROLOGICAL GUIDE FOR

ARIES—March 21–April 19
TAURUS—April 20–May 20
GEMINI—May 21–June 20
CANCER—June 21–July 22
LEO—July 23–August 22
VIRGO—August 23–September 22
LIBRA—September 23–October 22
SCORPIO—October 23–November 21
SAGITTARIUS—November 22–December 21
CAPRICORN—December 22–January 19
AQUARIUS—January 20–February 18
PISCES—February 19–March 20

IN 2002

CHANCE TO WIN A PERSONALIZED HOROSCOPE FOR A FULL YEAR!

Enter the Sydney Omarr Horoscope Sweepstakes!

No purchase necessary. Details below. Open only to U.S. residents age 18 and up

Name _____

Address_____

City_____ State_____ Zip_____

Mail to:
Sydney Omarr Horoscope Sweepstakes
c/o Penguin Putnam Inc.
375 Hudson St., 5th floor
New York, NY 10014
All entries must be postmarked by August 31, 2001 and received by September 8, 2001.

1. NO PURCHASE NECESSARY TO ENTER OR WIN A PRIZE. To enter the Sydney Omarr Horoscope Sweepstakes, complete this official entry form or, on a 3" x 5" piece of paper, write your name and complete address. Mail your entry to: Sydney Omarr Horoscope Sweepstakes; c/o Penguin Putnam Inc.; 375 Hudson St., 5th floor; New York, NY 10014. Enter as often as you wish, but mail each entry in a separate envelope. No mechanically reproduced or computer generated entries allowed. All entries must be postmarked by 8/31/2001 and received by 9/8/2001 to be eligible. Not responsible for late, lost, damaged, incomplete, illegible, postage due or misdirected mail entries.

2. Winners will be selected from all eligible entries in a random drawing on or about 9/14/01, by Penguin Putnam Inc., whose decisions are final and binding. Odds of winning are dependent upon the number of entries received. Winners will be notified by mail and may be required to execute an affidavit of eligibility and release which must be returned within 14 days of notification or an alternate winner will be selected.

3. One (1) Grand Prize winner will receive a personalized one-year horoscope from an astrologer chosen by Sydney Omarr or Penguin Putnam Inc. One (1) Second Prize winner will receive a personalized one-month horoscope from an astrologer chosen by Sydney Omarr or Penguin Putnam Inc. Estimated aggregate value of Grand Prize and Second Prize: $250. If there is an insufficient number of entries, Penguin Putnam Inc. reserves the right not to award the prizes.

4. Sweepstakes open to residents of the U.S. 18 years of age or older, except employees and the immediate families of Penguin Putnam Inc., its affiliated companies, advertising and promotion agencies. Void in Puerto Rico, and wherever else prohibited by law. No cash substitutions, transfers or assignments of prizes are allowed. In event of unavailability, sponsor may substitute a prize of equal or greater value. Limit one prize per person, household or family. All Federal, State, and Local laws apply. Taxes, if any, are the sole responsibility of the prize winners. Winners consent to the use of their name and/or photos or likenesses for advertising purposes without additional compensation (except where prohibited). By accepting this prize, winners release Penguin Putnam Inc., its affiliated companies, advertising and promotion agencies from any and all liability for any loss, harm, injuries, damages, cost or expense arising out of participation in this Sweepstakes or the acceptance, use or misuse of the prize.

5. For the names of the prize-winners, send a self-addressed, stamped envelope after 9/28/01 to : SYDNEY OMARR HOROSCOPE SWEEPSTAKES WINNERS, Penguin Putnam Inc., 375 Hudson St., 5th floor, New York, NY 10014.

SYDNEY OMARR'S

DAY-BY-DAY ASTROLOGICAL GUIDE FOR

VIRGO

August 23–September 22

2002

A SIGNET BOOK

SIGNET
Published by New American Library, a division of
Penguin Putnam Inc., 375 Hudson Street,
New York, New York 10014, U.S.A.
Penguin Books Ltd, 27 Wrights Lane,
London W8 5TZ, England
Penguin Books Australia Ltd, Ringwood,
Victoria, Australia
Penguin Books Canada Ltd, 10 Alcorn Avenue,
Toronto, Ontario, Canada M4V 3B2
Penguin Books (N.Z.) Ltd, 182–190 Wairau Road,
Auckland 10, New Zealand

Penguin Books Ltd, Registered Offices:
Harmondsworth, Middlesex, England

First published by Signet, an imprint of New American Library,
a division of Penguin Putnam Inc.

First Printing, June 2001
10 9 8 7 6 5 4 3 2 1

Sydney Omarr is syndicated worldwide by
Los Angeles Times Syndicate.

 REGISTERED TRADEMARK—MARCA REGISTRADA

Printed in the United States of America

CONTENTS

INTRODUCTION

Your Cosmic Code

Are you ready for the excitement and challenges of the year 2002? We've cracked the mystery of the human genome, but there's another code that's been used to map the human personality since ancient times. Like your genetic imprint, your astrology chart is uniquely "you." It is a map of your moment in time, which has its own code, based on the position of the sun, moon, and planets at the time and place you were born. What is especially intriguing is that this system can offer specific, practical guidance, even when using only *one* of the elements of the code, your *sun sign*. Though you share that sun sign with others, there are many ways to use it every day to find a more fulfilling lifestyle. Your sun sign "map" can help you find success, attract love, look for a better job, have a healthier body, and even take the vacation of your dreams or decorate your home.

Just knowing the other person's sun sign can give you many clues to how to make your relationship a happy one. You can troubleshoot problems in advance and, if they crop up, find a way to make them work for you. In this year's edition of *Sydney Omarr's Guides,* you'll learn what's best for you and how your sign relates, positively and negatively, with every other sign under the sun.

"For every thing there is a season" could be the theme song of astrology. Will 2002 be the time to charge forward or proceed with caution, to change

1

careers or stick with the job at hand, to fall in love? We'll deal in many ways with the question of timing—when are the potentially difficult times (which also present positive challenges), when can you expect delays and potential misunderstandings, when are the best times to take risks? You'll be able to get your life "on track" and chart your course with full knowledge of the shoals ahead.

For those who are new to astrology or would like to know more about it, there is basic information to give you an inside look at how astrology works. Then you can look up the other planets in your horoscope to find out how each contributes to your unique personality.

Astrologers have been quick to embrace the new technology of the twenty-first century, especially since sophisticated astrological computer programs have eliminated the tedious work of casting a chart and deliver beautiful chart printouts. Now anyone with access to the Internet can view their astrology chart at a free Internet site or buy the same programs professional astrologers use. We'll show you where to do this in chapters devoted especially to Internet resources. We'll also give you Sydney Omarr's updated "Yellow Pages" of the best places for books, tapes, and further astrological studies.

As we explore our inner cosmos via astrology, we are still searching for the same things that always have made life worth living: love, meaningful work, and fulfilling relationships. With Sydney Omarr's astonishingly accurate day-by-day forecasts, you can use your cosmic link to the universe to enhance every aspect of your life. So here's hoping you use your star power wisely and well for a productive and happy 2002!

CHAPTER 1

The Coming Trends of 2002!

We're at the beginning of a decisive decade, when many issues are coming to the forefront simultaneously: global expansion, territorial disputes, space travel, biotechnology breakthroughs, overpopulation, dangers of nuclear warfare, and environmental crises. Here are the key planets calling the shots and the trends to watch in 2002.

This year is a "bridge" year, when there are no dramatic shifts in the atmosphere (that comes next year). So it is more a time of consolidation, of taking stock and making plans for the future. The slow-moving planet Pluto is our guide to the hottest trends. Pluto brings about a heightened consciousness and transformation of matters related to the sign it is passing through. Now in Sagittarius, Pluto is emphasizing everything associated with this sign to prepare us philosophically and spiritually for things to come.

Perhaps the most pervasive sign of Pluto in Sagittarius is globalization in all its forms, which has become a main theme of the past few years. We are re-forming boundaries, creating new forms of travel that will definitely include space travel. At this writing, the $60 billion space station is under way, a joint venture between the United States, Russia, Japan, Europe, and Canada. It is scheduled for completion in 2006 and will be one of the brightest objects in the sky.

In true Sagittarius fashion, Pluto will shift our emphasis away from acquiring wealth to a quest for the meaning of it all, as upward strivers discover that money and power are not enough. Sagittarius is the sign of linking everything together; therefore the trend will be to find ways to interconnect on spiritual, philosophical, and intellectual levels.

Pluto in Sagittarius's spiritual emphasis has already filtered down to our home lives. Home altars and private sanctuaries are becoming a part of our personal environment. The oriental art of feng shui has moved westward, giving rise to a more harmonious, spiritual atmosphere in offices and homes, which also promotes luck and prosperity.

Sagittarians are known for their love of animals, and we have never been more pet-happy. Look for extremes related to animal welfare, such as vegetarianism, which will become even more popular and widespread as a lifestyle. As habitats are destroyed, the care, feeding, and control of wild animals will become a larger issue, especially where there are deer, bears, and coyotes in the back yard.

The Sagittarian love of the outdoors combined with Pluto's power has already promoted extreme sports, especially those that require strong legs, like rock climbing, trekking, or snowboarding. Rugged, sporty all-terrain vehicles continue to be popular, as are zippy little scooters which help us get around in a fun way. Expect the trend toward more adventurous travel and fitness or sports-oriented vacations to accelerate: exotic hiking trips to unexplored territories, mountain-climbing expeditions, spa vacations, and sports-associated resorts are part of this trend.

Publishing, which is associated with Sagittarius, has been transformed by the new electronic media, with an enormous variety of books available in print. The Internet bookstore will continue to prosper under Pluto in Sagittarius. It is fascinating that the online bookstore Amazon.com took the Sagittarius-influenced name of the fierce female tribe of archer-warriors who went to the extreme of removing their right breasts to better shoot their arrows.

Who's Lucky? Make Hay, Cancer and Leo!

Good fortune, expansion, and big money opportunities are associated with the movement of Jupiter, the planet that embodies the principle of expansion. Jupiter has a twelve-year cycle, staying in each sign for approximately one year.

When Jupiter enters a sign, the fields associated with that sign usually provide excellent opportunities. Areas of speculation associated with the sign Jupiter is passing through will have the hottest market potential—the ones that currently arouse excitement and enthusiasm.

The flip side of Jupiter is that there are no limits . . . you can expand off the planet under a Jupiter transit, which is why the planet is often called the "Gateway to Heaven." If something is going to burst—such as an artery—or overextend or go over the top in some way, it could happen under a supposedly "lucky" Jupiter transit . . . so be aware.

This year, Jupiter will finish its journey through Cancer in August, when it moves into Leo. So sun sign Cancers and Leos and those with strong Cancer or Leo influence in their horoscopes should have abundant growth opportunities during the year. On the other hand, those born under Capricorn and Aquarius, the signs which occur at the opposite time of year, may have to work harder for success.

Jupiter in Cancer should bring opportunities in home-related industries, child care, the food and shelter industries, cruises, maternal issues, shipping and boating, and water sports. Look for further expansion in home-based business and telecommuting. Combining mothering with an active career will be a key issue for Gen-X women, who'll have a tug of war between family and career.

After Jupiter moves into Leo in August, people will

be looking for more fun in life, more joy, and more opportunities to play. We'll all want to be young again, and chances are that plastic surgery will enjoy a big boom time. Bring on the divas, as larger-than-life personalities take center stage. Look for more self-aggrandizement and self-adornment in flamboyant fashions with plenty of color, style, and piles of gold jewelry. This is an influence which encourages extravagance, showing off, and enjoying the best things in life. On a more serious note, child-raising will very much be on our minds, since the sign of Leo rules children. How will we raise children in a workaholic era? Since this Jupiter encourages love affairs and casual sex, the pull of family ties and responsibilities could be one of the biggest challenges this year.

Saturn Puts on the Brakes in Gemini

Saturn keywords are focus, time, commitment, accomplishment, discipline, and restriction. If Jupiter gives you a handout, then Saturn hands you the bill. With Saturn, nothing's free; you work for what you get, so it's always a good idea to find the areas (or houses) of your horoscope where Saturn is passing through, to learn where to focus your energy on lasting value. With Saturn, you must be sure to finish what you start, be responsible, put in the hard work, and stick with it.

This year, Saturn finishes up its two-year transit of Gemini. The normally light-spirited Geminis have had to deal with the serious, sobering influence of Saturn, just after they enjoyed the expansive period of Jupiter in Gemini in 2000 and 2001. Geminis have to back up the risks they took then and will be required to deliver on promises made. It'll be a powerful challenge for changeable Geminis, who must now pay the piper.

In the world at large, Saturn in Gemini is sure to affect communications. Talk must be followed up by action now. We'll be concerned with Gemini issues of lower education and literacy, reforming the lower educational system. Since Gemini is an air sign, which rules the lungs, there will be further controversy and restriction surrounding smoking and the tobacco industry.

Uranus and Neptune in Aquarius— The High-Tech Signs

Uranus and Neptune are pushing us into the future as they continue their long stays in Aquarius. Uranus overthrows the worn-out status quo and points us toward the future. It rules the sign of Aquarius, so it has been in its most powerful position since 1995, and has created radical breakthroughs in technology, as well as a concern with issues that involve all humanity. It is now preparing to move into Pisces, a sign associated with spirituality, imagination, and creativity. Its coming influence should begin to show up this year, with some dramatic changes in the arts beginning this summer.

Our lust for techno-toys should make this a gadget-crazed time, especially as Jupiter enters playful Leo, reinforcing this trend. Interactive forms of amusement and communication will rival television for our leisure. In fact, television may be on its way out as we opt for more exciting forms of entertainment.

While Jupiter remains in Cancer, the first half of the year, look for more Cancer-related products and events in the news: home furnishings, housing, child care, food products and merchandising, and a surge in restaurants, futuristic cruise ships, and new concepts in living quarters. After Jupiter moves into Leo, it forms an uneasy relationship with Neptune and Uranus on the opposite side of the zodiac, which could engender conflicts between individuals and society at large, between what "I" want and what "they" want.

7

There will be concern about how technology is negatively affecting personal lives and creativity.

Where there is Neptune, look for imagination and creativity, and since this is the planet of deception and illusion, scams and scandals continue, especially in the high-tech area associated with Aquarius. Neptune is also associated with hospitals, which are acquiring a Neptunian glamour, as well as cutting-edge technology. The atmosphere of many hospitals is already changing from the intimidating sterile surgical environment of the past to that of a health-promoting spa, with alternative therapies such as massage, diet counseling, and aromatherapy available. New procedures in plastic surgery, also a Neptunian glamour field, and antiaging therapies should restore the bloom and the body of youth, as Jupiter in Leo glorifies the ever-young.

CHAPTER 2

Planning Ahead in 2002— Timing Your Life for Luck, Prosperity, and Love!

It's no secret that some of the most powerful and famous people, from Julius Caesar to financier J. P. Morgan, from Ronald Reagan to Cher, have consulted astrologers before they made their moves. If astrology helps the rich and famous stay on course through life's ups and downs, why not put it to work for you?

Take control of your life by coordinating your schedule with the cosmos. For instance, if you know the dates that the mischievous planet Mercury will be creating havoc with communications, you'll back up that vital fax with a duplicate by Express Mail; you'll read between the lines of contracts and put off closing that deal until you have double-checked all the information. When Venus is in your sign, making you the romantic flavor of the month, you'll be at your most attractive. That would be a great time to update your wardrobe, revamp your image, or ask someone you'd like to know better to dinner. Venus helps you make that sales pitch and win over the competition.

To find out for yourself if there's truth to the saying "Timing is everything," mark your own calendar for love, career moves, vacations, and important events, using the following information and the tables in this chapter and the one titled "Look Up Your Planets,"

as well as the moon sign listings under your daily forecast. Here are the happenings to note on your agenda:

- Dates of your sun sign (high-energy period)
- The month previous to your sun sign (low-
  energy period)
- Dates of planets in your sign this year
- Full and new moons
  (Pay special attention when these fall in your
  sun sign.)
- Eclipses
- Moon in your sun sign every month, as well as
  moon in the opposite sign (listed in daily forecast)
- Mercury retrogrades
- Other retrograde periods

Your Personal Power Time

Every birthday starts a cycle of solar energy for you.
You should feel a new surge of vitality as the powerful
sun enters your sign. This is the time when predomi-
nant energies are most favorable to you. So go for it!
Start new projects; make your big moves. You'll get
the recognition you deserve now, when everyone is
attuned to your sun sign. Look in the tables in this
book to see if other planets will also be passing
through your sun sign at this time. Venus (love,
beauty), Mars (energy, drive), or Mercury (communication, mental sharpness) reinforce the sun and give
an extra boost to your life in the areas they affect.
Venus will rev up your social and love life, making
you seem especially attractive. Mars gives you extra
energy and drive. Mercury fuels your brain power and
helps you communicate. Jupiter signals an especially
lucky period of expansion.

There are two "down" times related to the sun.
During the month before your birthday period, when
you are winding up your annual cycle, you could be
feeling especially vulnerable and depleted, so get extra

rest, watch your diet, and don't overstress yourself. Use this time to gear up for a big "push" when the sun enters your sign.

Another "down" time is when the sun is in the opposite sign from your sun sign (six months from your birthday) and the prevailing energies are very different from yours. You may feel at odds with the world, and things might not come easily. You'll have to work harder for recognition, because people are not on your wavelength. However, this could be a good time to work on a team, in cooperation with others or behind the scenes.

How to Use the Moon's Phase and Sign

Working with the phases of the moon is as easy as looking up at the night sky. During the new moon, when both the sun and the moon are in the same sign, it's the best time to begin new ventures, especially the activities that are favored by that sign. You'll have powerful energies pulling you in the same direction. You'll be focused outward, toward action and doing. Postpone breaking off, terminating, deliberating, or reflecting, activities that require introspection and passive work.

Get your project under way during the first quarter, then go public at the full moon, a time of high intensity, when feelings come out into the open. This is your time to shine—to express yourself. Be aware, however, that because pressures are being released, other people are also letting off steam and confrontations are possible. So try to avoid arguments. Traditionally, astrologers often advise against surgery at this time, which could produce heavier bleeding.

During the last quarter of the new moon, you'll be most controlled. This is a winding-down phase, a time to cut off unproductive relationships and do serious thinking and inward-directed activities.

You'll feel some new and full moons more strongly than others, especially those new moons that fall in your sun sign and full moons in your opposite sign. Because that full moon happens at your low-energy time of year, it is likely to be an especially stressful time in a relationship, when any hidden problems or unexpressed emotions could surface.

Full and New Moons in 2002

New Moon in Capricorn—January 13
Full Moon in Leo—January 28
New Moon in Aquarius—February 12
Full Moon in Virgo—February 27
New Moon in Pisces—March 13
Full Moon in Libra—March 28
New Moon in Aries—April 12
Full Moon in Scorpio—April 27
New Moon in Taurus—May 12
Full Moon in Sagittarius (lunar eclipse)—May 26
New Moon in Gemini (solar eclipse)—June 10
Full Moon in Capricorn (lunar eclipse)—June 24
New Moon in Cancer—July 10
Full Moon in Aquarius—July 24
New Moon in Leo—August 8
Full Moon in Aquarius (second time)—August 22
New Moon in Virgo—September 6
Full Moon in Pisces—September 21
New Moon in Libra—October 6
Full Moon in Aries—October 21
New Moon in Scorpio—November 4
Full Moon in Taurus (lunar eclipse)—November 19
New Moon in Sagittarius (solar eclipse)—December 4
Full Moon in Gemini—December 19

Moon Sign Timing

To forecast the daily emotional "weather," to determine your monthly high and low days, or to synchronize your activities with the cycles and the sign of the moon, take note of the moon's daily sign under your daily forecast at the end of the book. Here are some of the activities favored and moods you are likely to encounter under each sign.

Moon in Aries

Get moving! The new moon in Aries is an ideal time to start new projects. Everyone is pushy, raring to go, and rather impatient and short-tempered. Leave details and follow-up for later. Competitive sports or martial arts are great ways to let off steam. Quiet types could use some assertiveness, but it's a great day for dynamos. Be careful not to step on too many toes.

Moon in Taurus

It's time to do solid, methodical tasks. This is the time to tackle follow-through or backup work. Lay the foundations for success. Make investments, buy real estate, do appraisals, and do some hard bargaining. Attend to your property—get out in the country. Spend some time in your garden. Enjoy creature comforts, music, a good dinner, and sensual lovemaking. Forget starting a diet.

Moon in Gemini

Talk means action today. Telephone, write a letter, fax! Make new contacts; stay in touch with steady customers. You can handle lots of tasks at once. A great day for mental activity of any kind. Don't try to pin people down—they, too, are feeling restless. Keep it light. Flirtations and socializing are good. Watch gossip—and don't give away secrets.

Moon in Cancer

This is a moody, sensitive, emotional time. People respond to personal attention and mothering. Stay at home; have a family dinner; call your mother. Nostalgia, memories, and psychic powers are heightened. You'll want to hang on to people and things (don't clean out your closets now). You could have some shrewd insights into what others really need and want now. Pay attention to dreams, intuition, and gut reactions.

Moon in Leo

Everybody is in a much more confident, warm, generous mood. It's a good day to ask for a raise, show what you can do, or dress like a star. People will respond to flattery; enjoy a bit of drama and theater. You may be extravagant—treat yourself royally, and show off a bit (but don't break the bank!). Be careful that you don't promise more than you can deliver!

Moon in Virgo

Do practical, down-to-earth chores. Review your budget. Make repairs. Be an efficiency expert. Not a day to ask for a raise. Have a health checkup. Revamp your diet. Buy vitamins or health food. Make your home spotless. Take care of details and piled-up chores. Reorganize your work and life so they run more smoothly and efficiently. Save money. Be prepared for others to be in a critical, faultfinding mood.

Moon in Libra

Attend to legal matters. Negotiate contracts. Arbitrate. Do things with your favorite partner. Socialize.

Be romantic. Buy a special gift, a beautiful object. Decorate yourself or your surroundings. Buy new clothes. Throw a party. Have an elegant, romantic evening. Smooth over any ruffled feathers. Avoid confrontations. Stick to civilized discussions.

Moon in Scorpio

This is a day to do things with passion. You'll have excellent concentration and focus. Try not to get too intense emotionally, however, and avoid sharp exchanges with loved ones. Others may tend to go to extremes, get jealous, and overreact. Great for troubleshooting, problem-solving, research, scientific work—and making love. Pay attention to psychic vibes.

Moon in Sagittarius

A great time for travel. Have philosophical discussions. Set long-range career goals. Work out, do sports, or buy athletic equipment. Others will be feeling upbeat, exuberant, and adventurous. Risk taking is favored—you may feel like taking a gamble, betting on the horses, visiting a local casino, or buying a lottery ticket. Teaching, writing, and spiritual activities also get the green light. Relax outdoors. Take care of animals.

Moon in Capricorn

You can accomplish a lot today, so get on the ball! Issues concerning your basic responsibilities, duties, family and parents could crop up. You'll be expected to deliver on promises now. Weed out the dead wood from your life. Get a dental checkup.

Moon in Aquarius

A great day for doing things with groups—clubs, meetings, outings, politics, and parties. Campaign for your candidate. Work for a worthy cause. Deal with larger issues that affect humanity: the environment and metaphysical questions. Buy a computer or an electronic gadget. Watch TV. Wear something outrageous. Try something you've never done before. Present an original idea. Don't stick to a rigid schedule—go with the flow. Take a class in meditation, mind control, or yoga.

Moon in Pisces

This can be a very creative day, so let your imagination work overtime. Film, theater, music, or ballet could inspire you. Spend some time alone, resting and reflecting, reading or writing poetry. Daydreams can also be profitable. Help those less fortunate or lend a listening ear to someone who may be feeling blue. Don't overindulge in self-pity or escapism, however. People are especially vulnerable to substance abuse now. Turn your thoughts to romance and someone special.

When the Planets Go Backward

All the planets, except for the sun and moon, have times when they appear to move backward—or retrograde—in the sky, or so it seems from our point of view on earth. At these times, planets do not work as they normally do, so it's best to "take a break" from that planet's energies in our life and do some work on an inner level.

Mercury Retrograde

Mercury goes retrograde most often, and its effects can be especially irritating. When it reaches a short distance ahead of the sun three times a year, it seems to move backward from our point of view. Astrologers often compare retrograde motion to the optical illusion that occurs when we ride on a train that passes another train traveling at a different speed—the second train appears to be moving in reverse.

What this means to you is that the Mercury-ruled areas of your life—analytical thought processes, communications, and scheduling—are subject to all kinds of confusion. Be prepared. People will change their minds, or renege on commitments. Communications equipment can break down. Schedules must be changed on short notice. People are late for appointments or don't show up at all. Traffic is terrible. Major purchases malfunction, don't work out, or get delivered in the wrong color. Letters don't arrive or are delivered to the wrong address. Employees will make errors that have to be corrected later. Contracts don't work out or must be renegotiated.

Since most of us can't put our lives on "hold" for nine weeks every year (three Mercury retrograde periods), we should learn to tame the trickster and make it work for us. The key is in the prefix "re-." This is the time to go back over things in your life. Reflect on what you've done during the previous months. Look for deeper insights, spot errors you've missed, and take time to review and reevaluate what has happened. This time is very good for inner spiritual work and meditations. *Re*st and *re*ward yourself—it's a good time to take a vacation, especially if you revisit a favorite place. *Re*organize your work and finish up projects that are backed up. Clean out your desk and closets. Throw away what you can't *re*cycle. If you must sign contracts or agreements, do so with a contingency clause that lets you *re*evaluate the terms later.

Postpone major purchases or commitments. Don't get married (unless you're *re*marrying the same person). Try not to rely on other people keeping appointments, contracts, or agreements to the letter—have several alternatives. Double-check and read between the lines. Don't buy anything connected with communications or transportation (if you must, be sure to cover yourself). Mercury retrograding through your sun sign will intensify its effect on your life.

If Mercury was retrograde when you were born, you may be one of the lucky people who don't suffer the frustrations of this period. If so, your mind probably works in a very intuitive, insightful way.

The sign Mercury is retrograding through can give you an idea of what's in store—as well as the sun signs that will be especially challenged.

MERCURY RETROGRADE PERIODS IN 2002

Mercury has three retrograde periods this year: from January 18 to February 8, from May 15 to June 8, and from September 14 to October 6.

Venus Retrograde

Retrograding Venus can cause your relationships to take a backward step, or it can make you extravagant and impractical. Shopping till you drop and buying what you cannot afford are trip-ups at this time. It's *not* a good time to redecorate—you'll hate the color of the walls later. Postpone getting a new hairstyle and try not to fall in love either. But if you wish to make amends in an already troubled relationship, make peaceful overtures at this time. (Note: there is no Mars retrograde period this year.)

VENUS RETROGRADE PERIOD IN 2002

Venus retrogrades from October 10 to November 21.

When Other Planets Retrograde

The slower-moving planets stay retrograde for months at a time (Saturn, Jupiter, Neptune, Uranus, and Pluto). When Saturn is retrograde, it's an uphill battle with self-discipline. You may feel more like hanging out at the beach than getting things done. Neptune retrograde promotes a dreamy escapism from reality, whereas Uranus retrograde may mean setbacks in areas where there have been sudden changes. Think of this as an adjustment period, a time to think things over and allow new ideas to develop. Pluto retrograde is a time to work on establishing proportion and balance in areas where there have been recent dramatic transformations.

When the planets start moving forward again, there's a shift in the atmosphere. Activities connected with each planet start moving ahead, and plans that were stalled get rolling. Make a special note of those days on your calendar and proceed accordingly.

Other Retrogrades in 2002

Jupiter is retrograde from November 2, 2001, until March 1, 2002. It turns retrograde again on December 4, 2002.

Saturn retrogrades from February 7 to October 11.
Uranus retrogrades from June 6 to November 3.
Neptune retrogrades from May 13 to October 20.
Pluto retrogrades from March 20 to August 16.

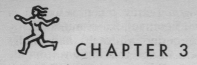

CHAPTER 3

Teach Yourself Astrology

Astrology is a powerful tool of inner transformation that can help you access your personal potential, to understand others, and to interpret events in your life and in the world at large. You don't have to be an expert in astrology to put it to work for you. In this chapter, we'll demystify the horoscope chart and walk you through the basic concepts, so you'll know a sign from a house and what the planets mean. Perhaps from here, you'll upgrade your knowledge with a computer program that calculates charts for everyone you know in a nanosecond, or you'll join an astrology class in your city, or you'll want to explore different techniques of astrology and go on to the asteroids and the fixed stars. The sky's the limit, literally. So let's take off!

The Basics: Signs, Houses, Constellations, and the Zodiac

Everyone knows what a sign is . . . or do they? A *sign* is literally a 30-degree portion of the zodiac, a circular belt of the sky. That is what is meant by a "sign of the zodiac." Things happen within a sign, but a sign does not *do* anything itself—that's the job of the planets. Each sign is simply a portion of celestial real estate and has certain unique characteristics described by four things: an *element* (earth, air, fire, water), a *quality* or mode (cardinal (active), fixed, mutable), by a *polarity* (masculine/feminine, yin/yang) and finally by a *position* in the sequence of zodiac signs.

The *signs* are named after *constellations,* patterns of stars on the zodiac which originally lit up the twelve divisions, like billboards. However, over the centuries, the constellations have shifted from our point of view here on earth. So the constellation which once marked a particular sign may now be in the territory of another sign. (Most Western astrologers use the twelve-equal-part division of the zodiac; however, there are some methods of astrology that still do use the constellations instead of the signs.) However, the *names* of the signs remain the same as their original place-markers.

Most people think of themselves in terms of their *sun sign,* which refers to the sign the sun seems to be passing through at a given moment, from our point of view here on earth. (Of course, we are the ones that are traveling around the sun.) For instance, "I'm an Aries" means that the sun was passing through Aries territory at your birth. However, there are nine other planets (plus asteroids, fixed stars, and sensitive points) which also form our total astrological personality, and some or many of these will be located in other signs. No one is completely "Aries," with all their astrological components in one sign! (Please note that, in astrology, the sun and moon are usually referred to as "planets," though of course they're not.)

Defining the Signs

What makes Aries the sign of go-getters and Taureans savvy with money? And Geminis talk a blue streak and Sagittarians footloose? Descriptions of the signs are not accidental; they are characterized by different combinations of four concepts we have already mentioned: the sign's element, quality, polarity, and position in the sequence of the zodiac.

Take the element of fire: it's associated with passion, heat. Then have it work in an active, energetic way. Give it a jolt of positive energy and place it first in line. And doesn't that sound like the active, me-first, driving, hotheaded, energetic Aries?

Then take the element of earth: it's practical, sensual, where things grow. Make it work in a fixed, stable way or mode. Give it the kind of energy that reacts to its surroundings, that settles in. Make it the consolidating force, coming right after the passionate beginning of Aries. Now you've got a good idea of how sensual, earthy Taurus operates.

Another way to grasp the idea is to pretend you're doing a magical puzzle based on the numbers that can divide into 12 (the total number of signs): 4, 3, and 2. There are 4 "building blocks" or elements, 3 ways a sign operates (qualities or modes), and 2 polarities. These alternate, in turn, around the zodiac, with a different combination coming up for each sign.

THE FOUR ELEMENTS

Here's how they add up. The *four elements* describe the physical concept of the sign. Is it fiery (dynamic), earthy (practical), airy (mental), or watery (emotional)? Divide the 12 signs by the 4 elements and you get 3 zodiac signs of each element: fire (Aries, Leo, Sagittarius); earth (Taurus, Virgo, Capricorn); air (Gemini, Libra, Aquarius); and water (Cancer, Scorpio, Pisces). These are the same elements that make up our planet: earth, air, fire, and water. But astrology uses the elements as *symbols* which link your body and psyche to the rhythms of the cosmos. If major planets in a horoscope are passing through fire signs, the person will be likely to have a warm, enthusiastic personality, able to fire up or motivate others. These are people who make ideas catch fire and spring into existence, but they also have hot tempers. Those with major planets in earth signs are the builders of the zodiac who follow through after the initiative of fire signs to make things happen. These people are solid, practical realists who enjoy material things and sensual pleasures. They are interested in ideas that can be used to achieve concrete results. With major planets in air signs, a person will be more mental, a good communicator. Following the consolidating earth signs, air people reach out to inspire others through the use of words, social contacts, discussion, and debate. Water sign people complete each four-element series, adding the ingredients of emotion, compassion, and imagination. These people are nonverbal communicators who attune themselves to their surroundings and react through the medium of feelings.

THE THREE QUALITIES

The second consideration when defining a sign is how it will operate. Will it take the initiative, or move slowly and deliberately, or adapt easily? Its *quality* (or modality) will tell. There are 3 qualities; therefore, after dividing 3 into 12 signs, it follows that there will be 4 signs of each quality: cardinal, fixed, and mutable.

Cardinal signs begin each season (Aries, Cancer, Libra, Capricorn). People with major planets in cardinal signs tend to be doers. They're active, always involved in projects. They are usually on the fast track to success, impatient to get things under way. Those with major planets in *fixed signs* (Taurus, Leo, Scorpio, Aquarius) move steadily and are always in control. Since these signs happen in the middle of a season, after the initial character of the season is established, it follows that people with major planets in fixed signs would tend to be more centered; they move more deliberately and do things more slowly but thoroughly. The fixed signs fall in parts of your horoscope where you take root and integrate your experiences. *Mutable signs* (Gemini, Virgo, Sagittarius, Pisces) embody the principle of distribution. Planets in these signs will break up the cycle, preparing the way for a change by distributing the energy to the next group. People with predominantly mutable planets are likely to be flexible, adaptable, and communicative. They can move in many directions easily, darting around obstacles.

THE TWO POLARITIES
In addition to an element and a quality, each sign has a *polarity,* either a positive or negative electrical charge that generates energy around the zodiac, like a giant battery. Polarity refers to opposites, which you could also define as masculine/feminine, yin/yang, active/reactive. In their zodiac positions, the six fire and air signs are positive, active, masculine, and yang in polarity. Therefore, planets in these signs will express their energy openly, expanding outward. The six earth and water signs are reactive, negative, and yin—in other words, nurturing and receptive in polarity, which allows the energy to develop and take shape.

All positive energy would be like a car without brakes. All negative energy would be like a stalled vehicle, going nowhere. So both polarities are needed in balanced proportion, to keep the zodiac in a state of equilibrium.

THE ORDER OF THE SIGNS
The specific order of the signs is vital to the balance of the zodiac and the transmission of energy around the cycle. Though each sign is quite different from its neighbors on either side, each seems to grow out of its predecessor like links in a chain, transmitting a synthesis of energy accumulated along the chain to the following sign, beginning with the fire-powered, active, positive, cardinal sign of Aries and ending with watery, mutable, reactive Pisces.

Houses of the Horoscope—
Where the Action Is

We come to the concept of *houses* as we set up a specific horoscope, which is a map of the heavens at a given moment in time. Picture the horoscope chart as a wheel with twelve spokes. In between each of the "spokes" is a section called a *house*. The wheel is stationary, however . . . the houses are always in the same place. Each house represents a different area of life and is influenced or "ruled" by a sign and a planet that are associated with that house. But besides the house's given "rulers," it is colored by the sign which is passing over the spoke (or cusp) at the moment when the horoscope chart is cast. In other words, the first house is naturally ruled by Aries and Mars; however, if Capricorn was the sign passing over the house at the time the chart was cast, it would have a Capricorn influence.

Numerically, the house order begins at the left center spoke (or the 9 position if you were reading a clock) and is read counterclockwise around the chart.

The First House—Home of Aries
and the Planet Mars

This is the house of "firsts"—the first impression you make, how you initiate matters, the image you choose to project. This is where you advertise yourself, where you project your personality. Planets that fall here will intensify the way you come across to others. Often the first house will project an entirely different type of energy from the sun sign. For instance, a Capricorn with Leo in the first house will come across as much more flamboyant than the average Capricorn. The sign on the cusp of this house is known as your *ascendant,* or *rising sign.*

The Second House—Home of Taurus and Venus

Here is your contact with the material world. In this house are your attitudes about money, possessions, finances, whatever belongs to you, and what you own, as well as your earning and spending capacity. On a deeper level, this house reveals your sense of self-worth, the inner values that draw wealth in various forms.

The Third House—Home of Gemini and Mercury

This house describes how you communicate with others—are you understood? Here you reach out to others nearby and interact with the immediate environment. This is how your thinking process works, the way you express your thoughts. In relationships, here are your first experiences with brothers and sisters, and how you handle people close to you, such as your neighbors or pals. It's also where you take short trips, write letters, or use the telephone. It shows how your mind works in terms of left-brain logical and analytical functions.

The Fourth House—Home of Cancer and the Moon

This house shows how you are nurtured and made to feel secure—your roots! Located at the bottom of the chart, the fourth house, like the home, shows the foundation of life, your deepest psychological underpinnings. Here is where you have the deepest confrontation with who you are, and how you make yourself feel secure. It shows your early home environment and the circumstances at the end of your life—your final "home"—as well as the place you call home now. Astrologers look here for information about the primary nurturers in your life.

The Fifth House—Home of Leo and the Sun

This is how you express yourself creatively—your idea of play. The Leo house is where the creative potential develops, where you show off your talents. It is also where you procreate, in the sense that your children are outgrowths of your creative ability. It most represents your inner childlike self, the part of you which finds joy in play. If inner security has been established by the time you reach this house, you are now free to have fun, romance, and love affairs—to give of yourself. This is also the place astrologers look for the playful kind of love affairs, flirtations, and brief romantic encounters (rather than long-term commitments).

The Sixth House—Home of Virgo and Mercury

Here is your "care and maintenance" department. It shows how you function in daily life, where you get things done, and where you determine how you look after others and fulfill service duties, such as taking care of pets. Here are your daily survival, your "job" (as opposed to your career, which is the domain of the tenth house), your diet, and your health and fitness regimens. Here is where you take care of your body and organize yourself to perform efficiently.

The Seventh House—Home of Libra and Venus

This house shows your attitude toward partners and those with whom you enter commitments, contracts, or agreements. This house has to do with your relationships—your close, intimate, one-on-one relationships (even your open enemies—those you "face off" with). Open hostilities, lawsuits, divorces, and marriages happen here. If the first house represents the "I," the seventh or opposite house represents the "not-I"—the complementary partner you attract by the way you come across. If you are having trouble with partnerships, consider what you are attracting by the interaction of your first and seventh house.

The Eighth House—Home of Scorpio and Pluto (also Mars)

This refers to how you merge with something or someone, and how you handle power and control. This is one of the most mysterious and powerful houses, where your energy transforms itself from "I" to "we." As you give up your personal power and control by uniting with something or someone, two kinds of energies merge and become something greater, leading to a regeneration of the self on a higher level. Here are your attitudes toward sex, shared resources, and taxes (what you share with the government). Because this house involves what belongs to others, you face issues of control and power struggles, or undergo a deep psychological transformation as you bond with another. Here you transcend yourself with dreams, drugs, and occult or psychic experiences that reflect the collective unconscious.

The Ninth House—Home of Sagittarius and Jupiter

Here is where you search for wisdom and higher knowledge—your belief system. While the third house represents the "lower mind," its opposite on the wheel, the ninth house, is the "higher mind." This is where you ask the "big" questions like "Why are we here?" The ninth house shows what you believe in. After the third house has explored what was close at hand, the ninth stretches out to broaden you with higher education and travel. Here you stretch spiritually with religious activity. Since you are concerned with how everything is related, you tend to take risks, break rules, and push boundaries. Here is where you express your ideas in a book or extensive thesis, where you pontificate, philosophize, or preach.

The Tenth House—Home of Capricorn and Saturn

Here is your public image and how you handle authority. Located directly overhead at the "high noon" position on the horoscope wheel, this house is associated with high-profile activities, where the world sees you. It deals with your career (but not your routine "job"), and your reputation. Here is where you go public and take on responsibilities (as opposed to the fourth house, where you stay home). This will affect the career you choose and your "public relations." This house is also associated with your father or the main authority figure in your life.

The Eleventh House—Home of Aquarius and Uranus

Here is your support system, how you relate to society and your goals. In this house, you extend your identity to belong to a group, a team, a club, a goal, or a belief system. You worry about being popular, winning the election, or making the team; you define what you really want, the kinds of friends you have, your political affiliations, and the kinds of groups you'll belong to. Here is where you become concerned with "what other people think," or you rebel against society. Here is where you could become a socially conscious humanitarian—or a party-going social butterfly. It's where you look to others to stimulate you and discover your kinship to the rest of humanity. The sign on the cusp of this house can help you understand what you gain and lose from friendships.

The Twelfth House—Home of Pisces and Neptune

Here is where the boundaries between yourself and others become blurred, where you become self-less. In your trip around the zodiac, you've gone from the "I" of self-assertion in the first house to the final house, symbolizing the dissolution that happens before rebirth. It's where accumulated experiences are processed in the unconscious. Spiritually oriented astrologers look to this house for evidence of past lives and karma. Places where we go for solitude or to do spiritual or reparatory work belong here, such as retreats, religious institutions, or hospitals. Here are also institutions such as prisons where we withdraw from society or are forced to withdraw because of antisocial behavior. Selfless giving through charitable acts is part of this house, as is helpless receiving or dependence on charity.

In your daily life, the twelfth house reveals your deepest intimacies, your best-kept secrets, especially those you hide from yourself, repressed deep in the unconscious. It is where we surrender a sense of a separate self to a deep feeling of wholeness, such as selfless service in religion or any activity that involves merging with the greater whole. Many sports stars have important planets in the twelfth house that enable them to play in the "zone," finding an inner, almost mystical, strength that transcends their limits.

The Planets Power Up Your Houses

Houses are stronger or weaker depending on how many planets are inhabiting them. If there are many planets occupying a given house, it follows that the activities of that house will be emphasized in your life. If the planet that rules the house naturally is also located there, this too adds power to the house.

Mapping Your Planets

The ten major planets (including the sun and moon) are the doers in your chart. The planets cause things to happen. They will play starring or supporting roles, depending on their positions in your horoscope. A planet in the first house, particularly one that's close to your rising sign, is sure to be a featured player. Planets that are grouped together usually operate together like a team, playing off each other, rather than expressing their energy singularly. A planet that stands alone, away from the others, is usually outstanding and sometimes calls the shots.

The best place for a planet is in the sign or signs it rules; the next best is in a sign where it is *exalted,* or especially harmonious. On the other hand, there are signs where a planet has to work harder to play its role. These are called the planet's *detriment* and *fall.* The sign opposite a planet's rulership, which embodies the opposite area of life, is its *detriment.* The sign opposite its exaltation is its *fall.* Though these terms may suggest unfortunate circumstances for the planet, that is not always true. In fact, a planet that is debilitated can actually be more complete, because it must stretch itself to meet the challenges of living in a more difficult sign. Like world leaders who've had to struggle for greatness, this planet may actually develop more strength and character.

Here's a list of the best places for each planet to be. Note that, as Uranus, Neptune, and Pluto were discovered, they replaced the traditional rulers of signs which best complemented their energies.

ARIES—Mars.
TAURUS—Venus, in its most sensual form.
GEMINI—Mercury in its communicative role.
CANCER—the moon.
LEO—the sun.

VIRGO—Also Mercury, this time in its more critical capacity.

LIBRA—Also Venus, in its more aesthetic, judgmental form.

SCORPIO—Pluto, replacing the sign's original ruler, Mars.

SAGITTARIUS—Jupiter.

CAPRICORN—Saturn.

AQUARIUS—Uranus, replacing Saturn, its original ruler.

PISCES—Neptune, replacing Jupiter, its original ruler.

A person who has many planets in exalted signs is lucky indeed, for here is where the planet can accomplish the most and be its most influential and creative.

SUN—Exalted in Aries, where its energy creates action.

MOON—Exalted in Taurus, where instincts and reactions operate on a highly creative level.

MERCURY—Exalted in Aquarius, where it can reach analytical heights.

VENUS—Exalted in Pisces, a sign whose sensitivity encourages love and creativity.

MARS—Exalted in Capricorn, a sign that puts energy to work productively.

JUPITER—Exalted in Cancer, where it encourages nurturing and growth.

SATURN—At home in Libra, where it steadies the scales of justice and promotes balanced, responsible judgment.

URANUS—Powerful in Scorpio, where it promotes transformation.

NEPTUNE—Especially favored in Cancer, where it gains the security to transcend to a higher state.

PLUTO—Exalted in Pisces, where it dissolves the old cycle, to make way for transition to the new.

The Sun and the Moon

Since the sun is always the first consideration, it is important to treat it as the star of the show. It is your conscious ego and it is always center stage, even when sharing a house or a sign with several other planets. This is why sun sign astrology works for so many people.

The sun rules the sign of Leo, gaining strength through the pride, dignity, and confidence of the fixed-fire personality. It is exalted in "me-first" Aries. In its detriment, Aquarius, the sun-ego is strengthened through group participation and social consciousness, rather than through self-centeredness. (Note how many Aquarius people are involved in politics, social work, and public life. They are following the demands of their sun sign to be spokesperson for a group.) In its fall, Libra, the sun needs the strength of a partner—an "other"—to enhance its own balance and self-expression.

As the sun represents your outer light, the moon represents the inner "you," your deep emotional nature. We go into more detail about the moon and its influence in your life and moods in a separate chapter in this book. Read it for details about this all-important planet.

Each of the other eight planets is colored by the sign it is passing through. For example, Mercury, the planet that rules the way you communicate, will express itself in a dynamic, headstrong way if it was passing through the sign of Aries when you were born. You will speak differently if it was passing through the slower, more patient sign of Taurus. And so on through the list. Here's a rundown of the planets and how they behave in every sign.

The Personal Planets—Mercury, Venus, and Mars

These planets work in your immediate personal life.

Mercury affects how you communicate and how your mental processes work. Are you a quick study who grasps information rapidly, or do you learn more slowly and thoroughly? How is your concentration? Can you express yourself easily? Are you a good writer? All these questions can be answered by your Mercury placement.

Venus shows what you react to. What turns you on? What appeals to you aesthetically? Are you charming to others? Are you attractive to look at? Your taste, your refinement, your sense of balance and proportion are all Venus-ruled.

Mars is your outgoing energy, your drive and ambition. Do you reach out for new adventures? Are you assertive? Are you motivated? Self-confident? Hot-tempered? How you channel your energy and drive is revealed by your Mars placement.

Mercury Communicates

Since Mercury never travels far from the sun, read Mercury in your sun sign, then the signs preceding and following it. Then decide which reflects the way your mind works.

Mercury in Aries

Your mind is very active and assertive. You never hesitate to say what you think or shy away from a battle. In fact, you may relish a verbal confrontation. Tact is not your strong point, so you may have to learn not to trip over your tongue.

Mercury in Taurus

Though you may be a slow learner, you have good concentration and mental stamina. You want to make your ideas really happen. You'll attack a problem methodically and consider every angle thoroughly, never jumping to conclusions. You'll stick with a subject until you master it.

Mercury in Gemini

A wonderful communicator with great facility for expressing yourself both verbally and in writing. You talk and talk, love gathering all kinds of information. You probably finish other people's sentences and talk with hand gestures. You can talk to anybody anytime and probably have phone and e-mail bills to prove it. You read anything from sci-fi to Shakespeare and might need an extra room just for your book collection. Though you learn fast, you may lack focus and discipline. Watch a tendency to jump from subject to subject.

Mercury in Cancer

You rely on intuition more than logic. Your mental processes are usually colored by your emotions, so you may seem shy or hesitant to voice your opinions. However, this placement gives you the advantage of great imagination and empathy in the way you communicate with others.

Mercury in Leo

You are enthusiastic and very dramatic in the way you express yourself. You like to hold the attention of groups and could be a great public speaker. Your mind thinks big, so you'd prefer to deal with the overall picture rather than with the details.

Mercury in Virgo

This is one of the best places for Mercury. It should give you critical ability, attention to details, and thorough analysis. Your mind focuses on the practical side of things. This type of thinking is very well suited to being a teacher or an editor.

Mercury in Libra

You're either a born diplomat who smoothes over ruffled feathers or a talented debater. However, since you're forever weighing the pros and cons of a situation, you may vacillate when making decisions.

Mercury in Scorpio

This is an investigative mind which stops at nothing to get the answers. You may have a sarcastic, stinging wit or a gift for the cutting remark. There's always a grain of truth to your verbal sallies, thanks to your penetrating insight.

Mercury in Sagittarius

You're a super salesman with a tendency to expound. Though you are very broad-minded, you can be dogmatic when it comes to telling others what's good for them. You won't hesitate to tell the truth as you see it, so watch a tendency toward tactlessness. On the plus side, you have a great sense of humor. This position of Mercury is often considered by astrologers to be at a disadvantage because Sagittarius opposes Gemini, the sign Mercury rules, and squares off with Virgo, another Mercury-ruled sign. What often happens is that Mercury in Sagittarius oversteps its bounds and loses sight of the facts in a situation. Do a reality check before making promises that you may not be able to keep.

Mercury in Capricorn

This placement endows good mental discipline. You have a love of learning and a very orderly approach to your subjects. You will patiently plod through the facts and figures until you have mastered the tasks. You grasp structured situations easily, but may be short on creativity.

Mercury in Aquarius

With Uranus and Neptune in Aquarius now energizing your Mercury, you're sure to be on the cutting edge of new ideas. An independent, original thinker, you'll have more far-out ideas than the average person and be quick to check out any unusual opportunities. Your opinions are so well researched and grounded, in fact, that once your mind is made up, it is difficult to change.

Mercury in Pisces

You have the psychic intuitive mind of a natural poet. Learn to make use of your creative imagination. You may think in terms of helping others, but check a tendency to be vague and forgetful of details.

Venus Relates

Venus tells how you relate to others and to your environment. It shows where you receive pleasure, what you love to do. Find your Venus placement on the chart on pages 68–75 by looking for the year of your birth in the left-hand column. Then follow the line of that year across the page until you reach the time period of your birthday. The sign heading that column will be your Venus. If you were born on a day when Venus was changing signs, check the signs preceding or following that day to determine if that feels more like your Venus nature.

Venus in Aries

You can't stand to be bored, confined, or ordered around. But a good challenge, maybe even a rousing row, turns you on. Don't you pick a fight now and then just to get someone stirred up? You're attracted by the chase, not the catch, which could cause some problems in your love life, if the object of your affection becomes too attainable. You love someone who keeps you on your toes. You like to wear red and be first with the latest fashion. You'll spot a trend before anyone else.

Venus in Taurus

All your senses work in high gear. You love to be surrounded by glorious tastes, smells, textures, sounds, and visuals. Austere minimalism is not your style. Neither is being rushed. You like time to enjoy your pleasures. Soothing surroundings with plenty of creature comforts are your cup of tea. You like to feel secure in your nest, with no sudden jolts or surprises. You like familiar objects—in fact, you may hate to let anything or anyone go.

Venus in Gemini

You are a lively, sparkling personality who thrives in a situation that affords a constant variety and a frequent change of scenery. A varied social life is important to you, with plenty of stimulation and a chance to engage in some light flirtation. Commitment may be difficult, because playing the field is so much fun.

Venus in Cancer

An atmosphere where you feel protected, coddled, and mothered is best for you. You love to be surrounded by children in a cozy, homelike situation. You are attracted to those who are tender and nurturing, who make you feel secure and well provided for. You may be quite secretive about your emotional life or attracted to clandestine relationships.

Venus in Leo

First-class attention in large doses turns you on, and so do the glitter of real gold and the flash of mirrors. You like to feel like a star at all times, surrounded by your admiring audience. The side effect is that you may be attracted to flatterers and tinsel, while the real gold requires some digging.

Venus in Virgo

Everything neatly in its place? On the surface, you are attracted to an atmosphere where everything is in perfect order, but underneath are some basic, earthy urges. You are attracted to those who appeal to your need to teach, be of service, or play out a Pygmalion fantasy. You are at your best when you are busy doing something useful, helping someone improve.

Venus in Libra

"Elegance" and "harmony" are your key words. You can't abide an atmosphere of contention. Your taste tends toward the classic, with light harmonies of color— nothing clashing, trendy, or outrageous. You love doing things with a partner and should be careful to pick one who is decisive, but patient enough to let you weigh the pros and cons. And steer clear of argumentative types. It helps a lot if your partner is attractive and stylish, as well as charming, and appreciates the finer things in life.

Venus in Scorpio

Hidden mysteries intrigue you. In fact, anything that is too open and aboveboard is a bit of a bore. You surely have a stack of whodunits by the bed, along with an erotic magazine or two. You like to solve puzzles, and may also be fascinated with the occult, crime, or scientific research. Intense, all-or-nothing situations add spice to your life, and you love to ferret out the secrets of others. But you could get burned by your flair for living dangerously. The color black, spicy food, dark wood furniture, and heady perfume all get you in the right mood.

Venus in Sagittarius

If you are not actually a world traveler, your surroundings are sure to reflect your love of faraway places. You like a casual outdoor atmosphere and a dog or two to pet. There should be plenty of room for athletic equipment and suitcases. You're attracted to kindred souls who love to travel and who share your freedom-loving philosophy of life. Athletics, spiritual, or New Age pursuits could be other interests.

Venus in Capricorn

No fly-by-night relationships for you! You want substance in life and you are attracted to whatever will help you get where you are going. Status objects turn you on. And so do those who have a serious, responsible, businesslike approach, or who remind you of a beloved parent. It is characteristic of this placement to be attracted to someone of a different generation. Antiques, traditional clothing, and dignified behavior favor you.

Venus in Aquarius

This Venus wants to make friends more than to make love. You like to be in a group, particularly one pushing a worthy cause. In fact, fame of one sort or another is fascinating to you. You feel quite at home surrounded by people, but may remain detached from any intense commitment. Original ideas and unpredictable people attract you. You don't like everything to be planned out in advance, preferring spontaneity and delightful surprises.

Venus in Pisces

Venus is exalted in Pisces, which makes this one of the more desirable Venuses to have. This Venus loves to give of the self, and you'll find plenty of takers. Stray animals and people appeal to your heart and your pocketbook, but be careful to look at their motives realistically once in a while. You are extremely vulnerable to sob stories of all kinds. Fantasy, theater, and psychic or spiritual activities also speak to you.

Mars Moves and Shakes

Mars shows how you pursue your goals, whether you have energy to burn or proceed at a slow, steady pace. Or are you nervous, restless, unable to sit still? Mars will also show how you get angry. Will you explode, do a slow burn, or hold everything inside, then get revenge later?

To find your Mars, turn to the chart on pages 76–87. Then find your birth year in the left-hand column and trace the line across horizontally until you come to the column headed by the month of your birth. There you will find an abbreviation of your Mars sign. If the description of your Mars sign doesn't ring true, read the description of the signs preceding and following it. You may have been born on a day when Mars was changing signs, and your Mars would then be in the adjacent sign.

Mars in Aries

In the sign it rules, Mars shows its brilliant fiery nature. You have an explosive temper and can be quite impatient, but on the other hand, you possess tremen-

41

dous courage, energy, and drive. You'll let nothing stand in your way as you race to be first! Obstacles are met head-on and broken through by force. However, situations that require patience and persistence could make you explode in rage. You're a great starter, but not necessarily there at the finish.

Mars in Taurus

Slow, steady, concentrated energy gives you staying power. You've got great stamina and you never give up. Your tactic is to wear away obstacles with your persistence. Often you come out a winner because you've had the patience to hang in there. When angered, you do a slow burn.

Mars in Gemini

You can't sit still for long. This Mars craves variety. You often have two or more things going on at once. It's all an amusing game to you. Your life can get very complicated, which only adds spice and stimulation. What drives you into a nervous, hyper state? Boredom, sameness, routine, and confinement. You can do wonderful things with your hands, and you have a way with words.

Mars in Cancer

You rarely attack head-on. Instead, you'll keep things to yourself, make plans in secret, and always cover your actions. This might be interpreted by some as manipulative, but it's really your method of self-protection. You get furious when anyone knows too much about you, though you do like to know all about others. Your mothering and feeding instincts can be put to good use, if you work in food, hotel, or child-care-related businesses. You may have to overcome your fragile sense of security, which prompts you not to take risks and to get physically upset when criticized. Don't take things so personally!

Mars in Leo

You have a very dominant personality that takes center stage. Modesty is not one of your stellar traits, nor is taking a back seat, ever. You prefer giving the orders and have been known to make a dramatic scene if they are not obeyed. Properly used, this Mars confers leadership ability, endurance, and courage.

Mars in Virgo

You are the faultfinder of the zodiac, who notices every detail. Mistakes of any kind make you nervous, and you are sure you can do the job better than anyone else. You may worry, even if everything is going smoothly. Though you might not express anger directly, you sure can nag. You have definite likes and dislikes. You are certainly more industrious and detail-oriented than other signs. Your Mars energy is often most positively expressed in some kind of teaching role.

Mars in Libra

This Mars will have a passion for beauty, justice, and art. Generally, you will avoid confrontations at all costs. You prefer to spend your energy finding diplomatic solutions or weighing pros and cons. Your other techniques are passive aggression or exercising your well-known charm to get people to do what you want.

Mars in Scorpio

This is a powerful placement, so intense that it demands careful channeling into worthwhile activities. Otherwise, you could become obsessed with your sexuality or might

43

use your need for power and control to manipulate others. You are strong-willed, shrewd, and very private about your affairs, and you'll usually have a secret agenda behind your actions. Your great stamina, focus, and discipline would be excellent assets for careers in the military or medical fields, especially research or surgery. When angry, you don't get mad—you get even!

Mars in Sagittarius

This expansive Mars often propels people into sales, travel, athletics, or philosophy. Your energies function well when you are on the move. You have a hot temper and are inclined to say what you think before you consider the consequences. You shoot for high goals and talk endlessly about them, but you may be weak on groundwork. This Mars needs a solid foundation. Watch a tendency to take unnecessary risks.

Mars in Capricorn

This is an ambitious Mars with an excellent sense of timing. You have an eye for those who can be useful to you, and you may dismiss people ruthlessly when you're angry. But you drive yourself hard and deliver full value. This is a good placement for an executive. You'll aim for status and a high material position in life, and keep climbing despite the odds. A great Mars to have!

Mars in Aquarius

This is the most rebellious Mars. You seem to have a drive to assert yourself against the status quo. You may enjoy provoking people, shocking them out of traditional views. Or this placement could express itself in an offbeat sex life. Somehow you often find yourself in unconventional situations. You enjoy being a leader of an active avant-garde group, which pursues forward-looking studies, politics, or goals.

Mars in Pisces

This Mars is a good actor who knows just how to appeal to the sympathies of others. You create and project wonderful fantasies or use your sensitive antennae to crusade for those less fortunate. You get what you want through creating a veil of illusion and glamour. This is a good Mars for someone in the creative fields—a dancer, performer, or photographer—or for someone in motion pictures. Many famous film stars have this placement. Watch a tendency to manipulate by making others feel sorry for you.

Jupiter Expands

Jupiter is the planet in your horoscope that makes you want *more*. This big, bright, swirling mass of gases is associated with abundance, prosperity, and the kind of windfall you get without too much hard work. You're optimistic under Jupiter's influence, when anything seems possible. You'll travel, expand your mind with higher education, and publish to share your knowledge widely. But a strong Jupiter has its downside, too, because Jupiter's influence is neither discriminating nor disciplined. It represents the principle of growth without judgment, and could result in extravagance, weight gain, laziness, and carelessness, if not kept in check.

Be sure to look up your Jupiter in the tables in this book. When the current position of Jupiter is favorable, you may get that lucky break. This is a great time to try new things, take risks, travel, or get more education. Opportunities seem to open up easily, so take advantage of them.

Once a year, Jupiter changes signs. That means you are due for an expansive time every twelve years, when Jupiter travels through your sun sign. You'll also have "up" periods every four years, when Jupiter is in the same element as your sun sign.

Jupiter in Aries

You are the soul of enthusiasm and optimism. Your luckiest times are when you are getting started on an exciting project or selling an ideal that you really believe in. You may have to watch a tendency to be arrogant with those who do not share your enthusiasm. You follow your impulses, often ignoring budget or other commonsense limitations. To produce real, solid benefits, you'll need patience and follow-through wherever this Jupiter falls in your horoscope.

Jupiter in Taurus

You'll spend on beautiful material things, especially those that come from nature—items made of rare woods, natural fabrics, or precious gems, for instance. You can't have too much comfort or too many sensual pleasures. Watch a tendency to overindulge in good food, or to overpamper yourself with nothing but the best. Spartan living is not for you! You may be especially lucky in matters of real estate.

Jupiter in Gemini

You are the great talker of the zodiac, and you may be a great writer, too. But restlessness could be your weak point. You jump around, talk too much, and could be a jack-of-all-trades. Keeping a secret is especially difficult, so you'll also have to watch a tendency to spill the beans. Since you love to be at the center of a beehive of activity, you'll have a vibrant social life. Your best opportunities will come through your talent for language—speaking, writing, communicating, and selling.

Jupiter in Cancer

You are luckiest in situations where you can find emotional closeness or deal with basic security needs, such as food, nurturing, or shelter. You may be a great collector and you may simply love to accumulate things—you are the one who stashes things away for a rainy day. You probably have a very good memory and love children—in fact, you may have many children to care for. The food, hotel, child-care, and shipping businesses hold good opportunities for you.

Jupiter in Leo

You are a natural showman who loves to live in a larger-than-life way. Yours is a personality full of color that always finds its way into the limelight. You can't have too much attention or applause. Show biz is a natural place for you, and so is any area where you can play to a crowd. Exercising your flair for drama, your natural playfulness, and your romantic nature brings you good fortune. But watch a tendency to be overly extravagant or to monopolize center stage.

Jupiter in Virgo

You actually love those minute details others find boring. To you, they make all the difference between the perfect and the ordinary. You are the fine craftsman who spots every flaw. You expand your awareness by finding the most efficient methods and by being of service to others. Many will be drawn to medical or teaching fields. You'll also have luck in publishing, crafts, nutrition, and service professions. Watch out for a tendency to overwork.

Jupiter in Libra

This is an other-directed Jupiter that develops best with a partner, for the stimulation of others helps you grow. You are also most comfortable in harmonious, beautiful situations, and you work well with artistic people. You have a great sense of fair play and an ability to evaluate the pros and cons of a situation. You usually prefer to play the role of diplomat rather than adversary.

Jupiter in Scorpio

You love the feeling of power and control, of taking things to their limit. You can't resist a mystery, and your shrewd, penetrating mind sees right through to the heart of most situations and people. You have luck in work that provides for solutions to matters of life and death. You may be drawn to undercover work, behind-the-scenes intrigue, psychotherapy, the occult, and sex-related ventures. Your challenge will be to develop a sense of moderation and tolerance for other beliefs. This Jupiter can be fanatical. You may have luck in handling other people's money—insurance, taxes, and inheritance can bring you a windfall.

Jupiter in Sagittarius

Independent, outgoing, and idealistic, you'll shoot for the stars. This Jupiter compels you to travel far and wide, both physically and mentally, via higher education. You may have luck while traveling in an exotic place. You also have luck with outdoor ventures, exercise, and animals, particularly horses. Since you tend to be very open about your opinions, watch a tendency to be tactless and to exaggerate. Instead, use your wonderful sense of humor to make your point.

Jupiter in Capricorn

Jupiter is much more restrained in Capricorn, the sign of rules and authority. Here, Jupiter can make you overwork and heighten any ambition or sense of duty you may have. You'll expand in areas that advance your position, putting you farther up the social or corporate ladder. You are lucky working within the establishment in a very structured situation, where you can show off your ability to organize and reap rewards for your hard work.

Jupiter in Aquarius

This is another freedom-loving Jupiter, with great tolerance and originality. You are at your best when you are working for a humanitarian cause and in the company of many supporters. This is a good Jupiter for a political career. You'll relate to all kinds of people on all social levels. You have an abundance of original ideas, but you are best off away from routine and any situation that imposes rigid rules. You need mental stimulation!

Jupiter in Pisces

You are a giver whose feelings and pocketbook are easily touched by others, so choose your companions with care. You could be the original sucker for a hard-luck story. Better find a worthy hospital or charity to appreciate your selfless support. You have a great creative imagination and may attract good fortune in fields related to oil, perfume, pharmaceuticals, petroleum, dance, footwear, and alcohol. But beware of overindulgence in alcohol—focus on a creative outlet instead.

Saturn Brakes

Jupiter speeds you up with *lucky breaks,* then along comes Saturn to slow you down with the *disciplinary brakes.* Saturn has unfairly been called a malefic planet, one of the bad guys of the zodiac. On the contrary, Saturn is one of our best friends, the kind who tells you what you need to hear, even if it's not good news. Under a Saturn transit, we grow up, take responsibility for our lives, and emerge from whatever test this planet has in store, far wiser, more capable, and more mature.

When Saturn hits a critical point in your horoscope, you can count on an experience that will make you slow up, pull back, and reexamine your life. It is a call to eliminate what is not working and to shape up. By the end of its twenty-eight-year trip around the zodiac,

Saturn will have tested you in all areas of your life. The major tests happen in seven-year cycles, when Saturn passes over the *angles* of your chart—your rising sign, midheaven, descendant, and nadir. This is when the real life-changing experiences happen. But you are also in for a testing period whenever Saturn passes a *planet* in your chart or stresses that planet from a distance. Therefore, it is useful to check your planetary positions with the timetable of Saturn to prepare in advance, or at least to brace yourself.

When Saturn returns to its location at the time of your birth, at approximately age twenty-eight, you'll have your first Saturn return. At this time, a person usually takes stock or settles down to find his mission in life and assumes full adult duties and responsibilities.

Another way Saturn helps us is to reveal the karmic lessons from previous lives and give us the chance to overcome them. So look at Saturn's challenges as much-needed opportunities for self-improvement. Under a Jupiter influence, you'll have more fun, but Saturn gives you solid, long-lasting results.

Look up your natal Saturn in the tables in this book for clues on where you need work.

Saturn in Aries

Saturn here puts the brakes on Aries's natural drive and enthusiasm. You don't let anyone push you around and you know what's best for yourself. Following orders is not your strong point, and neither is diplomacy. You tend to be quick to go on the offensive in relationships, attacking first, before anyone attacks you. Because no one quite lives up to your standards, you often wind up doing everything yourself. You'll have to learn to cooperate and tone down self-centeredness.

Saturn in Taurus

A big issue is taking control of your cash flow. There will be lean periods that can be frightening, but you have the patience and endurance to stick them out and the methodical drive to prosper in the end. Learn to take a philosophical attitude like Ben Franklin, who had this placement and who said, "A penny saved is a penny earned."

Saturn in Gemini

You are a serious student of life, who may have difficulty communicating or sharing your knowledge. You may be shy, speak slowly, or have fears about communicating, like Eleanor Roosevelt. You dwell in the realms of science, theory, or abstract analysis, even when you are dealing with the emotions, like Sigmund Freud, who also had this placement.

Saturn in Cancer

Your tests come with establishing a secure emotional base. In doing so, you may have to deal with some very basic fears centering on your early home environment. Most of your Saturn tests will have emotional roots in those early childhood experiences. You may have difficulty remaining objective in terms of what you try to achieve, so it will be especially important for you to deal with negative feelings such as guilt, paranoia, jealousy, resentment, and suspicion. Galileo and Michaelangelo also navigated these murky waters.

Saturn in Leo

This is an authoritarian Saturn, a strict, demanding parent who may deny the pleasure principle in your zeal to see that rules are followed. Though you may feel guilty about taking the spotlight, you are very ambitious and loyal. You have to watch a tendency toward rigidity, also toward overwork and holding back affection. Joseph Kennedy and Billy Graham share this placement.

Saturn in Virgo

This is a cautious, exacting Saturn, intensely hard on yourself. Most of all, you give yourself the roughest time with your constant worries about every little detail, often making yourself sick. You may have difficulties setting priorities and getting the job done. Your tests will come in learning tolerance and understanding of others. Charles de Gaulle, Mae West, and Nathaniel Hawthorne had this meticulous Saturn.

Saturn in Libra

Saturn is exalted here, which makes this planet an ally. However, there are very likely to be commitment issues. You must learn to stand solidly on your own before you can have a successful relationship. You may choose very serious, older partners in life. You are extremely cautious as you deliberate every involvement—with good reason. It is best that you find an occupation that makes good use of your sense of duty and honor. Steer clear of fly-by-night situations. Both Khrushchev and Mao Tse-tung had this placement, too.

Saturn in Scorpio

You have great staying power. This Saturn tests you in situations involving control of others. You may feel drawn to some kind of intrigue or undercover work, like J. Edgar Hoover. Or there may be an air of mystery surrounding your life and death, like Marilyn Monroe and Robert Kennedy, who had this placement. There are lessons to be learned from your sexual involvements. Often sex is used for manipulation or is somehow out of the ordinary. The Roman emperor Caligula and the transvestite Christine Jorgensen are extreme cases.

Saturn in Sagittarius

Your challenges and lessons will come from tests of your spiritual and philosophical values, as happened to Martin Luther King and Gandhi. You are high-minded and sincere with this reflective, moral placement. Uncompromising in your ethical standards, you could become a benevolent despot.

Saturn in Capricorn

With the help of Saturn at maximum strength, your judgment will improve with age. And like Spencer Tracy's screen image, you'll be the gray-haired hero with a strong sense of responsibility. You advance in life slowly but steadily, always with a strong hand at the helm and an eye for the advantageous situation. Like Pat Robertson, you're likely to stand for conservative values. Negatively, you may be a loner, prone to periods of melancholy.

Saturn in Aquarius

Your tests come from relationships with groups. Do you care too much about what others think? Do you feel like an outsider, as Greta Garbo did? You may fear being different from others and therefore demean your own unique, forward-looking gifts, or like Lord Byron and Howard Hughes, take the opposite tack and rebel in the extreme. However, others with this placement have been able to apply discipline to accomplish great humanitarian goals, as Albert Schweitzer did.

Saturn in Pisces

Your fear of the unknown and the irrational may lead you to the safety and protection of an institution. You may go on the run like Jesse James, who had this placement, to avoid looking too deeply inside. Or you might go in the opposite, more positive direction and develop a disciplined psychoanalytic approach, which puts you more in control of your feelings. Some of you will take refuge in work with hospitals, charities, or religious institutions. Queen Victoria, who had this placement, symbolized an era when institutions of all kinds were sustained. Discipline applied to artistic work, especially poetry and dance, or spiritual work, such as yoga or meditation, might be helpful.

Uranus, Neptune, and Pluto Affect Your Whole Generation

These three planets remain in signs such a long time that a whole generation bears the imprint of the sign. Mass movements, great sweeping changes, fads that characterize a generation, even the issues of the conflicts and wars of the time are influenced by the "outer three." When one of these distant planets changes signs, there is a definite shift in the atmosphere, the feeling of the end of an era.

Since these planets are so far away from the sun—too distant to be seen by the naked eye—they pick up signals from the universe at large. These planetary receivers literally link the sun with distant energies, and then perform a similar function in your horoscope by linking your central character with intuitive, spiritual, transformative forces from the cosmos. Each planet has a special domain and will reflect this in the area of your chart where it falls.

Uranus Wakes You Up

There is nothing ordinary about this quirky green planet that seems to be traveling on its side, surrounded by a swarm of moons. Is it any wonder that astrologers assigned it to Aquarius, the most eccentric and gregarious sign? Uranus seems to wend its way around the sun, marching to its own tune.

Uranus's energy is electrical, happening in sudden flashes. It is not influenced by karma or past events, nor does it regard tradition, sex, or sentiment. The Uranian key words are "surprise" and "awakening." Uranus wakes you up, jolts you out of your comfortable rut. Suddenly, there's that flash of inspiration, that bright idea, a totally new approach that revolutionizes whatever you're doing. A Uranus event takes you by surprise, happens from out of the blue, for better or for worse. The Uranus place in your life is where you wake up to your own special qualities and become your own person, leaving the structures of Saturn behind.

Look up the sign of Uranus at the time of your birth. Then place it in the appropriate house in your chart and see where you follow your own tune.

Uranus in Aries

BIRTH DATES:
   March 31, 1927–November 4, 1927
   January 13, 1928—June 6, 1934
   October 10, 1934—March 28, 1935

Your generation is original, creative, pioneering. It developed the computer, the airplane, and the cyclotron. You let nothing hold you back from exploring the unknown and have a powerful mixture of fire and electricity behind you. Women of your generation were among the first to be liberated. You were the unforgettable style setters. You have a surprise in store for everyone. Like Yoko Ono, Grace Kelly, and Jacqueline Onassis, your life may be jolted by sudden and violent changes.

Uranus in Taurus

BIRTH DATES:
   June 6, 1934–October 10, 1934
   March 28, 1935–August 7, 1941
   October 5, 1941–May 15, 1942

World War II began during your generation. You are probably self-employed or would like to be. You have original ideas about making money, and you brace yourself for sudden changes of fortune. This Uranus can cause shakeups, particularly in finances, but it can also make you a born entrepreneur.

Uranus in Gemini

BIRTH DATES:
   August 7, 1941–October 5, 1941
   May 15, 1942–August 30, 1948
   November 12, 1948–June 10, 1949

You were the first children to be influenced by television. Now, in your adult years, your generation stocks up on answering machines, cordless phones, car phones, computers, and fax machines—any new way you can communicate. You have an inquiring mind, but your interests may be rather short-lived. This Uranus can be easily fragmented if there is no structure and focus.

Uranus in Cancer

BIRTH DATES:
   August 30, 1948–November 12, 1948
   June 10, 1949–August 24, 1955
   January 28, 1956–June 10, 1956

This generation came at a time when divorce was becoming commonplace, so your home image is unconventional. You may have an unusual relationship with your parents; you may have come from a broken home or an unconventional one. You'll have unorthodox ideas about parenting, intimacy, food, and shelter. You may also be interested in dreams, psychic phenomena, and memory work.

Uranus in Leo

BIRTH DATES:
August 24, 1955–January 28, 1956
June 10, 1956–November 1, 1961
January 10, 1962–August 10, 1962

This generation understands how to use electronic media. Many of your group are now leaders in the high-tech industries, and you also understand how to use the new media to promote yourself. Like Isadora Duncan, you may have a very eccentric kind of charisma and a life that is sparked by unusual love affairs. Your children, too, may have traits that are out of the ordinary. Where this planet falls in your chart, you'll have a love of freedom, be a bit of an egomaniac, and show the full force of your personality in a unique way, like tennis great Martina Navratilova.

Uranus in Virgo

BIRTH DATES:
November 1, 1961–January 10, 1962
August 10, 1962–September 28, 1968
May 20, 1969–June 24, 1969

You'll have highly individual work methods, and many will be finding newer, more practical ways to use computers. Like Einstein, who had this placement, you'll break the rules brilliantly. Your generation came at a time of student rebellions, the civil rights movement, and the general acceptance of health foods. Chances are, you're concerned about pollution and cleaning up the environment. You may also be involved with nontraditional healing methods. Heavyweight champ Mike Tyson has this placement.

Uranus in Libra

BIRTH DATES:
  September 28, 1968–May 20, 1969
  June 24, 1969–November 21, 1974
  May 1, 1975–September 8, 1975

Your generation will be always changing partners. Born during the era of women's liberation, you may have come from a broken home and have no clear image of what a marriage entails. There will be many sudden splits and experiments before you settle down. Your generation will be much involved in legal and political reforms and in changing artistic and fashion looks.

Uranus in Scorpio

BIRTH DATES:
  November 21, 1974–May 1, 1975
  September 8, 1975–February 17, 1981
  March 20, 1981–November 16, 1981

Interest in transformation, meditation, and life after death signaled the beginning of New Age consciousness. Your generation recognizes no boundaries, no limits, and no external controls. You'll have new attitudes toward death and dying, psychic phenomena, and the occult. Like Mae West and Casanova, you'll shock 'em sexually, too.

Uranus in Sagittarius

BIRTH DATES:
  February 17, 1981–March 20, 1981
  November 16, 1981–February 15, 1988
  May 27, 1988–December 2, 1988

Could this generation be the first to travel in outer space? An earlier generation with this placement included Charles Lindbergh—at that time, the first Zeppelins and the Wright Brothers were conquering the skies. Uranus here forecasts great discoveries, mind expansion, and long-distance travel. Like Galileo and Martin Luther, this generation will formulate new theories about the cosmos and man's relation to it.

Uranus in Capricorn

BIRTH DATES:
  December 20, 1904–January 30, 1912
  September 4, 1912–November 12, 1912
  February 15, 1988–May 27, 1988
  December 2, 1988–April 1, 1995
  June 9, 1995–January 12, 1996

This generation will challenge traditions with the help of electronic gadgets. During the mid-1990s, we got organized with the help of technology put to practical use. Home computers and handheld devices became widely used. Great leaders, who were movers and shakers of history, like Julius Caesar and Henry VIII, were born under this placement.

Uranus in Aquarius

BIRTH DATES:
  January 30, 1912–September 4, 1912
  November 12, 1912–April 1, 1919
  August 16, 1919–January 22, 1920
  April 1, 1995–June 9, 1995
  January 12, 1996–March 10, 2003

The last generation with this placement produced great innovative minds such as Leonard Bernstein and Orson Welles. Babies who are born now will become another radical breakthrough generation, much concerned with global issues that involve all humanity. Intuition, innovation, and sudden changes will continue to surprise everyone while Uranus is in its home sign.

Uranus in Pisces

BIRTH DATES:
  April 1, 1919–August 16, 1919
  January 22, 1920–March 31, 1927
  November 4, 1927–January 12, 1928
  March 10, 2003–May 28, 2010

Uranus in Pisces previously focused attention on the rise of electronic entertainment—radio and the cinema—and the secretiveness of Prohibition. This produced a generation of idealists exemplified by Judy Garland's theme, "Somewhere Over the Rainbow." Coming up next year will be the dramatic return of Uranus to Pisces, which should spark a wonderful spurt of creativity and innovation in the arts.

Neptune Takes You out of This World

Under Neptune's influence, you see what you want to see. But Neptune also encourages you to create, letting your fantasies and daydreams run free. Neptune is often maligned as the planet of illusions, drugs, and alcohol, where you can't bear to face reality. But it also embodies the energy of glamour, subtlety, mystery, and mysticism, and governs anything that takes you beyond the mundane world, including out-of-body experiences.

Neptune acts to break through your ordinary perceptions and take you to another level of reality, where you experience either confusion or ecstasy. Neptune's force can pull you off-course, the way this planet affects its neighbor, Uranus, but only if you allow this to happen. Those who use Neptune wisely can translate their daydreams into poetry, theater, design, or inspired moves in the business world, avoiding the tricky "con artist" side of this planet.

Find your Neptune listed below:

Neptune in Cancer

BIRTH DATES:
  July 19, 1901–December 25, 1901
  May 21, 1902–September 23, 1914
  December 14, 1914–July 19, 1915
  March 1916–May 2, 1916

Dreams of the homeland, idealistic patriotism, and glamorization of the nurturing assets of women characterized this time. You who were born here have unusual psychic ability and deep insights into the basic needs of others.

Neptune in Leo

BIRTH DATES:
  September 23, 1914–December 14, 1914
  July 19, 1915–March 19, 1916
  May 2, 1916–September 21, 1928
  February 19, 1929–July 24, 1929

Neptune here brought us the glamour and high living of the 1920s and the big spenders of that time. The Neptunian temptations of gambling, seduction, theater, and lavish entertaining distracted us from the realities of the age. Those born in this generation also made great advances in the arts.

Neptune in Virgo

BIRTH DATES:
September 21, 1928–February 19, 1929
July 24, 1929–October 3, 1942
April 17, 1943–August 2, 1943

Neptune in Virgo encompassed the Great Depression and World War II, while those born at this time later spread the gospel of health and fitness. This generation's devotion to spending hours at the office inspired the term "workaholic."

Neptune in Libra

BIRTH DATES:
October 3, 1942–April 17, 1943
August 2, 1943–December 24, 1955
March 12, 1956–October 19, 1956
June 15, 1957–August 6, 1957

Neptune in Libra produced the romantic generation who would later be extremely concerned with relating. As this generation matured, there was a new trend toward marriage and commitment. Racial and sexual equality become important issues, as they redesigned traditional relationship roles to suit modern times.

Neptune in Scorpio

BIRTH DATES:
December 24, 1955–March 12, 1956
October 19, 1956–June 15, 1957
August 6, 1957–January 4, 1970
May 3, 1970–November 6, 1970

Neptune in Scorpio ushered in a generation that would become interested in transformative power. Born in an

era that glamorized sex, drugs, rock and roll, and Eastern religion, they matured in a more sobering time of
AIDS, cocaine abuse, and New Age spirituality. As they
evolve, they will become active in healing the planet
from the results of the abuse of power.

Neptune in Sagittarius

BIRTH DATES:
   January 4, 1970–May 3, 1970
   November 6, 1970–January 19, 1984
   June 23, 1984–November 21, 1984

Neptune in Sagittarius was the time when space and astro-
naut travel became a reality. The Neptune influence glamorized new approaches to mysticism, religion, and mind
expansion. This generation will take a new approach to
spiritual life, with emphasis on visions, mysticism, and
clairvoyance.

Neptune in Capricorn

BIRTH DATES:
   January 19, 1984–June 23, 1984
   November 21, 1984–January 29, 1998

Neptune in Capricorn brought a time when delusions
about material power were first glamorized, then
dashed on the rocks of reality. It was also a time when
the psychic and occult worlds spawned a new category
of business enterprise, and sold services on television.

Neptune in Aquarius

BIRTH DATES:
   January 29, 1998–April 4, 2111

This should continue to be a time of breakthroughs, when
the creative influence of Neptune reaches a universal audi-

ence. This is a time of dissolving barriers, of globalization, when we truly become one world. Computer technology used for the creative arts, innovative drug therapies, and high-tech "highs" such as trance music are recent manifestations.

Pluto Transforms You

Pluto is a mysterious little planet with a strange elliptical orbit that occasionally runs inside the orbit of its neighbor Neptune. Because of its eccentric path, the length of time Pluto stays in any given sign can vary from thirteen to thirty-two years. It has covered only seven signs in the past century. Though it is a tiny planet, its influence is great. When Pluto zaps a strategic point in your horoscope, your life changes dramatically.

This little planet is the power behind the scenes; it affects you at deep levels of consciousness, causing events to come to the surface that will transform you and your generation. Nothing escapes, or is sacred, with this probing planet. The Pluto place in your horoscope is where you have invisible power (Mars governs the visible power), where you can transform, heal, and affect the unconscious needs of the masses. Pluto tells how your generation projects power, what makes it seem "cool" to others. And when Pluto changes signs, there's a whole new concept of what's cool.

Pluto in Gemini

BIRTH DATES:
Late 1800s–May 26, 1914

This was a time of mass suggestion and breakthroughs in communications, when many brilliant writers, such as Ernest Hemingway and F. Scott Fitzgerald, were born. Henry Miller, D. H. Lawrence, and James Joyce scandalized society by using explicit sexual images and language in their literature. "Muckraking" journalists exposed corruption. Pluto-ruled Scorpio President Theodore Roosevelt said, "Speak softly, but carry a big stick." This generation had an intense need to communicate and made major breakthroughs in knowledge. A compulsive restlessness and a thirst for a variety of experiences characterizes many of this generation.

Pluto in Cancer

BIRTH DATES:
  May 26, 1914–June 14, 1939

Dictators and mass media rose up to wield emotional power over the masses. Women's rights was a popular issue. Deep sentimental feelings, acquisitiveness, and possessiveness characterized these times and people. The great Hollywood stars who embodied the American image were born during this period: Grace Kelly, Esther Williams, Frank Sinatra, Lana Turner, etc.

Pluto in Leo

BIRTH DATES:
  June 14, 1939–August 19, 1957

The performing arts played on the emotions of the masses. Mick Jagger, John Lennon, and rock and roll were born at this time. So were "baby boomers" like Bill and Hillary Clinton. Those born here tend to be self-centered, powerful, and boisterous. This generation does its own thing, for better or for worse.

Pluto in Virgo

BIRTH DATES:
  August 19, 1957–October 5, 1971
  April 17, 1972–July 30, 1972

This is the "yuppie" generation that sparked a mass movement toward fitness, health, and career. A much more sober, serious, driven generation than the fun-loving Pluto in Leos. During this time, machines were invented to process detail work efficiently. Inventions took a practical turn, as answering machines, fax machines, car phones, and home office equipment contributed to transform the workplace.

Pluto in Libra

BIRTH DATES:
    October 5, 1971–April 17, 1972
    July 30, 1972–August 28, 1984

A mellower generation concerned with partnerships, working together, and finding diplomatic solutions to problems. Marriage is important to this generation, who will redefine it, combining traditional values with equal partnership. This was a time of women's liberation, gay rights, ERA, and legal battles over abortion, all of which transformed our ideas about relationships.

Pluto in Scorpio

BIRTH DATES:
    August 28, 1984–January 17, 1995

Pluto was in its ruling sign for a comparatively short period of time. In 1989, it was at its perihelion, or closest point to the sun and Earth. We have all felt the transforming power somewhere in our lives. This was a time of record achievements, destructive sexually transmitted diseases, nuclear power controversies, and explosive political issues. Pluto destroys in order to create new understanding—the phoenix rising from the ashes, which should be some consolation for those of you who felt Pluto's force before 1995. Sexual shockers were par for the course during these intense years, when black clothing, transvestites, body piercing, tattoos, and sexually explicit advertising pushed the boundaries of good taste.

Pluto in Sagittarius

BIRTH DATES:
January 17, 1995–January 27, 2008

During our current Pluto transit, we are being pushed to expand our horizons. For many of us, this will mean rolling down the information superhighway into the future. Another trend is to find deeper spiritual meaning in life. This is a time when spiritual emphasis will become pervasive, when religious convictions will exert more power in our political life as well.

Since Sagittarius is the sign that rules travel, there's a good possibility that Pluto, the planet of extremes, will make space travel a reality for some of us. Discovery of life on Mars, which traveled here on meteors, could transform our ideas about where we came from.

New dimensions in electronic publishing, concern with animal rights and the environment, and an increasing emphasis on extreme forms of religion are other signs of these times. Look for charismatic religious leaders to arise now. We'll also be developing far-reaching philosophies designed to elevate our lives with a new sense of purpose.

VENUS SIGNS 1901–2002

	Aries	Taurus	Gemini	Cancer	Leo	Virgo
1901	3/29–4/22	4/22–5/17	5/17–6/10	6/10–7/5	7/5–7/29	7/29–8/23
1902	5/7–6/3	6/3–6/30	6/30–7/25	7/25–8/19	8/19–9/13	9/13–10/7
1903	2/28–3/24	3/24–4/18	4/18–5/13	5/13–6/9	6/9–7/7	7/7–8/17
						9/6–11/8
1904	3/13–5/7	5/7–6/1	6/1–6/25	6/25–7/19	7/19–8/13	8/13–9/6
1905	2/3–3/6	3/6–4/9	7/8–8/6	8/6–9/1	9/1–9/27	9/27–10/21
	4/9–5/28	5/28–7/8				
1906	3/1–4/7	4/7–5/2	5/2–5/26	5/26–6/20	6/20–7/16	7/16–8/11
1907	4/27–5/22	5/22–6/16	6/16–7/11	7/11–8/4	8/4–8/29	8/29–9/22
1908	2/14–3/10	3/10–4/5	4/5–5/5	5/5–9/8	9/8–10/8	10/8–11/3
1909	3/29–4/22	4/22–5/16	5/16–6/10	6/10–7/4	7/4–7/29	7/29–8/23
1910	5/7–6/3	6/4–6/29	6/30–7/24	7/25–8/18	8/19–9/12	9/13–10/6
1911	2/28–3/23	3/24–4/17	4/18–5/12	5/13–6/8	6/9–7/7	7/8–11/8
1912	4/13–5/6	5/7–5/31	6/1–6/24	6/24–7/18	7/19–8/12	8/13–9/5
1913	2/3–3/6	3/7–5/1	7/8–8/5	8/6–8/31	9/1–9/26	9/27–10/20
	5/2–5/30	5/31–7/7				
1914	3/14–4/6	4/7–5/1	5/2–5/25	5/26–6/19	6/20–7/15	7/16–8/10
1915	4/27–5/21	5/22–6/15	6/16–7/10	7/11–8/3	8/4–8/28	8/29–9/21
1916	2/14–3/9	3/10–4/5	4/6–5/5	5/6–9/8	9/9–10/7	10/8–11/2
1917	3/29–4/21	4/22–5/15	5/16–6/9	6/10–7/3	7/4–7/28	7/29–8/21
1918	5/7–6/2	6/3–6/28	6/29–7/24	7/25–8/18	8/19–9/11	9/12–10/5
1919	2/27–3/22	3/23–4/16	4/17–5/12	5/13–6/7	6/8–7/7	7/8–11/8
1920	4/12–5/6	5/7–5/30	5/31–6/23	6/24–7/18	7/19–8/11	8/12–9/4
1921	2/3–3/6	3/7–4/25	7/8–8/5	8/6–8/31	9/1–9/25	9/26–10/20
	4/26–6/1	6/2–7/7				
1922	3/13–4/6	4/7–4/30	5/1–5/25	5/26–6/19	6/20–7/14	7/15–8/9
1923	4/27–5/21	5/22–6/14	6/15–7/9	7/10–8/3	8/4–8/27	8/28–9/20
1924	2/13–3/8	3/9–4/4	4/5–5/5	5/6–9/8	9/9–10/7	10/8–11/12
1925	3/28–4/20	4/21–5/15	5/16–6/8	6/9–7/3	7/4–7/27	7/28–8/21

Libra	Scorpio	Sagittarius	Capricorn	Aquarius	Pisces
8/23–9/17	9/17–10/12	10/12–1/16	1/16–2/9	2/9–3/5	3/5–3/29
			11/7–12/5	12/5–1/11	
10/7–10/31	10/31–11/24	11/24–12/18	12/18–1/11	2/6–4/4	1/11–2/6
					4/4–5/7
8/17–9/6	12/9–1/5			1/11–2/4	2/4–2/28
11/8–12/9					
9/6–9/30	9/30–10/25	1/5–1/30	1/30–2/24	2/24–3/19	3/19–4/13
		10/25–11/18	11/18–12/13	12/13–1/7	
10/21–11/14	11/14–12/8	12/8–1/1/06			1/7–2/3
8/11–9/7	9/7–10/9	10/9–12/15	1/1–1/25	1/25–2/18	2/18–3/14
	12/15–12/25	12/25–2/6			
9/22–10/16	10/16–11/9	11/9–12/3	2/6–3/6	3/6–4/2	4/2–4/27
			12/3–12/27	12/27–1/20	
11/3–11/28	11/28–12/22	12/22–1/15			1/20–2/4
8/23–9/17	9/17–10/12	10/12–11/17	1/15–2/9	2/9–3/5	3/5–3/29
			11/17–12/5	12/5–1/15	
10/7–10/30	10/31–11/23	11/24–12/17	12/18–12/31	1/1–1/15	1/16–1/28
				1/29–4/4	4/5–5/6
11/19–12/8	12/9–12/31		1/1–1/10	1/11–2/2	2/3–2/27
9/6–9/30	1/1–1/4	1/5–1/29	1/30–2/23	2/24–3/18	3/19–4/12
	10/1–10/24	10/25–11/17	11/18–12/12	12/13–12/31	
10/21–11/13	11/14–12/7	12/8–12/31		1/1–1/6	1/7–2/2
8/11–9/6	9/7–10/9	10/10–12/5	1/1–1/24	1/25–2/17	2/18–3/13
	12/6–12/30	12/31			
9/22–10/15	10/16–11/8	1/1–2/6	2/7–3/6	3/7–4/1	4/2–4/26
		11/9–12/2	12/3–12/26	12/27–12/31	
11/3–11/27	11/28–12/21	12/22–12/31		1/1–1/19	1/20–2/13
8/22–9/16	9/17–10/11	1/1–1/14	1/15–2/7	2/8–3/4	3/5–3/28
		10/12–11/6	11/7–12/5	12/6–12/31	
10/6–10/29	10/30–11/22	11/23–12/16	12/17–12/31	1/1–4/5	4/6–5/6
11/9–12/8	12/9–12/30		1/1–1/9	1/10–2/2	2/3–2/26
9/5–9/30	1/1–1/3	1/4–1/28	1/29–2/22	2/23–3/18	3/19–4/11
	9/31–10/23	10/24–11/17	11/18–12/11	12/12–12/31	
10/21–11/13	11/14–12/7	12/8–12/31		1/1–1/6	1/7–2/2
8/10–9/6	9/7–10/10	10/11–11/28	1/1–1/24	1/25–2/16	2/17–3/12
	11/29–12/31				
9/21–10/14	1/1	1/2–2/6	2/7–3/5	3/6–3/31	4/1–4/26
	10/15–11/7	11/8–12/1	12/2–12/25	12/26–12/31	
11/13–11/26	11/27–12/21	12/22–12/31		1/1–1/19	1/20–2/12
8/22–9/15	9/16–10/11	1/1–1/14	1/15–2/7	2/8–3/3	3/4–3/27
		10/12–11/6	11/7–12/5	12/6–12/31	

	Aries	Taurus	Gemini	Cancer	Leo	Virgo
1926	5/7–6/2	6/3–6/28	6/29–7/23	7/24–8/17	8/18–9/11	9/12–10/5
1927	2/27–3/22	3/23–4/16	4/17–5/11	5/12–6/7	6/8–7/7	7/8–11/9
1928	4/12–5/5	5/6–5/29	5/30–6/23	6/24–7/17	7/18–8/11	8/12–9/4
1929	2/3–3/7	3/8–4/19	7/8–8/4	8/5–8/30	8/31–9/25	9/26–10/19
	4/20–6/2	6/3–7/7				
1930	3/13–4/5	4/6–4/30	5/1–5/24	5/25–6/18	6/19–7/14	7/15–8/9
1931	4/26–5/20	5/21–6/13	6/14–7/8	7/9–8/2	8/3–8/26	8/27–9/19
1932	2/12–3/8	3/9–4/3	4/4–5/5	5/6–7/12	9/9–10/6	10/7–11/1
			7/13–7/27	7/28–9/8		
1933	3/27–4/19	4/20–5/28	5/29–6/8	6/9–7/2	7/3–7/26	7/27–8/20
1934	5/6–6/1	6/2–6/27	6/28–7/22	7/23–8/16	8/17–9/10	9/11–10/4
1935	2/26–3/21	3/22–4/15	4/16–5/10	5/11–6/6	6/7–7/6	7/7–11/8
1936	4/11–5/4	5/5–5/28	5/29–6/22	6/23–7/16	7/17–8/10	8/11–9/4
1937	2/2–3/8	3/9–4/13	7/7–8/3	8/4–8/29	8/30–9/24	9/25–10/18
	4/14–6/3	6/4–7/6				
1938	3/12–4/4	4/5–4/28	4/29–5/23	5/24–6/18	6/19–7/13	7/14–8/8
1939	4/25–5/19	5/20–6/13	6/14–7/8	7/9–8/1	8/2–8/25	8/26–9/19
1940	2/12–3/7	3/8–4/3	4/4–5/5	5/6–7/4	9/9–10/5	10/6–10/31
			7/5–7/31	8/1–9/8		
1941	3/27–4/19	4/20–5/13	5/14–6/6	6/7–7/1	7/2–7/26	7/27–8/20
1942	5/6–6/1	6/2–6/26	6/27–7/22	7/23–8/16	8/17–9/9	9/10–10/3
1943	2/25–3/20	3/21–4/14	4/15–5/10	5/11–6/6	6/7–7/6	7/7–11/8
1944	4/10–5/3	5/4–5/28	5/29–6/21	6/22–7/16	7/17–8/9	8/10–9/2
1945	2/2–3/10	3/11–4/6	7/7–8/3	8/4–8/29	8/30–9/23	9/24–10/18
	4/7–6/3	6/4–7/6				
1946	3/11–4/4	4/5–4/28	4/29–5/23	5/24–6/17	6/18–7/12	7/13–8/8
1947	4/25–5/19	5/20–6/12	6/13–7/7	7/8–8/1	8/2–8/25	8/26–9/18
1948	2/11–3/7	3/8–4/3	4/4–5/6	5/7–6/28	9/8–10/5	10/6–10/31
			6/29–8/2	8/3–9/7		
1949	3/26–4/19	4/20–5/13	5/14–6/6	6/7–6/30	7/1–7/25	7/26–8/19
1950	5/5–5/31	6/1–6/26	6/27–7/21	7/22–8/15	8/16–9/9	9/10–10/3
1951	2/25–3/21	3/22–4/15	4/16–5/10	5/11–6/6	6/7–7/7	7/8–11/9

Libra	Scorpio	Sagittarius	Capricorn	Aquarius	Pisces
10/6–10/29	10/30–11/22	11/23–12/16	12/17–12/31	1/1–4/5	4/6–5/6
11/10–12/8	12/9–12/31	1/1–1/7	1/8	1/9–2/1	2/2–2/26
9/5–9/28	1/1–1/3	1/4–1/28	1/29–2/22	2/23–3/17	3/18–4/11
	9/29–10/23	10/24–11/16	11/17–12/11	12/12–12/31	
10/20–11/12	11/13–12/6	12/7–12/30	12/31	1/1–1/5	1/6–2/2
8/10–9/6	9/7–10/11	10/12–11/21	1/1–1/23	1/24–2/16	2/17–3/12
	11/22–12/31				
9/20–10/13	1/1–1/3	1/4–2/6	2/7–3/4	3/5–3/31	4/1–4/25
	10/14–11/6	11/7–11/30	12/1–12/24	12/25–12/31	
11/2–11/25	11/26–12/20	12/21–12/31		1/1–1/18	1/19–2/11
8/21–9/14	9/15–10/10	1/1–1/13	1/14–2/6	2/7–3/2	3/3–3/26
		10/11–11/5	11/6–12/4	12/5–12/31	
10/5–10/28	10/29–11/21	11/22–12/15	12/16–12/31	1/1–4/5	4/6–5/5
11/9–12/7	12/8–12/31		1/1–1/7	1/8–1/31	2/1–2/25
9/5–9/27	1/1–1/2	1/3–1/27	1/28–2/21	2/22–3/16	3/17–4/10
	9/28–10/22	10/23–11/15	11/16–12/10	12/11–12/31	
10/19–11/11	11/12–12/5	12/6–12/29	12/30–12/31	1/1–1/5	1/6–2/1
8/9–9/6	9/7–10/13	10/14–11/14	1/1–1/22	1/23–2/15	2/16–3/11
	11/15–12/31				
9/20–10/13	1/1–1/3	1/4–2/5	2/6–3/4	3/5–3/30	3/31–4/24
	10/14–11/6	11/7–11/30	12/1–12/24	12/25–12/31	
11/1–11/25	11/26–12/19	12/20–12/31		1/1–1/18	1/19–2/11
8/21–9/14	9/15–10/9	1/1–1/12	1/13–2/5	2/6–3/1	3/2–3/26
		10/10–11/5	11/6–12/4	12/5–12/31	
10/4–10/27	10/28–11/20	11/21–12/14	12/15–12/31	1/1–4/4	4/6–5/5
11/9–12/7	12/8–12/31		1/1–1/7	1/8–1/31	2/1–2/24
9/3–9/27	1/1–1/2	1/3–1/27	1/28–2/20	2/21–3/16	3/17–4/9
	9/28–10/21	10/22–11/15	11/16–12/10	12/11–12/31	
10/19–11/11	11/12–12/5	12/6–12/29	12/30–12/31	1/1–1/4	1/5–2/1
8/9–9/6	9/7–10/15	10/16–11/7	1/1–1/21	1/22–2/14	2/15–3/10
	11/8–12/31				
9/19–10/12	1/1–1/4	1/5–2/5	2/6–3/4	3/5–3/29	3/30–4/24
	10/13–11/5	11/6–11/29	11/30–12/23	12/24–12/31	
11/1–11/25	11/26–12/19	12/20–12/31		1/1–1/17	1/18–2/10
8/20–9/14	9/15–10/9	1/1–1/12	1/13–2/5	2/6–3/1	3/2–3/25
		10/10–11/5	11/6–12/5	12/6–12/31	
10/4–10/27	10/28–11/20	11/21–12/13	12/14–12/31	1/1–4/5	4/6–5/4
11/10–12/7	12/8–12/31		1/1–1/7	1/8–1/31	2/1–2/24

	Aries	Taurus	Gemini	Cancer	Leo	Virgo
1952	4/10–5/4	5/5–5/28	5/29–6/21	6/22–7/16	7/17–8/9	8/10–9/3
1953	2/2–3/3	3/4–3/31	7/8–8/3	8/4–8/29	8/30–9/24	9/25–10/18
	4/1–6/5	6/6–7/7				
1954	3/12–4/4	4/5–4/28	4/29–5/23	5/24–6/17	6/18–7/13	7/14–8/8
1955	4/25–5/19	5/20–6/13	6/14–7/7	7/8–8/1	8/2–8/25	8/26–9/18
1956	2/12–3/7	3/8–4/4	4/5–5/7	5/8–6/23	9/9–10/5	10/6–10/31
			6/24–8/4	8/5–9/8		
1957	3/26–4/19	4/20–5/13	5/14–6/6	6/7–7/1	7/2–7/26	7/27–8/19
1958	5/6–5/31	6/1–6/26	6/27–7/22	7/23–8/15	8/16–9/9	9/10–10/3
1959	2/25–3/20	3/21–4/14	4/15–5/10	5/11–6/6	6/7–7/8	7/9–9/20
					9/21–9/24	9/25–11/9
1960	4/10–5/3	5/4–5/28	5/29–6/21	6/22–7/15	7/16–8/9	8/10–9/2
1961	2/3–6/5	6/6–7/7	7/8–8/3	8/4–8/29	8/30–9/23	9/24–10/17
1962	3/11–4/3	4/4–4/28	4/29–5/22	5/23–6/17	6/18–7/12	7/13–8/8
1963	4/24–5/18	5/19–6/12	6/13–7/7	7/8–7/31	8/1–8/25	8/26–9/18
1964	2/11–3/7	3/8–4/4	4/5–5/9	5/10–6/17	9/9–10/5	10/6–10/31
			6/18–8/5	8/6–9/8		
1965	3/26–4/18	4/19–5/12	5/13–6/6	6/7–6/30	7/1–7/25	7/26–8/19
1966	5/6–6/31	6/1–6/26	6/27–7/21	7/22–8/15	8/16–9/8	9/9–10/2
1967	2/24–3/20	3/21–4/14	4/15–5/10	5/11–6/6	6/7–7/8	7/9–9/9
					9/10–10/1	10/2–11/9
1968	4/9–5/3	5/4–5/27	5/28–6/20	6/21–7/15	7/16–8/8	8/9–9/2
1969	2/3–6/6	6/7–7/6	7/7–8/3	8/4–8/28	8/29–9/22	9/23–10/17
1970	3/11–4/3	4/4–4/27	4/28–5/22	5/23–6/16	6/17–7/12	7/13–8/8
1971	4/24–5/18	5/19–6/12	6/13–7/6	7/7–7/31	8/1–8/24	8/25–9/17
1972	2/11–3/7	3/8–4/3	4/4–5/10	5/11–6/11		
			6/12–8/6	8/7–9/8	9/9–10/5	10/6–10/30
1973	3/25–4/18	4/18–5/12	5/13–6/5	6/6–6/29	7/1–7/25	7/26–8/19
1974						
	5/5–5/31	6/1–6/25	6/26–7/21	7/22–8/14	8/15–9/8	9/9–10/2
1975	2/24–3/20	3/21–4/13	4/14–5/9	5/10–6/6	6/7–7/9	7/10–9/2
					9/3–10/4	10/5–11/9

Libra	Scorpio	Sagittarius	Capricorn	Aquarius	Pisces
9/4–9/27	1/1–1/2	1/3–1/27	1/28–2/20	2/21–3/16	3/17–4/9
	9/28–10/21	10/22–11/15	11/16–12/10	12/11–12/31	
10/19–11/11	11/12–12/5	12/6–12/29	12/30–12/31	1/1–1/5	1/6–2/1
8/9–9/6	9/7–10/22	10/23–10/27	1/1–1/22	1/23–2/15	2/16–3/11
	10/28–12/31				
9/19–10/13	1/1–1/6	1/7–2/5	2/6–3/4	3/5–3/30	3/31–4/24
	10/14–11/5	11/6–11/30	12/1–12/24	12/25–12/31	
11/1–11/25	11/26–12/19	12/20–12/31		1/1–1/17	1/18–2/11
8/20–9/14	9/15–10/9	1/1–1/12	1/13–2/5	2/6–3/1	3/2–3/25
		10/10–11/5	11/6–12/6	12/7–12/31	
10/4–10/27	10/28–11/20	11/21–12/14	12/15–12/31	1/1–4/6	4/7–5/5
11/10–12/7	12/8–12/31		1/1–1/7	1/8–1/31	2/1–2/24
9/3–9/26	1/1–1/2	1/3–1/27	1/28–2/20	2/21–3/15	3/16–4/9
	9/27–10/21	10/22–11/15	11/16–12/10	12/11–12/31	
10/18–11/11	11/12–12/4	12/5–12/28	12/29–12/31	1/1–1/5	1/6–2/2
8/9–9/6	9/7–12/31		1/1–1/21	1/22–2/14	2/15–3/10
9/19–10/12	1/1–1/6	1/7–2/5	2/6–3/4	3/5–3/29	3/30–4/23
	10/13–11/5	11/6–11/29	11/30–12/23	12/24–12/31	
11/1–11/24	11/25–12/19	12/20–12/31		1/1–1/16	1/17–2/10
8/20–9/13	9/14–10/9	1/1–1/12	1/13–2/5	2/6–3/1	3/2–3/25
		10/10–11/5	11/6–12/7	12/8–12/31	
10/3–10/26	10/27–11/19	11/20–12/13	2/7–2/25	1/1–2/6	4/7–5/5
			12/14–12/31	2/26–4/6	
11/10–12/7	12/8–12/31		1/1–1/6	1/7–1/30	1/31–2/23
9/3–9/26	1/1	1/2–1/26	1/27–2/20	2/21–3/15	3/16–4/8
	9/27–10/21	10/22–11/14	11/15–12/9	12/10–12/31	
10/18–11/10	11/11–12/4	12/5–12/28	12/29–12/31	1/1–1/4	1/5–2/2
8/9–9/7	9/8–12/31		1/1–1/21	1/22–2/14	2/15–3/10
9/18–10/11	1/1–1/7	1/8–2/5	2/6–3/4	3/5–3/29	3/30–4/23
	10/12–11/5	11/6–11/29	11/30–12/23	12/24–12/31	
	11/25–12/18	12/19–12/31		1/1–1/16	1/17–2/10
10/31–11/24					
8/20–9/13	9/14–10/8	1/1–1/12	1/13–2/4	2/5–2/28	3/1–3/24
		10/9–11/5	11/6–12/7	12/8–12/31	
			1/30–2/28	1/1–1/29	
10/3–10/26	10/27–11/19	11/20–12/13	12/14–12/31	3/1–4/6	4/7–5/4
			1/1–1/6	1/7–1/30	1/31–2/23
11/10–12/7	12/8–12/31				

VENUS SIGNS 1901–2002

	Aries	Taurus	Gemini	Cancer	Leo	Virgo
1976	4/8–5/2	5/2–5/27	5/27–6/20	6/20–7/14	7/14–8/8	8/8–9/1
1977	2/2–6/6	6/6–7/6	7/6–8/2	8/2–8/28	8/28–9/22	9/22–10/17
1978	3/9–4/2	4/2–4/27	4/27–5/22	5/22–6/16	6/16–7/12	7/12–8/6
1979	4/23–5/18	5/18–6/11	6/11–7/6	7/6–7/30	7/30–8/24	8/24–9/17
1980	2/9–3/6	3/6–4/3	4/3–5/12 6/5–8/6	5/12–6/5 8/6–9/7	9/7–10/4	10/4–10/30
1981	3/24–4/17	4/17–5/11	5/11–6/5	6/5–6/29	6/29–7/24	7/24–8/18
1982	5/4–5/30	5/30–6/25	6/25–7/20	7/20–8/14	8/14–9/7	9/7–10/2
1983	2/22–3/19	3/19–4/13	4/13–5/9	5/9–6/6	6/6–7/10 8/27–10/5	7/10–8/27 10/5–11/9
1984	4/7–5/2	5/2–5/26	5/26–6/20	6/20–7/14	7/14–8/7	8/7–9/1
1985	2/2–6/6	6/7–7/6	7/6–8/2	8/2–8/28	8/28–9/22	9/22–10/16
1986	3/9–4/2	4/2–4/26	4/26–5/21	5/21–6/15	6/15–7/11	7/11–8/7
1987	4/22–5/17	5/17–6/11	6/11–7/5	7/5–7/30	7/30–8/23	8/23–9/16
1988	2/9–3/6	3/6–4/3	4/3–5/17 5/27–8/6	5/17–5/27 8/28–9/22	9/7–10/4 9/22–10/16	10/4–10/29
1989	3/23–4/16	4/16–5/11	5/11–6/4	6/4–6/29	6/29–7/24	7/24–8/18
1990	5/4–5/30	5/30–6/25	6/25–7/20	7/20–8/13	8/13–9/7	9/7–10/1
1991	2/2–3/18	3/18–4/13	4/13–5/9	5/9–6/6	6/6–7/11 8/21–10/6	7/11–8/21 10/6–11/9
1992	4/7–5/1	5/1–5/26	5/26–6/19	6/19–7/13	7/13–8/7	8/7–8/31
1993	2/2–6/6	6/6–7/6	7/6–8/1	8/1–8/27	8/27–9/21	9/21–10/16
1994	3/8–4/1	4/1–4/26	4/26–5/21	5/21–6/15	6/15–7/11	7/11–8/7
1995	4/22–5/16	5/16–6/10	6/10–7/5	7/5–7/29	7/29–8/23	8/23–9/16
1996	2/9–3/6	3/6–4/3	4/3–8/7	8/7–9/7	9/7–10/4	10/4–10/29
1997	3/23–4/16	4/16–5/10	5/10–6/4	6/4–6/28	6/28–7/23	7/23–8/17
1998	5/3–5/29	5/29–6/24	6/24–7/19	7/19–8/13	8/13–9/6	9/6–9/30
1999	2/21–3/18	3/18–4/12	4/12–5/8	5/8–6/5	6/5–7/12 8/15–10/7	7/12–8/15 10/7–11/9
2000	4/6–5/1	5/1–5/25	5/25–6/13	6/13–7/13	7/13–8/6	8/6–8/31
2001	2/2–6/6	6/6–7/5	7/5–8/1	8/1–8/26	8/26–9/20	9/20–10/15
2002	3/7–4/1	4/1–4/25	4/25–5/20	5/20–6/14	6/14–7/10	7/10–8/7

Libra	Scorpio	Sagittarius	Capricorn	Aquarius	Pisces
9/1–9/26	9/26–10/20	1/1–1/26	1/26–2/19	2/19–3/15	3/15–4/8
		10/20–11/14	11/14–12/8	12/9–1/4	
10/17–11/10	11/10–12/4	12/4–12/27	12/27–1/20/78		1/4–2/2
8/6–9/7	9/7–1/7			1/20–2/13	2/13–3/9
9/17–10/11	10/11–11/4	1/7–2/5	2/5–3/3	3/3–3/29	3/29–4/23
		11/4–11/28	11/28–12/22	12/22–1/16/80	
10/30–11/24	11/24–12/18	12/18–1/11/81			1/16–2/9
8/18–9/12	9/12–10/9	10/9–11/5	1/11–2/4	2/4–2/28	2/28–3/24
			11/5–12/8	12/8–1/23/82	
10/2–10/26	10/26–11/18	11/18–12/12	1/23–3/2	3/2–4/6	4/6–5/4
			12/12–1/5/83		
11/9–12/6	12/6–1/1/84			1/5–1/29	1/29–2/22
9/1–9/25	9/25–10/20	1/1–1/25	1/25–2/19	2/19–3/14	3/14–4/7
		10/20–11/13	11/13–12/9	12/10–1/4	
10/16–11/9	11/9–12/3	12/3–12/27	12/28–1/19		1/4–2/2
8/7–9/7	9/7–1/7			1/20–2/13	2/13–3/9
9/16–10/10	10/10–11/3	1/7–2/5	2/5–3/3	3/3–3/28	3/28–4/22
		11/3–11/28	11/28–12/22	12/22–1/15	
10/29–11/23	11/23–12/17	12/17–1/10			1/15–2/9
8/18–9/12	9/12–10/8	10/8–11/5	1/10–2/3	2/3–2/27	2/27–3/23
			11/5–12/10	12/10–1/16/90	
10/1–10/25	10/25–11/18	11/18–12/12	1/16–3/3	3/3–4/6	4/6–5/4
			12/12–1/5		
11/9–12/6	12/6–12/31	12/31–1/25/92		1/5–1/29	1/29–2/22
8/31–9/25	9/25–10/19	10/19–11/13	1/25–2/18	2/18–3/13	3/13–4/7
			11/13–12/8	12/8–1/3/93	
10/16–11/9	11/9–12/2	12/2–12/26	12/26–1/19		1/3–2/2
8/7–9/7	9/7–1/7			1/19–2/12	2/12–3/8
9/16–10/10	10/10–11/13	1/7–2/4	2/4–3/2	3/2–3/28	3/28–4/22
		11/3–11/27	11/27–12/21	12/21–1/15	
10/29–11/23	11/23–12/17	12/17–1/10/97			1/15–2/9
8/17–9/12	9/12–10/8	10/8–11/5	1/10–2/3	2/3–2/27	2/27–3/23
			11/5–12/12	12/12–1/9	
9/30–10/24	10/24–11/17	11/17–12/11	1/9–3/4	3/4–4/6	4/6–5/3
11/9–12/5	12/5–12/31	12/31–1/24		1/4–1/28	1/28–2/21
8/31–9/24	9/24–10/19	10/19–11/13	1/24–2/18	2/18–3/12	3/13–4/6
			11/13–12/8	12/8	
10/15–11/8	11/8–12/2	12/2–12/26	12/26/01–	12/8/00–	1/3–2/2
			1/19/02	1/3/01	
8/7–9/7	9/7–1/7/03		1/26/01–1/18	1/18–2/11	2/11–3/7

How to Use the Mars, Jupiter, and Saturn Tables

Find the year of your birth on the left side of each column. The dates when the planet entered each sign are listed on the right side of each column. (Signs are abbreviated to three letters.) Your birthday should fall on or between each date listed, and your planetary placement should correspond to the earlier sign of that period.

MARS SIGNS 1901–2002

Year	Month	Day	Sign	Year	Month	Day	Sign
1901	MAR	1	Leo	1905	JAN	13	Scp
	MAY	11	Vir		AUG	21	Sag
	JUL	13	Lib		OCT	8	Cap
	AUG	31	Scp		NOV	18	Aqu
	OCT	14	Sag		DEC	27	Pic
	NOV	24	Cap	1906	FEB	4	Ari
1902	JAN	1	Aqu		MAR	17	Tau
	FEB	8	Pic		APR	28	Gem
	MAR	19	Ari		JUN	11	Can
	APR	27	Tau		JUL	27	Leo
	JUN	7	Gem		SEP	12	Vir
	JUL	20	Can		OCT	30	Lib
	SEP	4	Leo		DEC	17	Scp
	OCT	23	Vir	1907	FEB	5	Sag
	DEC	20	Lib		APR	1	Cap
1903	APR	19	Vir		OCT	13	Aqu
	MAY	30	Lib		NOV	29	Pic
	AUG	6	Scp	1908	JAN	11	Ari
	SEP	22	Sag		FEB	23	Tau
	NOV	3	Cap		APR	7	Gem
	DEC	12	Aqu		MAY	22	Can
1904	JAN	19	Pic		JUL	8	Leo
	FEB	27	Ari		AUG	24	Vir
	APR	6	Tau		OCT	10	Lib
	MAY	18	Gem		NOV	25	Scp
	JUN	30	Can	1909	JAN	10	Sag
	AUG	15	Leo		FEB	24	Cap
	OCT	1	Vir		APR	9	Aqu
	NOV	20	Lib		MAY	25	Pic

	JUL	21	Ari		AUG	19	Can
	SEP	26	Pic		OCT	7	Leo
	NOV	20	Ari	1916	MAY	28	Vir
1910	JAN	23	Tau		JUL	23	Lib
	MAR	14	Gem		SEP	8	Scp
	MAY	1	Can		OCT	22	Sag
	JUN	19	Leo		DEC	1	Cap
	AUG	6	Vir	1917	JAN	9	Aqu
	SEP	22	Lib		FEB	16	Pic
	NOV	6	Scp		MAR	26	Ari
	DEC	20	Sag		MAY	4	Tau
1911	JAN	31	Cap		JUN	14	Gem
	MAR	14	Aqu		JUL	28	Can
	APR	23	Pic		SEP	12	Leo
	JUN	2	Ari		NOV	2	Vir
	JUL	15	Tau	1918	JAN	11	Lib
	SEP	5	Gem		FEB	25	Vir
	NOV	30	Tau		JUN	23	Lib
1912	JAN	30	Gem		AUG	17	Scp
	APR	5	Can		OCT	1	Sag
	MAY	28	Leo		NOV	11	Cap
	JUL	17	Vir		DEC	20	Aqu
	SEP	2	Lib	1919	JAN	27	Pic
	OCT	18	Scp		MAR	6	Ari
	NOV	30	Sag		APR	15	Tau
1913	JAN	10	Cap		MAY	26	Gem
	FEB	19	Aqu		JUL	8	Can
	MAR	30	Pic		AUG	23	Leo
	MAY	8	Ari		OCT	10	Vir
	JUN	17	Tau		NOV	30	Lib
	JUL	29	Gem	1920	JAN	31	Scp
	SEP	15	Can		APR	23	Lib
1914	MAY	1	Leo		JUL	10	Scp
	JUN	26	Vir		SEP	4	Sag
	AUG	14	Lib		OCT	18	Cap
	SEP	29	Scp		NOV	27	Aqu
	NOV	11	Sag	1921	JAN	5	Pic
	DEC	22	Cap		FEB	13	Ari
1915	JAN	30	Aqu		MAR	25	Tau
	MAR	9	Pic		MAY	6	Gem
	APR	16	Ari		JUN	18	Can
	MAY	26	Tau		AUG	3	Leo
	JUL	6	Gem		SEP	19	Vir

	NOV	6	Lib		APR	7	Pic
	DEC	26	Scp		MAY	16	Ari
1922	FEB	18	Sag		JUN	26	Tau
	SEP	13	Cap		AUG	9	Gem
	OCT	30	Aqu		OCT	3	Can
	DEC	11	Pic		DEC	20	Gem
1923	JAN	21	Ari	1929	MAR	10	Can
	MAR	4	Tau		MAY	13	Leo
	APR	16	Gem		JUL	4	Vir
	MAY	30	Can		AUG	21	Lib
	JUL	16	Leo		OCT	6	Scp
	SEP	1	Vir		NOV	18	Sag
	OCT	18	Lib		DEC	29	Cap
	DEC	4	Scp	1930	FEB	6	Aqu
1924	JAN	19	Sag		MAR	17	Pic
	MAR	6	Cap		APR	24	Ari
	APR	24	Aqu		JUN	3	Tau
	JUN	24	Pic		JUL	14	Gem
	AUG	24	Aqu		AUG	28	Can
	OCT	19	Pic		OCT	20	Leo
	DEC	19	Ari	1931	FEB	16	Can
1925	FEB	5	Tau		MAR	30	Leo
	MAR	24	Gem		JUN	10	Vir
	MAY	9	Can		AUG	1	Lib
	JUN	26	Leo		SEP	17	Scp
	AUG	12	Vir		OCT	30	Sag
	SEP	28	Lib		DEC	10	Cap
	NOV	13	Scp	1932	JAN	18	Aqu
	DEC	28	Sag		FEB	25	Pic
1926	FEB	9	Cap		APR	3	Ari
	MAR	23	Aqu		MAY	12	Tau
	MAY	3	Pic		JUN	22	Gem
	JUN	15	Ari		AUG	4	Can
	AUG	1	Tau		SEP	20	Leo
1927	FEB	22	Gem		NOV	13	Vir
	APR	17	Can	1933	JUL	6	Lib
	JUN	6	Leo		AUG	26	Scp
	JUL	25	Vir		OCT	9	Sag
	SEP	10	Lib		NOV	19	Cap
	OCT	26	Scp		DEC	28	Aqu
	DEC	8	Sag	1934	FEB	4	Pic
1928	JAN	19	Cap		MAR	14	Ari
	FEB	28	Aqu		APR	22	Tau

	JUN	2	Gem		AUG	19	Vir
	JUL	15	Can		OCT	5	Lib
	AUG	30	Leo		NOV	20	Scp
	OCT	18	Vir	1941	JAN	4	Sag
	DEC	11	Lib		FEB	17	Cap
1935	JUL	29	Scp		APR	2	Aqu
	SEP	16	Sag		MAY	16	Pic
	OCT	28	Cap		JUL	2	Ari
	DEC	7	Aqu	1942	JAN	11	Tau
1936	JAN	14	Pic		MAR	7	Gem
	FEB	22	Ari		APR	26	Can
	APR	1	Tau		JUN	14	Leo
	MAY	13	Gem		AUG	1	Vir
	JUN	25	Can		SEP	17	Lib
	AUG	10	Leo		NOV	1	Scp
	SEP	26	Vir		DEC	15	Sag
	NOV	14	Lib	1943	JAN	26	Cap
1937	JAN	5	Scp		MAR	8	Aqu
	MAR	13	Sag		APR	17	Pic
	MAY	14	Scp		MAY	27	Ari
	AUG	8	Sag		JUL	7	Tau
	SEP	30	Cap		AUG	23	Gem
	NOV	11	Aqu	1944	MAR	28	Can
	DEC	21	Pic		MAY	22	Leo
1938	JAN	30	Ari		JUL	12	Vir
	MAR	12	Tau		AUG	29	Lib
	APR	23	Gem		OCT	13	Scp
	JUN	7	Can		NOV	25	Sag
	JUL	22	Leo	1945	JAN	5	Cap
	SEP	7	Vir		FEB	14	Aqu
	OCT	25	Lib		MAR	25	Pic
	DEC	11	Scp		MAY	2	Ari
1939	JAN	29	Sag		JUN	11	Tau
	MAR	21	Cap		JUL	23	Gem
	MAY	25	Aqu		SEP	7	Can
	JUL	21	Cap		NOV	11	Leo
	SEP	24	Aqu		DEC	26	Can
	NOV	19	Pic	1946	APR	22	Leo
1940	JAN	4	Ari		JUN	20	Vir
	FEB	17	Tau		AUG	9	Lib
	APR	1	Gem		SEP	24	Scp
	MAY	17	Can		NOV	6	Sag
	JUL	3	Leo		DEC	17	Cap

1947	JAN	25	Aqu		MAR	20	Tau
	MAR	4	Pic		MAY	1	Gem
	APR	11	Ari		JUN	14	Can
	MAY	21	Tau		JUL	29	Leo
	JUL	1	Gem		SEP	14	Vir
	AUG	13	Can		NOV	1	Lib
	OCT	1	Leo		DEC	20	Scp
	DEC	1	Vir	1954	FEB	9	Sag
1948	FEB	12	Leo		APR	12	Cap
	MAY	18	Vir		JUL	3	Sag
	JUL	17	Lib		AUG	24	Cap
	SEP	3	Scp		OCT	21	Aqu
	OCT	17	Sag		DEC	4	Pic
	NOV	26	Cap	1955	JAN	15	Ari
1949	JAN	4	Aqu		FEB	26	Tau
	FEB	11	Pic		APR	10	Gem
	MAR	21	Ari		MAY	26	Can
	APR	30	Tau		JUL	11	Leo
	JUN	10	Gem		AUG	27	Vir
	JUL	23	Can		OCT	13	Lib
	SEP	7	Leo		NOV	29	Scp
	OCT	27	Vir	1956	JAN	14	Sag
	DEC	26	Lib		FEB	28	Cap
1950	MAR	28	Vir		APR	14	Aqu
	JUN	11	Lib		JUN	3	Pic
	AUG	10	Scp		DEC	6	Ari
	SEP	25	Sag	1957	JAN	28	Tau
	NOV	6	Cap		MAR	17	Gem
	DEC	15	Aqu		MAY	4	Can
1951	JAN	22	Pic		JUN	21	Leo
	MAR	1	Ari		AUG	8	Vir
	APR	10	Tau		SEP	24	Lib
	MAY	21	Gem		NOV	8	Scp
	JUL	3	Can		DEC	23	Sag
	AUG	18	Leo	1958	FEB	3	Cap
	OCT	5	Vir		MAR	17	Aqu
	NOV	24	Lib		APR	27	Pic
1952	JAN	20	Scp		JUN	7	Ari
	AUG	27	Sag		JUL	21	Tau
	OCT	12	Cap		SEP	21	Gem
	NOV	21	Aqu		OCT	29	Tau
	DEC	30	Pic	1959	FEB	10	Gem
1953	FEB	8	Ari		APR	10	Can

	JUN	1	Leo		NOV	14	Cap
	JUL	20	Vir		DEC	23	Aqu
	SEP	5	Lib	1966	JAN	30	Pic
	OCT	21	Scp		MAR	9	Ari
	DEC	3	Sag		APR	17	Tau
1960	JAN	14	Cap		MAY	28	Gem
	FEB	23	Aqu		JUL	11	Can
	APR	2	Pic		AUG	25	Leo
	MAY	11	Ari		OCT	12	Vir
	JUN	20	Tau		DEC	4	Lib
	AUG	2	Gem	1967	FEB	12	Scp
	SEP	21	Can		MAR	31	Lib
1961	FEB	5	Gem		JUL	19	Scp
	FEB	7	Can		SEP	10	Sag
	MAY	6	Leo		OCT	23	Cap
	JUN	28	Vir		DEC	1	Aqu
	AUG	17	Lib	1968	JAN	9	Pic
	OCT	1	Scp		FEB	17	Ari
	NOV	13	Sag		MAR	27	Tau
	DEC	24	Cap		MAY	8	Gem
1962	FEB	1	Aqu		JUN	21	Can
	MAR	12	Pic		AUG	5	Leo
	APR	19	Ari		SEP	21	Vir
	MAY	28	Tau		NOV	9	Lib
	JUL	9	Gem		DEC	29	Scp
	AUG	22	Can	1969	FEB	25	Sag
	OCT	11	Leo		SEP	21	Cap
1963	JUN	3	Vir		NOV	4	Aqu
	JUL	27	Lib		DEC	15	Pic
	SEP	12	Scp	1970	JAN	24	Ari
	OCT	25	Sag		MAR	7	Tau
	DEC	5	Cap		APR	18	Gem
1964	JAN	13	Aqu		JUN	2	Can
	FEB	20	Pic		JUL	18	Leo
	MAR	29	Ari		SEP	3	Vir
	MAY	7	Tau		OCT	20	Lib
	JUN	17	Gem		DEC	6	Scp
	JUL	30	Can	1971	JAN	23	Sag
	SEP	15	Leo		MAR	12	Cap
	NOV	6	Vir		MAY	3	Aqu
1965	JUN	29	Lib		NOV	6	Pic
	AUG	20	Scp		DEC	26	Ari
	OCT	4	Sag	1972	FEB	10	Tau

Year	Mon	Day	Sign		Year	Mon	Day	Sign
	MAR	27	Gem		1978	JAN	26	Can
	MAY	12	Can			APR	10	Leo
	JUN	28	Leo			JUN	14	Vir
	AUG	15	Vir			AUG	4	Lib
	SEP	30	Lib			SEP	19	Scp
	NOV	15	Scp			NOV	2	Sag
	DEC	30	Sag			DEC	12	Cap
1973	FEB	12	Cap		1979	JAN	20	Aqu
	MAR	26	Aqu			FEB	27	Pic
	MAY	8	Pic			APR	7	Ari
	JUN	20	Ari			MAY	16	Tau
	AUG	12	Tau			JUN	26	Gem
	OCT	29	Ari			AUG	8	Can
	DEC	24	Tau			SEP	24	Leo
1974	FEB	27	Gem			NOV	19	Vir
	APR	20	Can		1980	MAR	11	Leo
	JUN	9	Leo			MAY	4	Vir
	JUL	27	Vir			JUL	10	Lib
	SEP	12	Lib			AUG	29	Scp
	OCT	28	Scp			OCT	12	Sag
	DEC	10	Sag			NOV	22	Cap
1975	JAN	21	Cap			DEC	30	Aqu
	MAR	3	Aqu		1981	FEB	6	Pic
	APR	11	Pic			MAR	17	Ari
	MAY	21	Ari			APR	25	Tau
	JUL	1	Tau			JUN	5	Gem
	AUG	14	Gem			JUL	18	Can
	OCT	17	Can			SEP	2	Leo
	NOV	25	Gem			OCT	21	Vir
1976	MAR	18	Can			DEC	16	Lib
	MAY	16	Leo		1982	AUG	3	Scp
	JUL	6	Vir			SEP	20	Sag
	AUG	24	Lib			OCT	31	Cap
	OCT	8	Scp			DEC	10	Aqu
	NOV	20	Sag		1983	JAN	17	Pic
1977	JAN	1	Cap			FEB	25	Ari
	FEB	9	Aqu			APR	5	Tau
	MAR	20	Pic			MAY	16	Gem
	APR	27	Ari			JUN	29	Can
	JUN	6	Tau			AUG	13	Leo
	JUL	17	Gem			SEP	30	Vir
	SEP	1	Can			NOV	18	Lib
	OCT	26	Leo		1984	JAN	11	Scp

	AUG	17	Sag				
	OCT	5	Cap				
	NOV	15	Aqu				
	DEC	25	Pic				
1985	FEB	2	Ari				
	MAR	15	Tau				
	APR	26	Gem				
	JUN	9	Can				
	JUL	25	Leo				
	SEP	10	Vir				
	OCT	27	Lib				
	DEC	14	Scp				
1986	FEB	2	Sag				
	MAR	28	Cap				
	OCT	9	Aqu				
	NOV	26	Pic				
1987	JAN	8	Ari				
	FEB	20	Tau				
	APR	5	Gem				
	MAY	21	Can				
	JUL	6	Leo				
	AUG	22	Vir				
	OCT	8	Lib				
	NOV	24	Scp				
1988	JAN	8	Sag				
	FEB	22	Cap				
	APR	6	Aqu				
	MAY	22	Pic				
	JUL	13	Ari				
	OCT	23	Pic				
	NOV	1	Ari				
1989	JAN	19	Tau				
	MAR	11	Gem				
	APR	29	Can				
	JUN	16	Leo				
	AUG	3	Vir				
	SEP	19	Lib				
	NOV	4	Scp				
	DEC	18	Sag				
1990	JAN	29	Cap				
	MAR	11	Aqu				
	APR	20	Pic				
	MAY	31	Ari				

	JUL	12	Tau
	AUG	31	Gem
	DEC	14	Tau
1991	JAN	21	Gem
	APR	3	Can
	MAY	26	Leo
	JUL	15	Vir
	SEP	1	Lib
	OCT	16	Scp
	NOV	29	Sag
1992	JAN	9	Cap
	FEB	18	Aqu
	MAR	28	Pic
	MAY	5	Ari
	JUN	14	Tau
	JUL	26	Gem
	SEP	12	Can
1993	APR	27	Leo
	JUN	23	Vir
	AUG	12	Lib
	SEP	27	Scp
	NOV	9	Sag
	DEC	20	Cap
1994	JAN	28	Aqu
	MAR	7	Pic
	APR	14	Ari
	MAY	23	Tau
	JUL	3	Gem
	AUG	16	Can
	OCT	4	Leo
	DEC	12	Vir
1995	JAN	22	Leo
	MAY	25	Vir
	JUL	21	Lib
	SEP	7	Scp
	OCT	20	Sag
	NOV	30	Cap
1996	JAN	8	Aqu
	FEB	15	Pic
	MAR	24	Ari
	MAY	2	Tau
	JUN	12	Gem
	JUL	25	Can

	SEP	9	Leo		NOV	26	Aqu
	OCT	30	Vir	2000	JAN	4	Pic
1997	JAN	3	Lib		FEB	12	Ari
	MAR	8	Vir		MAR	23	Tau
	JUN	19	Lib		MAY	3	Gem
	AUG	14	Scp		JUN	16	Can
	SEP	28	Sag		AUG	1	Leo
	NOV	9	Cap		SEP	17	Vir
	DEC	18	Aqu		NOV	4	Lib
1998	JAN	25	Pic		DEC	23	Scp
	MAR	4	Ari	2001	FEB	14	Sag
	APR	13	Tau		SEP	8	Cap
	MAY	24	Gem		OCT	27	Aqu
	JUL	6	Can		DEC	8	Pic
	AUG	20	Leo	2002	JAN	18	Ari
	OCT	7	Vir		MAR	1	Tau
	NOV	27	Lib		APR	13	Gem
1999	JAN	26	Scp		MAY	28	Can
	MAY	5	Lib		JUL	13	Leo
	JUL	5	Scp		AUG	29	Vir
	SEP	2	Sag		OCT	15	Lib
	OCT	17	Cap		DEC	1	Scp

JUPITER SIGNS 1901–2002

1901	JAN	19	Cap	1911	DEC	10	Sag
1902	FEB	6	Aqu	1913	JAN	2	Cap
1903	FEB	20	Pic	1914	JAN	21	Aqu
1904	MAR	1	Ari	1915	FEB	4	Pic
	AUG	8	Tau	1916	FEB	12	Ari
	AUG	31	Ari		JUN	26	Tau
1905	MAR	7	Tau		OCT	26	Ari
	JUL	21	Gem	1917	FEB	12	Tau
	DEC	4	Tau		JUN	29	Gem
1906	MAR	9	Gem	1918	JUL	13	Can
	JUL	30	Can	1919	AUG	2	Leo
1907	AUG	18	Leo	1920	AUG	27	Vir
1908	SEP	12	Vir	1921	SEP	25	Lib
1909	OCT	11	Lib	1922	OCT	26	Scp
1910	NOV	11	Scp	1923	NOV	24	Sag

1924	DEC	18	Cap	1955	JUN	13	Leo
1926	JAN	6	Aqu		NOV	17	Vir
1927	JAN	18	Pic	1956	JAN	18	Leo
	JUN	6	Ari		JUL	7	Vir
	SEP	11	Pic		DEC	13	Lib
1928	JAN	23	Ari	1957	FEB	19	Vir
	JUN	4	Tau		AUG	7	Lib
1929	JUN	12	Gem	1958	JAN	13	Scp
1930	JUN	26	Can		MAR	20	Lib
1931	JUL	17	Leo		SEP	7	Scp
1932	AUG	11	Vir	1959	FEB	10	Sag
1933	SEP	10	Lib		APR	24	Scp
1934	OCT	11	Scp		OCT	5	Sag
1935	NOV	9	Sag	1960	MAR	1	Cap
1936	DEC	2	Cap		JUN	10	Sag
1937	DEC	20	Aqu		OCT	26	Cap
1938	MAY	14	Pic	1961	MAR	15	Aqu
	JUL	30	Aqu		AUG	12	Cap
	DEC	29	Pic		NOV	4	Aqu
1939	MAY	11	Ari	1962	MAR	25	Pic
	OCT	30	Pic	1963	APR	4	Ari
	DEC	20	Ari	1964	APR	12	Tau
1940	MAY	16	Tau	1965	APR	22	Gem
1941	MAY	26	Gem		SEP	21	Can
1942	JUN	10	Can		NOV	17	Gem
1943	JUN	30	Leo	1966	MAY	5	Can
1944	JUL	26	Vir		SEP	27	Leo
1945	AUG	25	Lib	1967	JAN	16	Can
1946	SEP	25	Scp		MAY	23	Leo
1947	OCT	24	Sag		OCT	19	Vir
1948	NOV	15	Cap	1968	FEB	27	Leo
1949	APR	12	Aqu		JUN	15	Vir
	JUN	27	Cap		NOV	15	Lib
	NOV	30	Aqu	1969	MAR	30	Vir
1950	APR	15	Pic		JUL	15	Lib
	SEP	15	Aqu		DEC	16	Scp
	DEC	1	Pic	1970	APR	30	Lib
1951	APR	21	Ari		AUG	15	Scp
1952	APR	28	Tau	1971	JAN	14	Sag
1953	MAY	9	Gem		JUN	5	Scp
1954	MAY	24	Can		SEP	11	Sag

1972	FEB	6	Cap	1986	FEB	20	Pic
	JUL	24	Sag	1987	MAR	2	Ari
	SEP	25	Cap	1988	MAR	8	Tau
1973	FEB	23	Aqu		JUL	22	Gem
1974	MAR	8	Pic		NOV	30	Tau
1975	MAR	18	Ari	1989	MAR	11	Gem
1976	MAR	26	Tau		JUL	30	Can
	AUG	23	Gem	1990	AUG	18	Leo
	OCT	16	Tau	1991	SEP	12	Vir
1977	APR	3	Gem	1992	OCT	10	Lib
	AUG	20	Can	1993	NOV	10	Scp
	DEC	30	Gem	1994	DEC	9	Sag
1978	APR	12	Can	1996	JAN	3	Cap
	SEP	5	Leo	1997	JAN	21	Aqu
1979	FEB	28	Can	1998	FEB	4	Pic
	APR	20	Leo	1999	FEB	13	Ari
	SEP	29	Vir		JUN	28	Tau
1980	OCT	27	Lib		OCT	23	Ari
1981	NOV	27	Scp	2000	FEB	14	Tau
1982	DEC	26	Sag		JUN	30	Gem
1984	JAN	19	Cap	2001	JUL	14	Can
1985	FEB	6	Aqu				

SATURN SIGNS 1903–2002

1903	JAN	19	Aqu	1916	OCT	17	Leo
1905	APR	13	Pic		DEC	7	Can
	AUG	17	Aqu	1917	JUN	24	Leo
1906	JAN	8	Pic	1919	AUG	12	Vir
1908	MAR	19	Ari	1921	OCT	7	Lib
1910	MAY	17	Tau	1923	DEC	20	Scp
	DEC	14	Ari	1924	APR	6	Lib
1911	JAN	20	Tau		SEP	13	Scp
1912	JUL	7	Gem	1926	DEC	2	Sag
	NOV	30	Tau	1929	MAR	15	Cap
1913	MAR	26	Gem		MAY	5	Sag
1914	AUG	24	Can		NOV	30	Cap
	DEC	7	Gem	1932	FEB	24	Aqu
1915	MAY	11	Can		AUG	13	Cap

Year	Month	Day	Sign		Year	Month	Day	Sign
	NOV	20	Aqu			FEB	21	Gem
1935	FEB	14	Pic		1973	AUG	1	Can
1937	APR	25	Ari		1974	JAN	7	Gem
	OCT	18	Pic			APR	18	Can
1938	JAN	14	Ari		1975	SEP	17	Leo
1939	JUL	6	Tau		1976	JAN	14	Can
	SEP	22	Ari					
1940	MAR	20	Tau			JUN	5	Leo
1942	MAY	8	Gem		1977	NOV	17	Vir
1944	JUN	20	Can		1978	JAN	5	Leo
1946	AUG	2	Leo			JUL	26	Vir
1948	SEP	19	Vir		1980	SEP	21	Lib
1949	APR	3	Leo		1982	NOV	29	Scp
	MAY	29	Vir		1983	MAY	6	Lib
1950	NOV	20	Lib			AUG	24	Scp
1951	MAR	7	Vir		1985	NOV	17	Sag
	AUG	13	Lib		1988	FEB	13	Cap
1953	OCT	22	Scp			JUN	10	Sag
1956	JAN	12	Sag			NOV	12	Cap
	MAY	14	Scp		1991	FEB	6	Aqu
	OCT	10	Sag		1993	MAY	21	Pic
1959	JAN	5	Cap			JUN	30	Aqu
1962	JAN	3	Aqu		1994	JAN	28	Pic
1964	MAR	24	Pic		1996	APR	7	Ari
	SEP	16	Aqu		1998	JUN	9	Tau
	DEC	16	Pic			OCT	25	Ari
1967	MAR	3	Ari		1999	MAR	1	Tau
1969	APR	29	Tau		2000	AUG	10	Gem
1971	JUN	18	Gem			OCT	16	Tau
1972	JAN	10	Tau		2001	APR	21	Gem

CHAPTER 4

Crack the Astrology Code— Decipher Those Mysterious Glyphs on Your Chart

The first time you look at a horoscope, you'll realize that astrology has a code all its own, written in strange-looking characters which represent the planets and signs. These symbols, or *glyphs,* are used by astrologers worldwide and by computer astrology programs. So, if you want to progress in astrology enough to read a horoscope, there's no way around it . . . you've got to know the meaning of the glyphs.

Besides enabling you to read a horoscope chart, learning the astrology code can help you interpret the meaning of the signs and planets, because each glyph contains a minilesson in what its planet or sign represents. And since there are only twelve signs and ten planets (not counting a few asteroids and other space creatures some astrologers use), they're a lot easier to learn than, say, Chinese!

Here's a code cracker for the glyphs, beginning with the glyphs for the planets. To those who already know their glyphs, don't just skim over the chapter! There are hidden meanings to discover, so test your glyphese.

The Glyphs for the Planets

The glyphs for the planets are easy to learn. They're simple combinations of the most basic visual elements: the circle, the semicircle or arc, and the cross. However, each component of a glyph has a special meaning in relation to the others, which adds up to create the total meaning of the symbol.

The circle, which has no beginning or end, is one of the oldest symbols of spirit or spiritual forces. All of the early diagrams of the heavens—spiritual territory—are shown in circular form. The never-ending line of the circle is the perfect symbol for eternity. The semicircle or arc is an incomplete circle, symbolizing the receptive, finite soul, which contains spiritual potential in the curving line.

The vertical line of the cross symbolizes movement from heaven to earth. The horizontal line describes temporal movement, here and now, in time and space. Combined in a cross, the vertical and horizontal planes symbolize manifestation in the material world.

The Sun Glyph ⊙

The sun is always shown by this powerful solar symbol, a circle with a point in the center. The center point is you, your spiritual center, and the symbol represents your infinite personality incarnating (the point) into the finite cycles of birth and death.

The sun has been represented by a circle or disk since ancient Egyptian times, when the solar disk represented the sun god, Ra. Some archaeologists believe the great stone circles found in England were centers of sun worship. This particular version of the symbol was brought into common use in the sixteenth century, after German occultist and scholar Cornelius Agrippa (1486–1535) wrote a book called *Die Occulta Philosophia,* which became accepted as the standard work in its field. Agrippa collected many medieval astrological and magical symbols in this book, which have been used by astrologers since then.

The Moon Glyph ☽

The moon glyph is the most recognizable symbol on a chart, a left-facing arc stylized into the crescent moon. As part of a circle, the arc symbolizes the potential fulfillment of the entire circle, the life force that is still incomplete. Therefore, it is the ideal representation of the reactive, receptive, emotional nature of the moon.

The Mercury Glyph ☿

Mercury contains all three elemental symbols, the crescent, the circle, and the cross in vertical order. This is the "Venus with a hat" glyph (compare with the symbol of Venus). With another stretch of the imagination, can't you see the winged cap of Mercury the messenger? Think of the upturned crescent as antennae that tune in and transmit messages from the sun, reminding you that Mercury is the way you communicate, the way your mind works. The upturned arc is receiving energy into the spirit or solar circle, which will later be translated into action on the material plane, symbolized by the cross. All the elements are equally sized because Mercury is neutral; it doesn't play favorites! This planet symbolizes objective, detached, unemotional thinking.

The Venus Glyph ♀

Here the relationship is between two components, the circle or spirit and the cross of matter. Spirit is elevated over matter, pulling it upward. Venus asks, "What is beautiful? What do you like best? What do you love to have done to you?" Consequently,

Venus determines both your ideal of beauty and what feels good sensually. It governs your own allure and power to attract, as well as what attracts and pleases you.

The Mars Glyph ♂

In this glyph, the cross of matter is stylized into an arrowhead pointed up and outward, propelled by the circle of spirit. With a little imagination, you can visualize it as the shield and spear of Mars, the ancient god of war. You can deduce that Mars embodies your spiritual energy projected into the outer world. It's your assertiveness, your initiative, your aggressive drive, what you like to do to others, your temper. If you know someone's Mars, you know whether they'll blow up when angry or do a slow burn. Your task is to use your outgoing Mars energy wisely and well.

The Jupiter Glyph ♃

Jupiter is the basic cross of matter, with a large stylized crescent perched on the left side of the horizontal, temporal plane. You might think of the crescent as an open hand, because one meaning of Jupiter is "luck," what's handed to you. You don't work for what you get from Jupiter; it comes to you, if you're open to it.

The Jupiter glyph might also remind you of a jumbo jet plane with a huge tail fin, about to take off. This is the planet of travel, mental and spiritual, of expanding your horizons via new ideas, new spiritual dimensions, and new places. Jupiter embodies the optimism and enthusiasm of the traveler about to embark on an exciting adventure.

The Saturn Glyph ♄

Flip Jupiter over and you've got Saturn. (This might not be immediately apparent, because Saturn

91

is usually stylized into an "h" form like the one shown here.) The principle it expresses is the opposite of Jupiter's expansive tendencies. Saturn pulls you back to earth—the receptive arc is pushed down underneath the cross of matter. Before there are any rewards or expansion, the duties and obligations of the material world must be considered. Saturn says, "Stop, wait, finish your chores before you take off!"

Saturn's glyph also resembles the scythe of old "Father Time." Saturn was first known as Chronos, the Greek god of time, for time brings all matter to an end. When it was the most distant planet (before the discovery of Uranus), Saturn was believed to be the place where time stopped. After the soul departed from Earth, it journeyed back to the outer reaches of the universe and finally stopped at Saturn, or at "the end of time."

The Uranus Glyph ♅

The glyph for Uranus is often stylized to form a capital "H" after Sir William Herschel, who discovered the planet. But the more esoteric version curves the two pillars of the H into crescent antennae, or "ears," like satellite disks receiving signals from space. These are perched on the horizontal material line of the cross (matter) and pushed from below by the circle of the spirit. To many sci-fi fans, Uranus looks like an orbiting satellite.

Uranus channels the highest energy of all, the white electrical light of the universal spiritual force which holds the cosmos together. This pure electrical energy is gathered from all over the universe. Because Uranian energy doesn't follow any ordinary celestial drumbeat, it can't be controlled or predicted (which is also true of those who are strongly influenced by this eccentric planet). In the symbol, this energy is manifested through the balance of polarities (the two opposite arms of the glyph) like the two polarized wires of a light bulb.

The Neptune Glyph Ψ

Neptune's glyph is usually stylized to look like a trident, the weapon of the Roman god Neptune. However, on a more esoteric level, it shows the large, upturned crescent of the soul pierced through by the cross of matter. Neptune nails down, or materializes, soul energy, bringing impulses from the soul level into manifestation. That is why Neptune is associated with imagination or "imagining in," making an image of the soul. Neptune works through feeling, sensitivity, and a mystical capacity to bring the divine into the earthly realm.

The Pluto Glyph ♀

Pluto is written two ways. One is a composite of the letters PL, the first two letters of the word "Pluto" and coincidentally the initials of Percival Lowell, one of the planet's discoverers. The other, more esoteric symbol is a small circle above a large open crescent which surmounts the cross of matter. This depicts Pluto's power to regenerate—imagine a new little spirit emerging from the sheltering cup of the soul. Pluto rules the forces of life and death—after this planet has passed a sensitive point in your chart, you are transformed, reborn in some way.

Sci-fi fans might visualize this glyph as a small satellite (the circle) being launched. It was shortly after Pluto's discovery that we learned how to harness the nuclear forces that made space exploration possible. Pluto rules the transformative power of atomic energy, which totally changed our lives and from which there is no turning back.

The Glyphs for the Signs

On an astrological chart, the glyph for the sign will appear after that of the planet. For example, when you see the moon glyph followed first by a number and then by another glyph representing the sign, this means that the moon was passing over a certain degree of that astrological sign at the time of the chart. On the dividing lines between the segments or "houses" on your chart, you'll find the symbol for the sign that rules the house.

Because sun sign symbols do not contain the same basic geometric components of the planetary glyphs, we must look elsewhere for clues to their meanings. Many have been passed down from ancient Egyptian and Chaldean civilizations with few modifications. Others have been adapted over the centuries. In deciphering many of the glyphs, you'll often find that the symbols reveal a dual nature of the sign, which is not always apparent in the usual sun sign descriptions. For instance, the Gemini glyph is similar to the Roman numeral for two, and reveals this sign's longing to discover a twin soul. The Cancer glyph may be interpreted as resembling either the nurturing breasts or the self-protective claws of the crab, both symbols associated with the contrasting qualities of this sign. Libra's glyph embodies the duality of the spirit balanced with material reality. The Sagittarius glyph shows that the aspirant must also carry along the earthly animal nature in his quest. The Capricorn sea goat is another symbol with dual emphasis. The goat climbs high, yet is always pulled back by the deep waters of the unconscious. Aquarius embodies the double waves of mental detachment, balanced by the desire for connection with others in a friendly way. And finally, the two fishes of Pisces, which are forever tied together, show the duality of the soul and the spirit that must be reconciled.

The Aries Glyph ♈

Since the symbol for Aries is the ram, this glyph is obviously associated with a ram's horns, which characterize one aspect of the Aries personality—an aggressive, me-first, leaping-headfirst attitude. But the symbol can be interpreted in other ways as well. Some astrologers liken it to a fountain of energy, which Aries people also embody. The first sign of the zodiac bursts on the scene eagerly, ready to go. Another analogy is to the eyebrows and nose of the human head, which Aries rules, and the thinking power that is initiated in the brain.

One theory of this symbol links it to the Egyptian god Amun, represented by a ram in ancient times. As Amun-Ra, this god was believed to embody the creator of the universe, the leader of all the other gods. This relates easily to the position of Aries as the leader (or first sign) of the zodiac, which begins at the spring equinox, a time of the year when nature is renewed.

The Taurus Glyph ♉

This is another easy glyph to draw and identify. It takes little imagination to decipher the bull's head with long curving horns. Like the bull, the archetypal Taurus is slow to anger, but ferocious when provoked, as well as stubborn, steady, and sensual. Another association is the larynx (and thyroid) of the throat area (ruled by Taurus) and the eustachian tubes running up to the ears, which coincide with the relationship of Taurus to the voice, song, and music. Many famous singers, musicians, and composers have prominent Taurus influences.

Many ancient religions involved a bull as the central figure in fertility rites or initiations, usually symbolizing the victory of man over his animal nature. Another possible origin is in the sacred bull of Egypt, who embodied the incarnate form of Osiris, god of death and resurrection. In early Christian imagery, the Taurean bull represented St. Luke.

The Gemini Glyph ♊

The standard glyph immediately calls to mind the Roman numeral II and the "twins" symbol for Gemini. In almost all drawings and images used for this sign, the relationship between two persons is emphasized. Usually one twin will be touching the other, which signifies communication, human contact, and the desire to share.

The top line of the Gemini glyph indicates mental communication, while the bottom line indicates shared physical space.

The most famous Gemini legend is that of the twin sons, Castor and Pollux, one of whom had a mortal father, while the other was the son of Zeus, king of the gods. When it came time for the mortal twin to die, his grief-stricken brother pleaded with Zeus, who agreed to let them spend half the year on earth in mortal form and half in immortal life, with the gods on Mt. Olympus. This reflects a basic duality of humankind, which possesses an immortal soul, yet is also subject to the limits of mortality.

The Cancer Glyph ♋

Two convenient images relate to the Cancer glyph. It is easiest to decode the curving claws of the Cancer symbol, the crab. Like the crab, Cancer's element is water. This sensitive sign also has a hard protective shell to protect its tender interior. The crab must be wily to escape predators, scampering sideways and hiding under rocks. The crab also responds to the cycles of the moon, as do all shellfish. The other image is that of two female breasts, which Cancer rules, showing that this is a sign that nurtures and protects others as well as itself.

In ancient Egypt, Cancer was also represented by

the scarab beetle, a symbol of regeneration and eternal life.

The Leo Glyph ♌

Notice that the Leo glyph seems to be an extension of Cancer's glyph, with a significant difference. In the Cancer glyph, the lines curve inward protectively, while the Leo glyph expresses energy outwardly and there is no duality in the symbol (or in Leo).

Lions have belonged to the sign of Leo since earliest times, and it is not difficult to imagine the king of beasts with his sweeping mane and curling tail from this glyph. The upward sweep of the glyph easily describes the positive energy of Leos: the flourishing tail, their flamboyant qualities. Another analogy, which is a stretch of the imagination, is that of a heart leaping up with joy and enthusiasm, very typical of Leo, which also rules the heart. In early Christian imagery, the Leo lion represented St. Mark.

The Virgo Glyph ♍

You can read much into this mysterious glyph. For instance, it could represent the initials of "Mary Virgin," or a young woman holding a stalk of wheat, or stylized female genitalia, all common interpretations. The "M" shape might also remind you that Virgo is ruled by Mercury. The cross beneath the symbol reveals the grounded, practical nature of this earth sign.

The earliest zodiacs link Virgo with the Egyptian goddess Isis, who gave birth to the god Horus after her husband Osiris had been killed, in the archetype of a miraculous conception. There are many ancient statues of Isis nursing her baby son, which are reminiscent of medieval Virgin and Child motifs. This sign has also been associated with the image of the Holy

Grail, when the Virgo symbol was substituted with a chalice.

The Libra Glyph ♎

It is not difficult to read the standard image for Libra, the scales, into this glyph. There is another meaning, however, that is equally relevant: the setting sun as it descends over the horizon. Libra's natural position on the zodiac wheel is the descendant or sunset position (as Aries's natural position is the ascendant, or rising sign). Both images relate to Libra's personality. Libra is always weighing pros and cons for a balanced decision. In the sunset image, the sun (male) hovers over the horizontal Earth (female) before setting. Libra is the space between these lines, harmonizing yin and yang, spiritual and material, male and female, ideal and real worlds. The glyph has also been linked to the kidneys, which are ruled by Libra.

The Scorpio Glyph ♏

With its barbed tail, this glyph is easy to identify with the sign of the Scorpion. It also represents the male sexual parts, over which the sign rules. However, some earlier Egyptian symbols for Scorpio represent it as an erect serpent. You can also draw the conclusion that Mars was once its ruler by the arrowhead.

Another image for Scorpio, which is not identifiable in this glyph, is the eagle. Scorpios can go to extremes, either soaring like the eagle or self-destructing like the scorpion. In early Christian imagery, which often used zodiacal symbols, the Scorpio eagle was chosen to symbolize the intense apostle St. John the Evangelist.

The Sagittarius Glyph ♐

This glyph is one of the easiest to spot and draw—an upward pointing arrow lifting up a cross. The arrow is pointing skyward, while the cross represents the four elements of the material world, which the arrow must convey. Elevating materiality into spirituality is an important Sagittarius quality, which explains why this sign is associated with higher learning, religion, philosophy, and travel—the aspiring professions. Sagittarians can also send barbed arrows of frankness in their pursuit of truth. (This is also the sign of the super-salesman.)

Sagittarius is symbolically represented by the centaur, a mythological creature who is half man, half horse, aiming his arrow toward the skies. Though Sagittarius is motivated by spiritual aspiration, it also must balance the powerful appetites of the animal nature. The centaur Chiron, a figure in Greek mythology, became a wise teacher who, after many adventures and world travels, was killed by a poisoned arrow.

The Capricorn Glyph ♑

One of the most difficult symbols to draw, this glyph may take some practice. It is a representation of the sea goat: a mythical animal that is a goat with a curving fish's tail. The goat part of Capricorn wants to leave the waters of the emotions and climb to the elevated areas of life. But the fish tail is the unconscious, the deep chaotic psychic level that draws the goat back. Capricorn is often trying to escape the deep, feeling part of life by submerging himself in work, steadily ascending to the top. To some people, the glyph represents a seated figure with a bent knee, a reminder that Capricorn governs the knee area of the body.

An interesting aspect of this glyph is the contrast of the sharp pointed horns of the symbol, which represent the penetrating, shrewd, conscious side of Capricorn, with the swishing tail, which represents its serpentine, unconscious, emotional force. One Capricorn legend, which dates from Roman times, tells of the earthy fertility god, Pan, who tried to save himself from uncontrollable sexual desires by jumping into the Nile. His upper body then turned into a goat, while the lower part became a fish. Later, Jupiter gave him a safe haven in the skies, as a constellation.

The Aquarius Glyph ≈

This ancient water symbol can be traced back to an Egyptian hieroglyph representing streams of life force. Symbolized by the water bearer, Aquarius is distributor of the waters of life—the magic liquid of regeneration. The two waves can also be linked to the positive and negative charges of the electrical energy that Aquarius rules, a sort of universal wavelength. Aquarius is tuned in intuitively to higher forces via this electrical force. The duality of the glyph could also refer to the dual nature of Aquarius, a sign that runs hot and cold, is friendly but also detached in the mental world of air signs.

In Greek legends, Aquarius is represented by Ganymede, who was carried to heaven by an eagle in order to become the cup bearer of Zeus and to supervise the annual flooding of the Nile. The sign later became associated with aviation and notions of flight.

The Pisces Glyph)(

Here is an abstraction of the familiar image of Pisces, two fishes swimming in opposite directions, yet bound together by a cord. The fishes represent the spirit, which yearns for the freedom of heaven, and the soul, which remains attached to the desires of the temporal world. During life on Earth, the spirit and the soul are bound together. When they complement each other, instead of pulling in opposite directions they facilitate the Pisces creativity. The ancient version of this glyph, taken from the Egyptians, had no connecting line, which was added in the fourteenth century.

In another interpretation, it is said that the left fish

indicates the direction of involution or the beginning of a cycle, while the right fish signifies the direction of evolution, the way to completion of a cycle. It's an appropriate grand finale for Pisces, the last sign of the zodiac.

CHAPTER 5

How Your Rising Sign Personalizes Your Horoscope

Have you ever wondered what makes your horoscope unique, how your chart could be different from that of anyone else born on your birthday? Yes, other babies who may have been born later or earlier on the same day, in the same hospital, as you were, will be sure to have most planets in the same signs as you do. Most of your high school class, in fact, will have several planets in the same signs as your planets, especially the slow-moving planets (Uranus, Neptune, Pluto) and very possibly Jupiter and Saturn, which usually spend a year or more in each sign.

What makes a horoscope truly "yours" is the rising sign (or ascendant), the sign that was coming up over the eastern horizon at the moment you were born. This sign establishes the exact horoscope of your birth time. In astrology, this is called the *rising sign*, often referred to as the ascendant. As the earth moves, a different sign rises every two hours.

If you have read the chapter in this book on houses, you'll know that the houses are twelve stationary divisions of the horoscope, which represent areas of life. The sign which is moving over the house describes that area of life. The rising sign marks the border of the first house, which represents your first presentation to the world, your physical body, and how you come across to others. It has been called your "shop window," the first impression you give to others. After the rising sign is determined, then each "house" will be influenced by the signs which follow it.

Once the rising sign is established, it becomes possible to analyze a chart accurately because the astrologer knows in which area of life (house) the planets will operate. For instance, if Mars is in Gemini and your rising sign is Taurus, then Mars will most likely be active in the second or financial house of your chart. If you were born later in the day and your rising sign is Virgo, then Mars will be positioned at the top of your chart, energizing your tenth house or career. That is why many astrologers insist on knowing the exact time of a client's birth, before they analyze a chart. The more exact your birthtime, the more accurately an astrologer can position the planets in your chart. This is important, because if you were born when the midportion of a sign was rotating over the horizon and a key planet—let's say Saturn—was in the early degrees of that sign, then it would already be over the horizon, located in the twelfth house, rather than the first. So the interpretation of your horoscope would be quite different: you would not have the serious Saturn influence in the way you come across to others, which would be the case if you were born an hour earlier. If a planet is near the ascendant, sometimes even a few minutes can make a big difference.

Your rising sign has an important relationship with your sun sign. Some will complement the sun sign; others hide it under a totally different mask, as if playing an entirely different role, so it is often difficult to guess the person's sun sign from outer appearances. For example, a Leo with a conservative Capricorn ascendant would come across as much less flamboyant than a Leo with a fiery Aries or Sagittarius ascendant. The exception is when the sun sign is reinforced by other planets; then, with other planets on its side, the sun may assert its personality much more strongly, overcoming the image of a contradictory rising sign. For example, a Leo with Venus and Jupiter also in

103

Leo might counteract the conservative image of the Capricorn ascendant, in the above example. However, in most cases, the ascendant is the ingredient most strongly reflected in the first impression you make.

Rising signs change every two hours with the Earth's rotation. Those born early in the morning when the sun was on the horizon will be most likely to project the image of their sun sign. These people are often called a "double Aries" or a "double Virgo," because the same sun sign and ascendant reinforce each other.

Look up your rising sign on the chart at the end of this chapter. Since rising signs change every two hours, it is important to know your birth time as close to the minute as possible. Even a few minutes' difference could change the rising sign and therefore the setup of your chart. If you are unsure about the exact time, but know within a few hours, check the following descriptions to see which is most like the personality you project.

Aries Rising—Fiery Emotions

You are the most aggressive version of your sun sign, with boundless energy which can be used productively, if it's channeled in the right direction. Watch a tendency to overreact emotionally and blow your top. You come across as openly competitive, a positive asset in business or sports. Be on guard against impatience, which could lead to head injuries. Your walk and bearing could have the telltale head-forward Aries posture. You may wear more bright colors, especially red, than others of your sign. You may also have a tendency to drive your car faster.

Taurus Rising—The Earth Mother

You'll exude a protective nurturing quality, even if you're male, which draws those in need of TLC and support. You're slow-moving, with a beautiful (or distinctive) speaking or singing voice that can be especially soothing or melodious. You probably surround yourself with comfort, good food, luxurious surroundings and sensual pleasures, and prefer welcoming others into your home to gadding about. You may have a talent for business, especially in trading, appraising, and real estate. This ascendant gives a well-padded or curvaceous physique, which gains weight easily. Women with this ascendant are naturally sexy in a bodacious way.

Gemini Rising—Expressive Talents

You're naturally sociable, with lighter, more ethereal mannerisms than others of your sign, especially if you're female. You love to communicate with people and express your ideas and feelings easily. You may have writing or public speaking talent. Like Drew Barrymore, you may thrive on a constantly changing scenario with a varied cast of characters, though you may be far more sympathetic and caring than you project. You will probably travel widely, changing partners and jobs several times (or juggling two at once). Physically, you should cultivate a calm, tranquil atmosphere, because your nerves are quite sensitive.

Cancer Rising—Sensitive Antennae

Like billionaire Bill Gates, you are naturally acquisitive, possessive, private, a moneymaker. You easily pick up others' needs and feelings, a great gift in business, the arts, and personal relationships, but guard against overreacting or taking things too personally, especially during full moon periods. Find creative outlets for your natural nurturing gifts, such as helping the less fortunate, particularly children. Your insights would be useful in psychology, your desire to feed and care for others in the restaurant, hotel, or child care industry. You may be especially fond of wearing romantic old clothes, collecting antiques, and of course, good food. Since your body may retain fluids, pay attention to your diet. To relax, escape to places near water.

Leo Rising—The Scene Player

You may come across as more poised than you really feel; however, you play it to the hilt, projecting a proud royal presence. This ascendant gives you a natural flair for drama, like Marilyn Monroe. You'll also project a much more outgoing, optimistic, sunny personality than others of your sign. You take care to please your public by always projecting your best star quality, probably tossing a luxuriant mane of hair or, if you're female, dazzling with a spectacular jewelry collection. Since you may have a strong parental nature, you could well be the regal family matriarch or patriarch.

Virgo Rising—Cool and Calculating

Virgo rising masks your inner nature with a practical, analytical outer image. You seem neat, orderly, more particular than others of your sign. Others in your life may feel they must live up to your high standards. Though at times you may be openly critical, this masks a well-meaning desire to have only the best for loved ones. Your sharp eye for details could be used in the financial world, or your literary skills could draw you to teaching or publishing. The healing arts, health care, service-oriented professions attract many with this Virgo emphasis in their chart. Like Madonna, you're likely to take good care of yourself, with great attention to health, diet, and exercise. Physically, you may have a very sensitive digestive system.

Libra Rising—The Charmer

Libra rising makes you appear as a charmer, more of a social, public person than others of your sign. Your private life will extend beyond your home and family to include an active social life. You may tend to avoid confrontations in relationships, preferring to smooth the way or negotiate diplomatically, rather than give in to an emotional reaction. Because you are interested in all aspects of a situation, you may be slow to reach decisions. Physically, you'll have good proportions and pleasing symmetry. You're likely to have pleasing, if not beautiful, facial features. You move gracefully, and you have a winning smile and good taste in your clothes and home decor. Legal, diplomatic, or public relations professions could draw your interest. Men with Libra rising, like Bill Clinton and John F. Kennedy, have charming smiles and easy social manner that charms the ladies.

Scorpio Rising—Magnetic Power

Even when you're in the public eye, like Jacqueline Kennedy Onassis, you never lose your intriguing air of mystery and sense of underlying power. You can be a master manipulator, always in control and moving comfortably in the world of power. Your physical impression comes across as intense, and many of you have remarkable eyes, with a direct, penetrating gaze. But you'll never reveal your private agenda, and you tend to keep your true feelings under wraps (watch a tendency toward paranoia). You may have an interesting romantic history with secret love affairs. Many of you heighten your air of mystery by wearing black. You're happiest near water and should provide yourself with a seaside retreat.

Sagittarius Rising—The Wanderer

You travel with this ascendant. You may also be a more outdoor, sportive type, with an athletic, casual, outgoing air. Your moods are camouflaged with cheerful optimism or a philosophical attitude. Though you don't hesitate to speak your mind, you can also laugh at your troubles or crack a joke more easily than others of your sign, like Candice Bergen, who is best known for her comedy role as the outspoken "Murphy Brown." This ascendant can also draw you to the field of higher education or to spiritual life. You'll seem to have less attachment to things and people and may travel widely. Your strong, fast legs are a physical bonus.

Capricorn Rising—Serious Business

This rising sign makes you come across as serious, goal-oriented, disciplined, and careful with cash. You are not one of the zodiac's big spenders, though you might splurge occasionally on items with good investment value. You're the traditional, conservative type in dress and environment, and you might come across as quite formal and businesslike. You'll function well in a structured or corporate environment where you can climb to the top. (You are always aware of who's the boss.) In your personal life, you could be a loner or a single parent who is "father and mother" to your children. Like Paul Newman, you're likely to prefer a quiet private life to living in the spotlight.

Aquarius Rising—One of a Kind

You come across as less concerned about what others think and could even be a bit eccentric. Your appearance is sure to be unique and memorable. You're more at ease with groups of people than others in your sign, and may be attracted to public life. Your appearance may be unique, either unconventional or unimportant to you. Those with the sun in a water sign (Cancer, Scorpio, Pisces) may exercise your nurturing qualities with a large group, an extended family, or a day care or community center. Audrey Hepburn and Princess Diana, who had this rising sign, were known for their unique charisma and work on behalf of worthy causes.

Pisces Rising—Romantic Roles

Your creative, nurturing talents are heightened and so is your ability to project emotional drama. And your dreamy eyes and poetic air bring out the protective instinct in others. You could be attracted to the arts, especially theater, dance, film, or photography, or to psychology or spiritual or charity work. You are happiest when you are using your creative ability to help others, as Robert Redford has done. Since you are vulnerable to mood swings, it is especially important for you to find interesting, creative work where you can express your talents and boost your self-esteem. Accentuate the positive and be wary of escapist tendencies, particularly involving alcohol or drugs, to which you are supersensitive.

RISING SIGNS—A.M. BIRTHS

	1 AM	2 AM	3 AM	4 AM	5 AM	6 AM	7 AM	8 AM	9 AM	10 AM	11 AM	12 NOON
Jan 1	Lib	Sc	Sc	Sc	Sag	Sag	Cap	Cap	Aq	Aq	Pis	Ar
Jan 9	Lib	Sc	Sc	Sag	Sag	Sag	Cap	Cap	Aq	Pis	Ar	Tau
Jan 17	Sc	Sc	Sc	Sag	Sag	Cap	Cap	Aq	Aq	Pis	Ar	Tau
Jan 25	Sc	Sc	Sag	Sag	Sag	Cap	Cap	Aq	Pis	Ar	Tau	Tau
Feb 2	Sc	Sc	Sag	Sag	Cap	Cap	Aq	Pis	Pis	Ar	Tau	Gem
Feb 10	Sc	Sag	Sag	Sag	Cap	Cap	Aq	Pis	Ar	Tau	Tau	Gem
Feb 18	Sc	Sag	Sag	Cap	Cap	Aq	Pis	Pis	Ar	Tau	Gem	Gem
Feb 26	Sag	Sag	Sag	Cap	Aq	Aq	Pis	Ar	Tau	Tau	Gem	Gem
Mar 6	Sag	Sag	Cap	Cap	Aq	Pis	Pis	Ar	Tau	Gem	Gem	Can
Mar 14	Sag	Cap	Cap	Aq	Aq	Pis	Ar	Tau	Tau	Gem	Gem	Can
Mar 22	Sag	Cap	Cap	Aq	Pis	Ar	Ar	Tau	Gem	Gem	Can	Can
Mar 30	Cap	Cap	Aq	Pis	Pis	Ar	Tau	Tau	Gem	Can	Can	Can
Apr 7	Cap	Cap	Aq	Pis	Ar	Ar	Tau	Gem	Gem	Can	Can	Leo
Apr 14	Cap	Aq	Aq	Pis	Ar	Tau	Tau	Gem	Gem	Can	Can	Leo
Apr 22	Cap	Aq	Pis	Ar	Ar	Tau	Gem	Gem	Can	Can	Leo	Leo
Apr 30	Aq	Aq	Pis	Ar	Tau	Tau	Gem	Can	Can	Can	Leo	Leo
May 8	Aq	Pis	Ar	Ar	Tau	Gem	Gem	Can	Can	Leo	Leo	Leo
May 16	Aq	Pis	Ar	Tau	Gem	Gem	Can	Can	Can	Leo	Leo	Vir
May 24	Pis	Ar	Ar	Tau	Gem	Gem	Can	Can	Leo	Leo	Leo	Vir
June 1	Pis	Ar	Tau	Gem	Gem	Can	Can	Can	Leo	Leo	Vir	Vir
June 9	Ar	Ar	Tau	Gem	Gem	Can	Can	Leo	Leo	Leo	Vir	Vir
June 17	Ar	Tau	Gem	Gem	Can	Can	Can	Leo	Leo	Vir	Vir	Vir
June 25	Tau	Tau	Gem	Gem	Can	Can	Leo	Leo	Leo	Vir	Vir	Lib
July 3	Tau	Gem	Gem	Can	Can	Can	Leo	Leo	Vir	Vir	Vir	Lib
July 11	Tau	Gem	Gem	Can	Can	Leo	Leo	Leo	Vir	Vir	Lib	Lib
July 18	Gem	Gem	Can	Can	Can	Leo	Leo	Vir	Vir	Vir	Lib	Lib
July 26	Gem	Gem	Can	Can	Leo	Leo	Vir	Vir	Vir	Lib	Lib	Lib
Aug 3	Gem	Can	Can	Can	Leo	Leo	Vir	Vir	Vir	Lib	Lib	Sc
Aug 11	Gem	Can	Can	Leo	Leo	Leo	Vir	Vir	Lib	Lib	Lib	Sc
Aug 18	Can	Can	Can	Leo	Leo	Vir	Vir	Vir	Lib	Lib	Sc	Sc
Aug 27	Can	Can	Leo	Leo	Leo	Vir	Vir	Lib	Lib	Lib	Sc	Sc
Sept 4	Can	Can	Leo	Leo	Leo	Vir	Vir	Vir	Lib	Lib	Sc	Sc
Sept 12	Can	Leo	Leo	Leo	Vir	Vir	Lib	Lib	Lib	Sc	Sc	Sag
Sept 20	Leo	Leo	Leo	Vir	Vir	Vir	Lib	Lib	Sc	Sc	Sc	Sag
Sept 28	Leo	Leo	Leo	Vir	Vir	Lib	Lib	Lib	Sc	Sc	Sag	Sag
Oct 6	Leo	Leo	Vir	Vir	Vir	Lib	Lib	Sc	Sc	Sc	Sag	Sag
Oct 14	Leo	Vir	Vir	Vir	Lib	Lib	Lib	Sc	Sc	Sag	Sag	Cap
Oct 22	Leo	Vir	Vir	Lib	Lib	Lib	Sc	Sc	Sc	Sag	Sag	Cap
Oct 30	Vir	Vir	Vir	Lib	Lib	Sc	Sc	Sc	Sag	Sag	Cap	Cap
Nov 7	Vir	Vir	Lib	Lib	Lib	Sc	Sc	Sc	Sag	Sag	Cap	Cap
Nov 15	Vir	Vir	Lib	Lib	Sc	Sc	Sc	Sag	Sag	Cap	Cap	Aq
Nov 23	Vir	Lib	Lib	Lib	Sc	Sc	Sag	Sag	Sag	Cap	Cap	Aq
Dec 1	Vir	Lib	Lib	Sc	Sc	Sc	Sag	Sag	Cap	Cap	Aq	Aq
Dec 9	Lib	Lib	Lib	Sc	Sc	Sag	Sag	Sag	Cap	Cap	Aq	Pis
Dec 18	Lib	Lib	Sc	Sc	Sc	Sag	Sag	Cap	Cap	Aq	Aq	Pis
Dec 28	Lib	Lib	Sc	Sc	Sag	Sag	Sag	Cap	Aq	Aq	Pis	Ar

RISING SIGNS—P.M. BIRTHS

	1 PM	2 PM	3 PM	4 PM	5 PM	6 PM	7 PM	8 PM	9 PM	10 PM	11 PM	12 MID-NIGHT
Jan 1	Tau	Gem	Gem	Can	Can	Can	Leo	Leo	Vir	Vir	Vir	Lib
Jan 9	Tau	Gem	Gem	Can	Can	Leo	Leo	Leo	Vir	Vir	Vir	Lib
Jan 17	Gem	Gem	Can	Can	Can	Leo	Leo	Vir	Vir	Vir	Lib	Lib
Jan 25	Gem	Gem	Can	Can	Leo	Leo	Leo	Vir	Vir	Lib	Lib	Lib
Feb 2	Gem	Can	Can	Can	Leo	Leo	Vir	Vir	Vir	Lib	Lib	Sc
Feb 10	Gem	Can	Can	Leo	Leo	Leo	Vir	Vir	Lib	Lib	Lib	Sc
Feb 18	Can	Can	Can	Leo	Leo	Vir	Vir	Vir	Lib	Lib	Sc	Sc
Feb 26	Can	Can	Leo	Leo	Leo	Vir	Vir	Lib	Lib	Lib	Sc	Sc
Mar 6	Can	Leo	Leo	Leo	Vir	Vir	Vir	Lib	Lib	Sc	Sc	Sc
Mar 14	Can	Leo	Leo	Vir	Vir	Vir	Lib	Lib	Lib	Sc	Sc	Sag
Mar 22	Leo	Leo	Leo	Vir	Vir	Lib	Lib	Lib	Sc	Sc	Sc	Sag
Mar 30	Leo	Leo	Vir	Vir	Vir	Lib	Lib	Sc	Sc	Sc	Sag	Sag
Apr 7	Leo	Leo	Vir	Vir	Lib	Lib	Lib	Sc	Sc	Sc	Sag	Sag
Apr 14	Leo	Vir	Vir	Vir	Lib	Lib	Sc	Sc	Sc	Sag	Sag	Cap
Apr 22	Leo	Vir	Vir	Lib	Lib	Lib	Sc	Sc	Sc	Sag	Sag	Cap
Apr 30	Vir	Vir	Vir	Lib	Lib	Sc	Sc	Sc	Sag	Sag	Cap	Cap
May 8	Vir	Vir	Lib	Lib	Lib	Sc	Sc	Sag	Sag	Sag	Cap	Cap
May 16	Vir	Vir	Lib	Lib	Sc	Sc	Sc	Sag	Sag	Cap	Cap	Aq
May 24	Vir	Lib	Lib	Lib	Sc	Sc	Sag	Sag	Sag	Cap	Cap	Aq
June 1	Vir	Lib	Lib	Sc	Sc	Sc	Sag	Sag	Cap	Cap	Aq	Aq
June 9	Lib	Lib	Lib	Sc	Sc	Sag	Sag	Sag	Cap	Cap	Aq	Pis
June 17	Lib	Lib	Sc	Sc	Sc	Sag	Sag	Cap	Cap	Aq	Aq	Pis
June 25	Lib	Lib	Sc	Sc	Sag	Sag	Sag	Cap	Cap	Aq	Pis	Ar
July 3	Lib	Sc	Sc	Sc	Sag	Sag	Cap	Cap	Aq	Aq	Pis	Ar
July 11	Lib	Sc	Sc	Sag	Sag	Sag	Cap	Cap	Aq	Pis	Ar	Tau
July 18	Sc	Sc	Sc	Sag	Sag	Cap	Cap	Aq	Aq	Pis	Ar	Tau
July 26	Sc	Sc	Sag	Sag	Sag	Cap	Cap	Aq	Pis	Ar	Tau	Tau
Aug 3	Sc	Sc	Sag	Sag	Cap	Cap	Aq	Aq	Pis	Ar	Tau	Gem
Aug 11	Sc	Sag	Sag	Sag	Cap	Cap	Aq	Pis	Ar	Tau	Tau	Gem
Aug 18	Sc	Sag	Sag	Cap	Cap	Aq	Pis	Pis	Ar	Tau	Gem	Gem
Aug 27	Sag	Sag	Sag	Cap	Cap	Aq	Pis	Ar	Tau	Tau	Gem	Gem
Sept 4	Sag	Sag	Cap	Cap	Aq	Pis	Pis	Ar	Tau	Gem	Gem	Can
Sept 12	Sag	Sag	Cap	Aq	Aq	Pis	Ar	Tau	Tau	Gem	Gem	Can
Sept 20	Sag	Cap	Cap	Aq	Pis	Pis	Ar	Tau	Gem	Gem	Can	Can
Sept 28	Cap	Cap	Aq	Aq	Pis	Ar	Tau	Tau	Gem	Gem	Can	Can
Oct 6	Cap	Cap	Aq	Pis	Ar	Ar	Tau	Gem	Gem	Can	Can	Leo
Oct 14	Cap	Aq	Aq	Pis	Ar	Tau	Tau	Gem	Gem	Can	Can	Leo
Oct 22	Cap	Aq	Pis	Ar	Ar	Tau	Gem	Gem	Can	Can	Leo	Leo
Oct 30	Aq	Aq	Pis	Ar	Tau	Tau	Gem	Can	Can	Can	Leo	Leo
Nov 7	Aq	Aq	Pis	Ar	Tau	Tau	Gem	Can	Can	Can	Leo	Leo
Nov 15	Aq	Pis	Ar	Tau	Gem	Gem	Can	Can	Can	Leo	Leo	Vir
Nov 23	Pis	Ar	Ar	Tau	Gem	Gem	Can	Can	Leo	Leo	Leo	Vir
Dec 1	Pis	Ar	Tau	Gem	Gem	Can	Can	Can	Leo	Leo	Vir	Vir
Dec 9	Ar	Tau	Tau	Gem	Gem	Can	Can	Leo	Leo	Leo	Vir	Vir
Dec 18	Ar	Tau	Gem	Gem	Can	Can	Can	Leo	Leo	Vir	Vir	Vir
Dec 28	Tau	Tau	Gem	Gem	Can	Can	Leo	Leo	Vir	Vir	Vir	Lib

CHAPTER 6

The Moon—Our Light Within

In some astrology-conscious lands, the moon is given as much importance in a horoscope as the sun. Astrologers often refer to these two bodies as the "lights," an apt term, since they shed the most light upon our personality in a horoscope reading. This also is a more technically appropriate description, since the sun and moon are not really planets, but a star and a satellite.

The most fascinating aspect of the moon is its connection with our emotional state. Our moods seem to wax and wane with the moon. Even the state of shell-fish, animals, and planets is affected by the moon phase. Imagine what would happen if the moon were somehow caused to change its orbit, perhaps by a bombarding asteroid. What would happen to the tides, to ocean and plant life, which respond to the moon, or to our own bodies, which are mostly water? Life on earth would be impossible!

As the closest celestial body, the moon represents your receptive, reflective, female, nurturing self. And it reflects who you were nurtured by—the "mother" or mother figure in your chart. In a man's chart, the moon position also describes his receptive, emotional, "yin" side, as well as the woman in his life who will have the deepest effect, usually his mother. (Venus reveals the kind of woman who attracts him physically.)

The sign the moon was passing through at birth reveals much about your inner life, your needs and secrets, as well as those of people you'd like to know better. You can learn what appeals to a person sub-consciously by knowing their moon sign, which reflects their instinctive, emotional nature.

It's well worth having an accurate chart cast to determine your moon sign. Since accurate moon tables are too extensive for this book, check through these descriptions to find the moon sign that feels most familiar.

The moon is more at home in some signs than others. It rules maternal Cancer and is exalted in Taurus—both comforting, home-loving signs where the natural emotional energies of the moon are easily and productively expressed. But when the moon is in the opposite signs—Capricorn or Scorpio—it leaves the comfortable nest and deals with emotional issues of power and achievement in the outside world. Those of you with the moon in these signs are more likely to find your emotional role more challenging in life.

Moon in Aries

You are an idealistic, impetuous person who falls in and out of love easily. This placement makes you both independent and ardent. You love a challenge, but could cool once your quarry is captured. You should cultivate patience and tolerance—or you might tend to gravitate toward those who treat you rough, just for the sake of challenge and excitement.

Moon in Taurus

You are a sentimental soul who is very fond of the good life and gravitates toward solid, secure relationships. You like displays of affection and creature comforts—all the tangible trappings of a cozy, safe, calm atmosphere. You are sensual and steady emotionally, but very stubborn and determined. You can't be pushed and tend to dislike changes. You should make an effort to broaden your horizons and to take a risk sometimes.

Moon in Gemini

You crave mental stimulation and variety in life, which you usually get through either an ever-varied social life, the excitement of flirtation, and/or multiple professional involvements. You may marry more than once and have a rather chaotic emotional life due to your difficulty with commitment and settling down. Be sure to find a partner who is as outgoing as you are. You will have to learn at some point to focus your energies because you tend to be somewhat fragmented—to do two things at once, to have two homes or even two lovers. If you can find a creative way to express your many-faceted nature, you'll be ahead of the game.

Moon in Cancer

This is the most powerful lunar position, which is sure to make a deep imprint on your character. Your needs are very much associated with your reaction to the needs of others. You are very sensitive and self-protective, though some of you may mask this with a hard shell. This placement also gives you an excellent memory, keen intuition, and an uncanny ability to perceive the needs of others. All of the lunar phases will affect you, especially full moons and eclipses, so you would do well to mark them on your calendar. Because you're happiest at home, you may work at home or turn your office into a second home, where you can nurture and comfort people. (You may tend to "mother the world.") With natural psychic, intuitive ability, you might be drawn to occult work in some way. Or you may get professionally involved with providing food and shelter to others.

Moon in Leo

This warm, passionate moon takes everything to heart. You are attracted to all that is noble, generous, and aristocratic in life (and may be a bit of a snob). You have an innate ability to take command emotionally, but you do need strong support, loyalty, and loud applause from those you love. You are possessive of your loved ones and your turf and will roar if anyone threatens to take over your territory.

Moon in Virgo

You are rather cool until you decide if others measure up. But once someone or something meets your ideal standards, you hold up your end of the arrangement perfectly. You may, in fact, drive yourself too hard to attain some notion of perfection. Try to be a bit easier on yourself and others. Don't always act the censor! You love to be the teacher and are drawn to situations where you can change others for the better, but sometimes you must learn to accept others for what they are—enjoy what you have!

Moon in Libra

A partnership-oriented moon—you may find it difficult to be alone or to do things alone. After you have learned emotional balance by leaning on yourself first, you can have excellent relationships. It is best for you to avoid extremes, however, which set your scales swinging and can make your love life precarious. You thrive in a rather conservative, traditional, romantic relationship, where you receive attention and flattery—but not possessiveness—from your partner. You'll be your most charming in an elegant, harmonious atmosphere.

Moon in Scorpio

This is a moon that enjoys and responds to intense, passionate feelings. You may go to extremes and have a very dramatic emotional life, full of ardor, suspicion, jealousy, and obsession. It would be much healthier to channel your need for power and control into meaningful work. This is a good position for anyone in the fields of medicine, police work, research, the occult, psychoanalysis, or intuitive work, because life-and-death situations don't faze you. However, you do take personal disappointments very hard.

Moon in Sagittarius

You take life's ups and downs with good humor and the proverbial grain of salt. You'll love 'em and leave 'em, taking off on a great adventure at a moment's notice. "Born free" could be your slogan. Attracted by the exotic, you have wanderlust mentally and physically. You may be too much in search of new mental and spiritual stimulation to ever settle down.

Moon in Capricorn

Are you ever accused of being too cool and calculating? You have an earthy side, but you take prestige and position very seriously. Your strong drive to succeed extends to your romantic life, where you will be devoted to improving your lifestyle, rising to the top. A structured situation where you can advance methodically makes you feel wonderfully secure. You may be attracted to someone older or very much younger or from a different social world. It may be difficult to look at the lighter side of emotional relationships; however, the "up" side of this moon in the sign of its detriment is that you tend to be very dutiful and responsible to those you care for.

Moon in Aquarius

You are a people collector with many friends of all backgrounds. You are happiest surrounded by people and may feel uneasy when left alone. Though you usually stay friends with lovers, intense emotions and demanding one-on-one relationships turn you off. You don't like anything to be too rigid or scheduled. Though tolerant and understanding, you can be emotionally unpredictable and may opt for an unconventional love life. With plenty of space, you will be able to sustain relationships with liberal, freedom-loving types.

Moon in Pisces

You are very responsive and empathetic to others, especially if they have problems or are the underdog. (Be on guard against attracting too many people with sob stories.) You'll be happiest if you can express your creative imagination in the arts or in the spiritual or healing professions. Because you may tend to escape in fantasies or overreact to the moods of others, you need an emotional anchor to help you keep a firm foothold in reality. Steer clear of too much escapism (especially in alcohol) or reclusiveness. Places near water soothe your moods. Working in a field that gives you emotional variety will also help you to be productive.

What Eclipses Do to Your Moods

In case we've been taking the moon for granted, the eclipse seasons, which occur about every six months, remind us how important the moon is for our survival. Perhaps that is why eclipses have always had an ominous reputation. Folklore all over the world blames eclipses for catastrophes such as birth defects, crop failures, and hurricanes. Villagers on the peninsula of Baja California paint their fruit trees red and wear red ribbons and underwear to deflect "evil rays." During the total eclipse of July 1991, everyone retreated safely indoors to follow the eclipse on television. In other native societies, people play drums and make loud noises to frighten off heavenly monsters believed to destroy the light of the sun and moon. Only the romantic Tahitians seem to have positive feelings about an eclipse. In this sensual tropical paradise, legend declares that the "lights" go out when the sun and moon make love and procreate the stars.

Ancient Chaldean astrologer-priests were the first to time eclipses accurately. They discovered that 6,585 days after an eclipse, another eclipse would happen. By counting ahead after all the eclipses in a given year, they could predict eclipses eighteen years into the future. This technique was practiced by navigators through the centuries, including Christopher Columbus, who used his knowledge of an upcoming lunar eclipse to extort food from the frightened inhabitants of Jamaica in 1504. In ancient Mexico, Mayan astronomer-priests also discovered that eclipses occur at regular intervals and recorded them with a hieroglyph of a serpent swallowing the sun.

What Causes an Eclipse?

A solar eclipse is the passage of the new moon directly across the face of the sun. It is a very exciting and awesome event, which causes the sky to darken suddenly. Though the effect lasts only a few minutes, it is enough to strike panic in the uninformed viewer.

A lunar eclipse happens when the full moon passes through the shadow of the Earth on the opposite side from the sun; as a result, the Earth blocks out the sun's light from reaching the moon. The moon must be in level alignment with the sun and Earth for a lunar eclipse to occur.

Conditions are ripe for an eclipse twice a year, when a full or a new moon is most likely to cross the path of the sun at two points known as the *nodes*.

What to Know About Nodes

To understand the nodes, visualize two rings, one inside the other. As you move the rings, you'll notice that the two circles intersect at opposite points. Now imagine one ring as the moon's orbit and the other as the sun's (as seen from Earth). The crossing points are called the moon's "nodes."

For an eclipse to happen, two conditions must be met. First, the path of the orbiting moon must be close enough to a node. Second, this must happen at a time when there is either a new or a full moon. (Not every new or full moon happens close enough to the nodes to create an eclipse.) The axis of the nodes is continually moving backward through the zodiac at the rate of about one and a half degrees per month; therefore, eclipses will eventually occur in every sign of the zodiac.

How Often Do Eclipses Occur?

Whenever the sun draws close to one of the nodes, any new or full moon happening near that time will create an eclipse. This "eclipse season" happens twice a year, approximately six months apart. There are at least four eclipses each year, and there can be as many as seven. In 2002, there will be five eclipses:

- Full Moon in Sagittarius (lunar eclipse)—May 26
- New Moon in Gemini (solar eclipse)—June 10
- Full Moon in Capricorn (lunar eclipse)—June 24

119

- Full Moon in Taurus (lunar eclipse)—November 19
- New Moon in Sagittarius (solar eclipse)—December 4

Eclipses Have Family Ties

One of the most interesting things about eclipses is that they have "families." Each eclipse is a member of a string of related eclipses that pop up regularly. As mentioned before, the ancient Chaldeans, who were the first great sky-watchers, discovered that eclipses recur in patterns, repeating themselves after approximately eighteen years plus nine to eleven days, in a cycle lasting a total of approximately 1,300 years. Much later, in the eleventh century A.D., these patterns became known as the "Saros Series." (In ancient Greek, "saros" means repetition.)

Because each Saros Series begins at a moment in time, the initial eclipse has a horoscope, and therefore a "personality" which goes through stages of development as the series of eclipses progresses over its 1,300-year lifetime. So as a Saros Series moves through your chart, it will produce an eclipse with a similar "personality" every eighteen years. In the interim, you'll experience eclipses belonging to other Saros Series, which will exhibit their own special family characteristics. Therefore, there can be no one generic interpretation for eclipses, since each affects your horoscope in a different way, according to the personality of its particular Saros Series.

What Is the Purpose of an Eclipse in My Life?

Eclipses can bring on milestone events in your life, if they aspect a key point in your horoscope. In general, they shake up the status quo, bringing hidden areas out into the open. During this time, problems you've been avoiding or have brushed aside can surface to demand your attention. A good coping strategy is to accept whatever comes up as a challenge. It could make a big difference in your life. And don't forget the power of your sense of humor. If you can laugh at something, you'll never be afraid of it.

Second-guessing the eclipses is easy if you have a copy of your horoscope calculated by a computer. (If you do not have a computer or an astrology program, there are several sites on the Internet which will calculate your chart free. See the listings in the resource chapter of this book.) This enables you to pinpoint the area of your life which will be affected. However, you can make an educated guess, by setting up a rough diagram on your own. If you'd like to find out which area of your life this year's eclipses are most likely to affect, follow these easy steps. First, you must know the time of day you were born and look up your rising sign listed in the tables in this book. Then set up an estimated horoscope by drawing a circle, then dividing it into four parts by making a cross directly through the center. Continue to divide each of the parts into thirds, as if you were dividing a cake, until you have twelve slices. Write your rising sign on the middle left-hand slice, which would be the 9 o'clock point, if you were looking at your watch. Then continue listing the signs counterclockwise, until you have listed all twelve signs of the zodiac on the "slices" of the chart.

You should now have a basic diagram of your horoscope chart (minus the planets, of course). Starting with your rising sign "slice," number each portion consecutively, working counterclockwise. Since this year's eclipses will fall in Gemini, Sagittarius, Taurus, and Capricorn, find the number of these slices or "houses" on the chart and read the following descriptions for the kinds of issues that are likely to be emphasized.

If an eclipse falls in your FIRST HOUSE—
Events cause you to examine the ways you are acting independently, pushing you to become more visible and to assert yourself. This is a time when you feel compelled to make your own decisions and do your own thing. There is an emphasis on how you are coming across to others. You may want to change your physical appearance, body image, or style of dress in some way. Under affliction, there might be illness or physical harm.

If an eclipse falls in your SECOND HOUSE—
This is the place where you consider all matters of security. You consolidate your resources, earn money, acquire property, and decide what you value and what you want to own. On a deeper level, this house reveals your sense of self-worth, the inner values that draw wealth in various forms.

If an eclipse falls in your THIRD HOUSE—
Here you communicate, reach out to others, express your ideas, and explore different courses of action. You may feel especially restless, and have confrontations with neighbors or siblings. In your search for more knowledge, you may decide to improve your skills, get more education, or sign up for a course that interests you, which could ultimately alter your lifestyle. Local transportation, especially your car, might be affected by an eclipse here.

If an eclipse falls in your FOURTH HOUSE—
Here is where you put down roots and establish your home base. You'll consider what home really means to you. Issues involving parents, the physical setup or location of your home, or your immediate family demand your attention. You may be especially concerned with parenting or relationships with your own mother. You may consider moving your home to a new location or leaving home, untying family ties.

If an eclipse falls in your FIFTH HOUSE—

Here is where you express yourself, either through your personal talents or through procreating children. You are interested in making your special talents visible. This is also the house of love affairs and the romantic aspect of life, where you flirt, have fun, and enjoy the excitement of love. Hobbies and crafts, the ways you explore the playful child within, fall in this area.

If an eclipse falls in your SIXTH HOUSE—

This is your care and maintenance department, where you take care of your health, organize your life, and set up a daily routine. It is also the place where you perfect your skills and add polish to your life. The chores you do every day, the skills you learn, and the techniques you use fall here. If something doesn't "work" in your life, an eclipse is sure to bring this to light. If you've been neglecting your health, diet, and fitness, you'll probably pay the consequences during an eclipse. Or you may be faced with work that requires much routine organization and steady effort, rather than creative ability. Or you may be required to perform services for others. (In ancient astrology, this was the place of slavery!)

If an eclipse falls in your SEVENTH HOUSE—

This is the area of committed relationships, of those which involve legal agreements, of working in a close relationship with another. Here you'll be dealing with how you relate and what you'll be willing to give up for the sake of a marriage or partnership. Eclipses here can put extra pressure on a relationship and, if it's not working, precipitate a breakup. Lawsuits and open enemies also reside here.

If an eclipse falls in your EIGHTH HOUSE—

This area is concerned with power and control. Consider what you are willing to give up in order that something might happen. Power struggles, intense relationships, and a desire to penetrate a deeper mystery belong here. Debts, loans, financial matters that involve another party, and wheeling and dealing also come into focus. So does sex, where you surrender your individual power to create a new life together. Matters involving birth and death are also involved here.

If an eclipse falls in your NINTH HOUSE—
Here is where you look at the Big Picture: how everything relates to form a pattern. You'll seek information that helps you find meaning in life: higher education, religion, travel, and global issues. Eclipses here can push you to get out of your rut, explore something you've never done before, and expand your horizons.

If an eclipse falls in your TENTH HOUSE—
This is the high-profile point in your chart. Here is where you consider how society looks at you, and what your position is in the outside world. You'll be concerned about whether you receive proper credit for your work and if you're recognized by higher-ups. Promotions, raises, and other forms of recognition can be given or denied. Your standing in your career or community can be challenged, or you'll get publicly acknowledged for achieving a goal. An eclipse here can make you famous . . . or burst your balloon if you've been too ambitious or neglecting other areas of your life.

If an eclipse falls in your ELEVENTH HOUSE—
Your relationship with groups of people comes under scrutiny during an eclipse—whom you are identified with, whom you socialize with, and how well you are accepted by other members of your team. Activities of clubs, political parties, networking, and social inter-

actions become important. You'll be concerned about what other people think: "Do they like me?" "Will I make the team, or win the election?"

If an eclipse falls in your TWELFTH HOUSE—
This is the time when the focus turns to your inner life. An especially favorable eclipse here might bring you great insight and inspiration. Or events may happen which cause you to retreat from public life. Here is where we go to be alone, or to do spiritual or reparative work in retreats, hospitals, religious institutions, or psychotherapy. Here is where you deliver selfless service, through charitable acts. Good aspects from an eclipse could promote an ability to go with the flow, to rise above the competition and find an inner, almost mystical strength that enables you to connect with the deepest needs of others.

What Is the Best Thing to Do During an Eclipse?

When the natural rhythms of the sun and moon are disturbed, it's best to postpone important activities. Be sure to mark eclipse days on your calendar, especially if the eclipse falls in your birth sign. This year, Gemini, Sagittarius, Taurus, and Capricorn should take special note of the conscious and unconscious feelings that arise or are suppressed. With lunar eclipses, some possibilities could be a break from attachments, or the healing of an illness or substance abuse which had been triggered by the subconscious. The temporary event could be a healing time, when you gain perspective. During solar eclipses, when you could be in a highly subjective state, pay attention to the hidden subconscious patterns that surface, the emotional truth that is revealed in your feelings at this time.

The effect of the eclipse can reverberate for some time, often months after the event. But it is especially important to stay cool and make no major moves during the period known as the shadow of the eclipse, which begins about a week before as the energy begins to crescendo and lasts until at least three days after the eclipse, when the emotional atmosphere simmers down. After three days, the daily rhythms should be back to normal and you can proceed with business as usual.

The most positive way to view eclipses is as very special times, when we can receive great insight through a changed perspective. By blocking out the emotional pressure of the full moon, a lunar eclipse could be a time of reason, rather than confusion, a time when we can take a break from our problems. A solar eclipse, when the new moon blocks out the sun (or ego), could be a time when the moon's most positive qualities are expressed, bringing us a feeling of oneness, nurturing, and compassion.

CHAPTER 7

Astro-Mating—An Element-ary Guide to Love

How many people turn to astrology for the light it can shed on their love life! Probably the question astrologers hear most is: What sign is best for me in love? Or: I'm a Taurus and my lover is a Gemini—what are our prospects? Each sun sign does have certain predictable characteristics in love, and by comparing the sun signs, you can reach a better understanding of the dynamics of the relationship. However, it is very easy to oversimplify. Just because someone's sun sign is said to be "incompatible" is no reason why the relationship can't work out. A true in-depth comparison involves far more than just the sun sign. An astrologer considers the interrelationships of all the planets and houses (where they fall in your respective horoscopes). There are several bonds between planets that can offset any difficulties between sun signs. It's worthwhile to analyze them to learn more about your relationship. You can do this by making a very simple chart which compares the moon, Mars, and Venus, as well as the sun signs of the partners in a relationship. You can find the signs for Mars and Venus in the tables in this book. Unfortunately the moon tables are too long for a book of this size—so it might be worth your while to consult an astrological ephemeris (a book of planetary tables) in your local library or to have a computer chart cast to find out the moon placement.

Simply look up the signs of Mars and Venus (and

the Moon, if possible) for each person and list them, with the sun sign, next to each other, then add the *element* of each sign. The Earth signs are Taurus, Virgo, Capricorn. The Air signs are Gemini, Libra, Aquarius. The Fire signs are Aries, Leo, Sagittarius. And the Water signs are Cancer, Scorpio, Pisces.

Example:

ROMEO'S PLANETS:

SUN	MOON	MARS	VENUS
Aries/Fire	Leo/Fire	Scorpio/Water	Taurus/Earth

JULIET'S PLANETS:

SUN	MOON	MARS	VENUS
Pisces/Water	Leo/Fire	Aries/Fire	Aquarius/Air

As a rule of thumb, signs of the *same element* or *complementary elements* (fire with air and earth with water) get along best. So, after comparing this couple's planets, you can see that this particular Romeo and Juliet could have some challenges ahead.

The Lunar Link—Here's the Person You *Need*

The planet in your chart which governs your emotions is the moon. (Note: the moon is not technically a planet, but is usually referred to as one by astrologers.) So you would naturally take this into consideration when evaluating a potential romantic partnership. If a person's moon is in a good relationship to your sun, moon, Venus, or Mars, preferably in the same sign or element, you should relate well on some emotional level. Your needs will be compatible: you'll understand each other's feelings without much effort. If the moon is in a compatible element, such as earth with water or fire with air, you may have a few adjustments, but you will be able to make them easily. With a water-fire or earth-air combination, you'll have to make a considerable effort to understand where the other is coming from emotionally.

It's worth having a computer chart done, just to find the position of your moon. (Since the moon changes signs every two days, the tables are too long to print in this book.)

The Venus Attraction—Here's the One You *Want*

Venus is what you respond to, so if you and your partner have a good Venus aspect, you should have much in common. You'll enjoy doing things together. The same type of lovemaking will turn you both on. You'll have no trouble pleasing each other.

Look up both partners' Venus placements in the charts on page 69. Your lover's Venus in the same sign or a sign of the *same element* as your own Venus, Mars, moon, or sun is best. Second best is a sign of a compatible element (earth with water, air with fire). Venus in water with air, or earth with fire means that you may have to make a special effort to understand what appeals to each other. And you'll have to give each other plenty of space to enjoy activities that don't particularly appeal to you. By the way, this chart can work not only for lovers, but for any relationship where compatibility of tastes is important to you.

The Mars Connection—This One Lights Your Fire!

Mars positions reveal your sexual energy . . . how often you like to make love, for instance. It also shows your temper . . . do you explode or do a slow burn? Here you'll find out if your partner is direct, aggressive, and hot-blooded or more likely to take the cool, mental approach. Mutually supportive partners have their Mars working together in the same or complementary elements. But *any* contacts between Mars and Venus in two charts can strike sexy sparks. Even the difficult aspects, such as your partner's Mars three or six signs away from your sun, Mars, or Venus, can be sexually stimulating. Who doesn't get turned on by a challenge from time to time? On the other hand, the easy-flowing Mars relationships can drift into soporific dullness.

The Solar Bond

The sun is the focus of our personality and therefore the most powerful component involved. Each pair of sun signs has special lessons to teach and learn from each other. There is a negative side to the most ideal couple and a positive side to the unlikeliest match. Each has an up- and a downside. You'll find a comparison of your sun sign with every other one in the "pairs" section of the individual sun sign chapters in this book. If the forecast for you and your beloved (or business associate) seems like an uphill struggle, take heart! Such legendary lovers as Juan and Eva Peron, Ronald and Nancy Reagan, Harry and Bess Truman, Julius Caesar and Cleopatra, Billy and Ruth Graham, and George and Martha Washington are among the many who have made successful partnerships between supposedly incompatible sun signs.

Try astro-mating these hot celebrity couples for practice. Look up their planets in the "planet" tables in this book and discover the secret of their cosmic attraction. (Some may not be an "item" by the time this is published. Maybe you can figure out what went wrong!)

ARIES Matthew Broderick (3/21/62) and ARIES Sarah Jessica Parker (3/24/65)
PISCES Tea Leoni (2/25/66) and LEO David Duchovny (8/7/61)

ARIES Warren Beatty (3/30/37) and GEMINI Annette Bening (5/29/58)

ARIES Al Gore (3/31/48) and LEO Tipper Gore (8/19/48)

ARIES Alec Baldwin (4/3/58) and SAGITTARIUS Kim Basinger (12/8/53)

TAURUS Barbra Streisand (4/24/42) and CANCER James Brolin (7/18/40)

TAURUS Uma Thurman (4/29/70) and SCORPIO Ethan Hawke (11/6/70)

TAURUS Carmen Electra (4/20/72) and TAURUS Dennis Rodman (5/13/61)

GEMINI Liz Hurley (6/10/65) and VIRGO Hugh Grant (9/9/60)

GEMINI Angelina Jolie (6/4/75) and LEO Billy Bob Thornton (8/4/55)

GEMINI Nicole Kidman (6/21/67) and CANCER Tom Cruise (7/3/62)

LEO Jennifer Lopez (7/24/70) and SCORPIO Sean "Puffy" Combs (11/4/69)

LEO Arnold Schwarzenegger (7/30/47) and SCORPIO Maria Shriver (11/6/55)

LEO Whitney Houston (8/9/53) and AQUARIUS Bobby Brown (2/5/69)

LEO Melanie Griffith (8/9/57) and LEO Antonio Banderas (8/10/60)

LIBRA Michael Douglas (9/25/44) and LIBRA Catherine Zeta-Jones (9/25/69)

TAURUS Jessica Lange (4/20/49) and SCORPIO Sam Shepard (11/5/43)

SCORPIO Hillary Clinton (10/26/47) and LEO Bill Clinton (8/19/46)

PISCES Kurt Russell (3/17/51) and SCORPIO Goldie Hawn (11/21/45)

SCORPIO Prince Charles (11/14/48) and CANCER Camilla Parker Bowles (7/17/47)

SAGITTARIUS Brad Pitt (12/18/63) and AQUARIUS Jennifer Aniston (2/11/69)

CAPRICORN Diane Sawyer (12/22/45) and SCORPIO Mike Nichols (11/6/46)

AQUARIUS Oprah Winfrey (1/29/54) and PISCES Stedman Graham (3/6/51)

Now it's time to do a bit of astro-mating of your own! Do you have what it takes to seduce these celebrity hunks? Check your sun, moon, Mars, and Venus with theirs!

Prince William (6/21/82)

SUN: Cancer (water)
MOON: Cancer (water)
MARS: Libra (air)
VENUS: Taurus (earth)

Russell Crowe (4/7/64)

SUN: Aries (fire)
MOON: Aquarius (air)
MARS: Aries (fire)
VENUS: Gemini (earth)

Jude Law (12/29/72)

SUN: Capricorn (earth)
MOON: Scorpio (water)
MARS: Scorpio (water)
VENUS: Sagittarius (fire)

Leonardo DiCaprio (11/11/74)

SUN: Scorpio (water)
MOON: Libra (air)
MARS: Scorpio (water)
VENUS: Scorpio (water)

Matt Damon (10/8/70)

SUN: Libra (air)
MOON: Gemini (air)
MARS: Aquarius (air)
VENUS: Libra (air)

George Clooney (5/6/61)

SUN: Taurus (earth)
MOON: Capricorn (earth)
MARS: Leo (fire)
VENUS: Aries (fire)

Richard Gere (8/31/49)

SUN: Virgo (earth)
MOON: Sagittarius (fire)
MARS: Cancer (water)
VENUS: Libra (air)

Hugh Grant (9/9/60)

SUN: Virgo (earth)
MOON: Taurus (earth)
MARS: Gemini (air)
VENUS: Libra (air)

Kevin Costner (1/18/55)

SUN: Capricorn (earth)
MOON: Sagittarius (fire)
MARS: Aries (fire)
VENUS: Sagittarius (fire)

Mel Gibson (1/3/56)

SUN: Capricorn (earth)
MOON: Virgo (earth)
MARS: Scorpio (water)
VENUS: Aquarius (air)

Fabio (3/15/61)

SUN: Pisces (water)
MOON: Pisces (water)
MARS: Cancer (water)
VENUS: Aries (fire)

Brad Pitt (12/18/63)

SUN: Sagittarius (fire)
MOON: Capricorn (earth)
MARS: Capricorn (earth)
VENUS: Capricorn (earth)

Johnny Depp (6/9/63)

SUN: Gemini (air)
MOON: Capricorn (earth)
MARS: Virgo (earth)
VENUS: Taurus (earth)

Keanu Reeves (9/2/64)

SUN: Virgo (earth)
MOON: Leo (fire)
MARS: Cancer (water)
VENUS: Cancer (water)

Joaquin Phoenix (10/28/74)

SUN: Scorpio (water)
MOON: Aries (fire)
MARS: Scorpio (water)
VENUS: Scorpio (water)

CHAPTER 8

Ask the Expert—Should You Have a Personal Reading?

Though you can learn much about yourself and others from studying astrology yourself, there comes a time when you might want the objective opinion of a professional astrologer. Done by a qualified astrologer, the personal reading can be an empowering experience if you want to reach your full potential, size up a lover or business situation, or find out what the future has in store. There are so many options for readings today, however, that sorting through them can be a daunting task. Besides face-to-face consultations, there are readings by mail, phone, tape, and Internet. There are astrologers who are specialists in certain areas, such as finance or medical astrology. And unfortunately, there are many questionable practitioners who range from streetwise gypsy fortunetellers to unscrupulous scam artists. The following basic guidelines can help you sort out your options to find the reading that's right for you.

The One-on-One Reading

Nothing compares to a one-on-one consultation with a professional astrologer who has analyzed thousands of charts and can pinpoint the potential in yours. During your reading, you can get your specific questions answered. For instance, how to get along better with your mate or coworker. There are many astrologers who now combine their skills with training in psychology and are well suited to help you examine your alternatives.

To give you an accurate reading, an astrologer needs certain information from you, such as the date, time, and place where you were born. (A horoscope can be cast about anyone or anything that has a specific time and place.) Most astrologers will then enter this information into a computer, which will calculate a chart in seconds. From the resulting chart, the astrologer will do an interpretation.

If you don't know your exact birth time, you can usually locate it at the Bureau of Vital Statistics at the city hall or county seat of the state where you were born. If you still have no success in getting your time of birth, some astrologers can estimate an approximate birth time by using past events in your life to determine the chart. This technique is called *rectification*.

How to Find a Good Astrologer

Your first priority should be to choose a qualified astrologer. Rather than relying on word of mouth or grandiose advertising claims, choose your astrologer with the same care as any trusted adviser such as a doctor, lawyer, or banker. Unfortunately, anyone can claim to be an astrologer—to date, there is no licensing of astrologers or established professional criteria. However, there are nationwide organizations of serious, committed astrologers that can help you in your search.

Good places to start your investigation are organizations such as the American Federation of Astrologers or the National Council for Geocosmic Research (NCGR), which offer a program of study and certification. If you live near a major city, there is sure to be an active NCGR chapter or astrology club in your area—many are listed in astrology magazines available at your local newsstand. In response to many requests for referrals, the NCGR has compiled a directory of professional astrologers, which includes a glossary of terms and an explanation of specialties within the astrological field. Contact the NCGR headquarters (see Chapter 10, "The Sydney Omarr Yellow Pages") for information.

Be Aware of When to Beware

As a potentially lucrative freelance business, astrology has always attracted self-styled experts who may not have the knowledge or the counseling experience to give a helpful reading. These astrologers can range from the well-meaning amateur to the charlatan or street-corner gypsy who has for many years given astrology a bad name. Be very wary of astrologers who claim to have occult powers or who make pretentious claims of celebrated clients or miraculous achievements. You can often tell from the initial phone conversation if the astrologer is legitimate. He or she should ask for your birthday time and place and conduct the conversation in a professional manner. Any astrologer who gives a reading based only on your sun sign is highly suspect.

When you arrive at the reading, the astrologer should be prepared. The consultation should be conducted in a private, quiet place. The astrologer should be interested in your problems of the moment. A good reading involves feedback on your part, so if the reading is not relating to your concerns, you should let the astrologer know. You should feel free to ask questions and get clarifications of technical terms. The more you actively participate, rather than expecting the astrologer to carry the reading or come forth with oracular predictions, the more meaningful your experience will be. An astrologer should help you validate your current experience and be frank about possible negative happenings, but suggest a positive course of action.

In their approach to a reading, some astrologers may be more literal, others more intuitive. Those who have had counseling training may take a more psychological approach. Though some astrologers may seem to have an almost psychic ability, extrasensory perception or any other parapsychological talent is not essential. A very accurate picture can be drawn from the data in your horoscope chart.

An astrologer may do several charts for each client, including one for the time of birth and a "progressed chart," showing the evolution from birth to the present time. According to your individual needs, there are many other possibilities, such as a chart for a different location, if you are contemplating a change of place. Relationships between any two people, things, or events can be interpreted with a chart which compares one partner's horoscope with the other's. A composite chart, which uses the midpoint between planets in two individual charts to describe the relationship, is another commonly used device.

An astrologer will be particularly interested in transits—times when planets will pass over the planets or sensitive points in your birth chart, which signal important events in your life.

Many astrologers offer tape-recorded readings, another option to consider. In this case, you'll be mailed a taped reading based on your birth chart. This type of reading is more personal than a computer printout and can give you valuable insights, though it is not equivalent to a live dialogue with the astrologer, when you can discuss your specific interests and issues of the moment.

Phone Readings—Real or Phony?

Telephone readings come in two varieties, a dial-in taped reading, usually recorded in advance by an astrologer or a live consultation with an "astrologer" on the other end of the line. The taped readings are general daily or weekly forecasts, applied to all members of your sign and charged by the minute. The quality depends on the astrologer. *One caution*: Be aware that these readings can run up quite a telephone bill, especially if you get into the habit of calling every day. Be sure that you are aware of the per-minute cost of each call beforehand.

Live telephone readings also vary with the expertise of the astrologer. Ideally, the astrologer at the other end of the line enters your birth data into a computer, which calculates your chart. This chart will then be referred to during the consultation. The advantage of a live telephone reading is that your individual chart is used and you can ask about a specific problem. However, before you invest in any reading, be sure that your astrologer is qualified and that you fully understand in advance how much you will be charged. There should be no unpleasant financial surprises later.

About Computer Readings

Companies which offer computer programs (such as ACS, Matrix, Astrolabe) also offer a variety of computer-generated horoscope readings. These can be quite comprehensive, offering a beautiful printout of the chart plus many pages of detailed information about each planet and aspect of the chart. You can then study it at your convenience. Of course, the interpretations will be general, since there is no personal input from you, and may not cover your immediate concerns. Since computer-generated horoscopes are much lower in cost than live consultations, you might consider them as either a supplement or preparation for an eventual live reading. You'll then be more familiar with your chart and able to plan specific questions in advance. They also make a terrific gift for astrology fans. There are several companies in our "Yellow Pages" chapter which offer computerized readings prepared by reputable astrologers.

Whichever option you decide to pursue, may your reading be an empowering one!

CHAPTER 9

The "In" Sites Online

If you're curious to see a copy of your chart (or someone else's), want to study astrology in depth, or chat with another astrology fan, log on to the Internet! There you'll find a whole new world of astrology waiting for a click of your mouse. Thousands of astrological sites offer you everything from chart services to chat rooms to individual readings. Even better, you'll find *free* software, *free* charts, and *free* articles to download. You can virtually get an education in astrology from your computer screen, share your insights with new astrology-minded pals in a chat room or on a mailing list, then later meet them in person at one of the hundreds of conferences around the world.

The following sites were chosen for general interest from vast numbers of astrology-oriented places on the Net. Many have their own selection of links to other sites for further exploration. *One caveat*: Though these sites were selected with longevity in mind, the Internet is a volatile place where sites can disappear or change without notice. Therefore, some of our sites may have changed addresses, names, or content by the time this book is published.

Free Charts

Astrolabe Software at *http://www.alabe.com* distributes some of the most creative and user-friendly programs now available, like "Solar Fire," a favorite of top astrologers. Visitors to their site are greeted with a chart of the time you log on. You can get your chart calculated, with a mini-interpretation, e-mailed to you.

For an instant chart, surf to this address: *http:// www.astro.ch* and check into ASTRODIENST, one of the first and best astrology sites on the Internet. Its world atlas will give you the accurate longitude and latitude of your birthplace for setting up your horoscope. You can print out your chart in a range of easy-to-read formats. One handy feature for beginners: The planetary placement is listed in words, rather than glyphs, alongside the chart (a real help for those who haven't yet learned to read the astrology glyph).

There are many other attractions at this site, such as a list of your astro-twins (famous people born on your birthdate). The site even sorts the "twins" to feature those who also have your identical rising sign. You can then click on their names and get instant charts of your famous sign-mates.

Free Software

Software manufacturers on the Web are generous with free downloads of demo versions of their software. You may then calculate charts using their data. This makes sense if you're considering investing serious money in astrology software, and want to see how the program works in advance. You can preview ASTROLABE Software programs favored by many professional astrologers at *http://www.alabe.com*. Check out the latest demo of "Solar Fire," one of the most user-friendly astrology programs available—you'll be impressed.

For a Fully Functional Astrology Program:

Walter Pullen's amazingly complete ASTROLOG program is offered absolutely free at this site: *http:// www.magitech.com/~cruiser1/astrolog.htm*.

ASTROLOG is an ultrasophisticated program with all the features of much more expensive programs. It comes in versions for all formats—DOS, Windows, MAC, UNIX—and has some cool features such as a revolving globe and a constellation map. A "must" for those who want to get involved with astrology without paying big bucks for a professional-caliber program. Or for those who want to add ASTROLOG's unique features to their astrology software library. This program has it all!

Another good resource for software is Astro Computing Services. Their Web site has free demos of several excellent programs. Note especially their "Electronic Astrologer," one of the most effective and reasonably priced programs on the market. It's very easy to use, a bonus for nontechies. Go to *http://www.astrocom.com* for ACS software, books, readings, chart services, and software demos. At this writing, there are free new moon and full moon reports.

Surf to *http://www.astroscan.ca* for a free program called ASTROSCAN. Stunning graphics and ease of use make this a winner.

At Halloran Software's site, *http://www.halloran.com,* there are four levels of Windows astrology software from which to choose. The "Astrology for Windows" shareware program is available in unregistered demo form as a free download and in registered form for $26.50, at this writing. The calculations in this program may be all that an astrology hobbyist needs. The price for the full-service program is certainly reasonable.

Free Screen Saver and More

The Astrology Matrix offers a way to put your sign in view with a downloadable graphic screensaver. There are also many other diversions at this site, where you may consult the stars, the I Ching, the runes, and the tarot. Here's where to connect with news groups and online discussions. Their almanac helps you schedule the best day to sign on the dotted line, ask for a raise, or plant your rosebush. Address: *http://thenewage.com*.

Free Astrology Course

Schedule a long visit to *http://www.panplanet.com*, where you will find the Canopus Academy of Astrology, a site loaded with goodies. For the experienced astrologer, there is a collection of articles from top astrologers. They've done the work for you when it comes to picking the best astrology links on the Web, so be sure to check out those bestowed with the Canopus Award of Excellence.

Astrologer Linda Reid, an accomplished astrology teacher and author, offers a complete online curriculum for all levels of astrology study plus individual tutoring. To get your feet wet, Linda is offering an excellent beginners' course at this site, a terrific way to get off and running in astrology.

Visit an Astro-Mall

Surf to *http://www.astronet.com* for the Internet's equivalent of an Astrology Mall. ASTRONET offers interactive fun for everyone. At this writing, there's a special area for teenage astrology fans, access to popular astrology magazines like *American Astrology*, advice to the lovelorn, as well as a grab bag of horoscopes, featured guests, and a shopping area for books, reports, software, and even jewelry.

Swoon.com is another mall-like site aimed at dating, mating, and relating. It has fun features to spark up your love life, plenty of advice for the lovelorn, as well as links to all the popular fashion magazine astrology columns. Address: *http://www.swoon.com*.

Find An Astrologer Here

Metalog Directory of Astrology
http://www.astrologer.com

Looking for an astrologer in your local area? Perhaps you're planning a vacation in Australia or France and would like to meet astrologers or combine your activities with an astrology conference there? Go no further than this well-maintained resource. Here is an extensive worldwide list of astrologers and astrology sites. There is also an agenda of astrology conferences and seminars all over the world.

The A.F.A. Web Site
http://www.astrologers.com

This is the interesting Web site of the prestigious American Federation of Astrologers. The A.F.A. has a very similar address to the *Metalog Directory* and also has a directory of astrologers, restricted to those who meet their stringent requirements. Check out their correspondence course if you would like to study astrology in depth.

Tools Every Astrologer Needs Are Online

Internet Atlas
http://www.astro.ch/atlas

Find the geographic longitude and latitude and the correct time zone for any city worldwide. You'll need this information to calculate a chart.

The Exact Time, Anywhere in the World
http://www.timeticker.com

A fun site with fascinating graphics which give you the exact time anywhere in the world. Click on the world map and the correct time and zone for that place lights up.

Check the Weather Forecast
http://www.weathersage.com

More accurate than your local TV forecast is the Weathersage, which uses astrology to predict snowstorms and hurricanes. Get your long-range local forecast at this super site.

Celebrate the Queen's Birthday
http://www.zodiacal.com

A great jumping-off place for an astrology tour of the Internet, this site has a veritable Burke's Peerage of royal birthdays. There's a good selection of articles, plus tools such as a U.S. and world atlas and information on conferences, software, and tapes. The links at this site will send you off in the right direction.

Astrology World
http://astrology-world.com

Astrologer Deborah Houlding has gathered some of the finest European astrologers on this super Web site, as well as a comprehensive list of links and conferences.

Astrology Alive
http://www.astrologyalive.com

Barbara Schermer has one of the most innovative approaches to astrology. She was one of the first astrolo-

146

gers to go online, so there's always a "cutting edge" to this site. Great list of links.

National Council for Geocosmic Research (NCGR)
http://www.geocosmic.org

A key stop on any astrological tour of the Net. Here's where you can find local chapters in your area, get information on the NCGR testing and certification programs, and get a conference schedule. You can also order lecture tapes from their nationwide conferences, or get complete lists of conference topics to study at home. Good links to resources.

Where to Find Charts of the Famous

When the news is breaking, you can bet Lois Rodden will be the first to get accurate birthdays of the headline makers, and put up their charts on her Web site: *www.astrodatabank.com*. Rodden's research is astrology's most reliable source for data of the famous and infamous. Her Web site specializes in birthdays and charts of current newsmakers, political figures, and international celebrities. You can purchase her database program, a wonderful research tool, which gives you thousands of birthdays sorted into categories.

Another site with birthdays and charts of famous people to download is *http://www.astropro.com*.

You can get the sun and moon sign, plus a biography of the hottest new film stars here: *http://www.mrshowbiz.com*. Or go to *http://www.imdb.com* for a comprehensive list of film celebrities including bios, plus lists of famous couples from today and yesteryear.

Yet another good source for celebrity birthdates is *http://www.metamaze.com/bdays*. You can find some interesting offbeat newsmakers here.

For Astrology Books

National Clearinghouse for Astrology Books

A wide selection of books on all aspects of astrology, from basics to advanced. Many hard-to-find books. Surf to: *http://www.astroamerica.com.*

These addresses also have a good selection of astrology books, some which are unique to the site:
http://www.panplanet.com
http://thenewage.com
http://www.astrocom.com

Browse the huge astrology list of online bookstore Amazon.com at *http://www.amazon.com.*

Astrology Tapes at Pegasus Tapes
http://www.pegasustape.com

You can study at home with world-famous astrologers via audiocassette recordings from Pegasus Tapes. There's a great selection taped from conferences, classes, lectures, and seminars. An especially good source for astrologers who emphasize psychological and mythological themes.

For History and Mythology Buffs

Be sure to visit the astrology section of this gorgeous site, dedicated to the history and mythology of many traditions. One of the most beautifully designed sites we've seen. Address: *http://www.elore.com.*

The leading authority on the history of astrology, Robert Hand, has an excellent site which features his cutting-edge research. See what one of astrology's great teachers has to offer. Address: *http://www.robhand.com.*

The Project Hindsight group is devoted to restoring the astrology of the Hellenistic period (300 B.C. to about

600 A.D.), the primary source for all later Western astrology. Some fascinating articles for astrology fans. Address: *http://www.projecthindsight-tghp.com/index.html.*

C.U.R.A. is a European site for historical researchers. Address: *http://cura.free.fr.*

Readers interested in mythology should also check out *http://pantheon.org/mythical/* for stories of gods and goddesses.

Astrology Magazines

The Mountain Astrologer
http://www.mountainastrologer.com

A favorite magazine of astrology fans, *The Mountain Astrologer* has an interesting Web site featuring the latest news from an astrological point of view, plus feature articles from the magazine.

Financial Astrology

Find out how financial astrologers play the market. Here are hot picks, newsletters, specialized financial astrology software, and mutual funds run by astrology seers. Go to *www.afund.com* or *www.alphee.com* for tips and forecasts from two top financial astrologers.

CHAPTER 10

The Sydney Omarr Yellow Pages

Enter the world of astrology! If you want to find an astrology program for your computer, connect with other astrology fans, study advanced techniques, or buy books and tapes, consider this chapter "Astrology Central." Here you'll find the latest products and services available, as well as the top astrology organizations which hold meetings and conferences in your area.

There are organized groups of astrologers all over the country who are dedicated to promoting the image of astrology in the most positive way. The National Council for Geocosmic Research (NCGR) is one nationwide group that is dedicated to bringing astrologers together, promoting fellowship and high-quality education. Their accredited course system promotes a systematized study of all the different facets of astrology. Whether you'd like to know more about such specialties as financial astrology or techniques for timing events, or if you'd prefer the psychological or mythological approach, you'll find the leading experts at NCGR conferences.

Your computer can be a terrific tool for connecting with other astrology fans at all levels of expertise, as we explored in the Internet chapter in this book. Even if you are using a "dinosaur" from the 1980s, there are still calculation and interpretation programs available for DOS and MAC formats. They may not have all the bells and whistles or the exciting graphics, but they'll get the job done!

Newcomers to astrology should learn some of the basics, including the glyphs (astrology's special shorthand language) before you invest in a complex computer program. Use the chapter in this book to help you learn the symbols easily, so you'll be able to read the charts without consulting the "help" section of your program every time. Several programs, such as Astrolabe's "Solar Fire," have pop-up definitions to help you decipher the meanings of planets and aspects. Just click your mouse on a glyph or an icon on the screen, and a window with an instant definition appears.

You don't have to spend a fortune to get a perfectly adequate astrology program. In fact, if you are connected to the Internet, you can download one free. Astrology software is available at all price levels, from a sophisticated free application like *Astrology,* which you can download from a Web site, to inexpensive programs for under $100 such as Halloran's "Astrology for Windows," to the more expensive astrology programs such as "Winstar," "Solar Fire," or "Io" (for the Mac), which are used by serious students and professionals. Before you make an investment, it's a good idea to download a sample from the company's Web site or order a demo disk.

If you're baffled by the variety of software available, most of the companies on our list will be happy to help you find the right application for your needs.

Students of astrology who live in out-of-the-way places or are unable to fit classes into your schedule have several options. There are online courses offered at astrology Web sites, such as *www.panplanet.com,* and at the NCGR and AFA Web sites. Some astrology teachers will send you a series of audiotapes or you can order audiotaped seminars of recent conferences; other teachers offer correspondence courses that use their workbooks or computer printouts.

The Yellow Pages

Nationwide Astrology Organizations and Conferences

Contact these organizations for information on conferences, workshops, local meetings, conference tapes, and referrals:

National Council for Geocosmic Research

Educational workshops, tapes, conferences, and a directory of professional astrologers are available from this nationwide organization devoted to promoting astrological education. For a $35 annual membership fee, you get their excellent publications and newsletters, plus the opportunity to network with other astrology buffs at local chapter events (there are chapters in twenty states).

For general information about NCGR, contact:

NCGR
P.O. Box 38866
Los Angeles, CA 90038
Phone: 818-705-1678

Or visit their Web page, *http://www.geocosmic.org,* for updates and local events.

American Federation of Astrologers (A.F.A.)

One of the oldest astrological organizations in the United States, established in 1938. Conferences, conventions, and a correspondence course. Will refer you to an accredited A.F.A. astrologer.

A.F.A.
P.O. Box 22040
Tempe, AZ 85382

Phone: 602-838-1751
Fax: 602-838-8293

A.F.A.N. (Association for Astrological Networking)

(Nctworking, Legal Issues)
Did you know that astrologers are still being arrested for practicing in some states? AFAN provides support and legal information, and works toward improving the public image of astrology. Here are the people who will go to bat for astrology when it is attacked in the media. Everyone who cares about astrology should join!

A.F.A.N.
8306 Wilshire Blvd., Suite 537
Beverly Hills, CA 90211

ARC Directory

(Listing of astrologers worldwide)
2920 E. Monte Vista
Tucson, AZ 85716
Phone: 602-321-1114

Pegasus Tapes

(Lectures, conference tapes)
P.O. Box 419
Santa Ysabel, CA 92070

International Society for Astrological Research

(Lectures, workshops, seminars)
P.O. Box 38613
Los Angeles, CA 90038

ISIS Institute

(Newsletter, conferences, astrology tapes, catalog)
P.O. Box 21222
El Sobrante, CA 94820-1222
Phone: 888-322-4747
Fax: 510-222-2202

Astrology Software

Astrolabe

Box 1750-R
Brewster, MA 02631
Phone: 800-843-6682

Check out the latest version of their powerful "Solar Fire" software for Windows—it's a breeze to use and will grow with your increasing knowledge of astrology to the most sophisticated levels. This company also markets a variety of programs for all levels of expertise, a wide selection of computer astrology readings, and Mac programs. A good resource for innovative software as well as applications for older computers.

Matrix Software

407 N. State Street
Big Rapids, MI 49307
Phone: 800-PLANETS

A wide variety of software in all price ranges, demo disks, student and advanced levels, and lots of interesting readings. Check out "Winstar," their powerful professional software, if you're planning to study astrology seriously.

Astro Communications Services

Dept. AF693, PO Box 34487
San Diego, CA 92163-4487
Phone: 800-888-9983

Books, software for MAC and IBM compatibles, individual charts, and telephone readings. Find technical astrology materials here, such as "The American Ephemeris." They will calculate charts for you if you do not have a computer.

Air Software

115 Caya Avenue
West Hartford, CT 06110
Phone: 800-659-1247

Powerful, creative astrology software, like their millennium "Star Trax 2000." For beginners, check out "Father Time," which finds your best days. Or "Nostradamus," which answers all your questions. Financial astrology programs for stock market traders are a specialty.

Time Cycles Research—For Mac Users!!!

375 Willets Avenue
Waterford, CT 06385
Fax: 869-442-0625
E-mail: *astrology@timecycles.com*
Internet: *http://www.timecycles.com*

Where MAC users can find astrology software that's as sophisticated as it gets. If you have Mac, you'll love their beautiful graphic "IO Series" programs.

Astro-Cartography

(Charts for location changes)
Astro-Numeric Service Box 336-B
Ashland, OR 97520
Phone: 800-MAPPING

Astro-cartography is a sophisticated technique which superimposes an astrology chart on a map of the world. A fascinating study for serious students of astrology.

Astrology Magazines

In addition to articles by top astrologers, most have listings of astrology conferences, events, and local happenings.

AMERICAN ASTROLOGY
Dept. 4
P.O. Box 2021
Marion, OH 43306-8121

DELL HOROSCOPE
P.O. Box 53352
Boulder, CO 89321-3342

THE MOUNTAIN ASTROLOGER
P.O. Box 970
Cedar Ridge, CA 95924

Astrology Schools

Though there are many correspondence courses available through private teachers and astrological organizations, up until now, there has never been an accredited college of astrology. That is why the following address is so important.

Kepler College of Astrological Arts and Sciences

Kepler College, the first institution of its kind to combine an accredited liberal arts education with extensive astrological studies, is now in operation, after many years in planning. A degree-granting college that is also a center of astrological studies has long been the dream of the astrological community and will be a giant step forward in providing credibility to the profession. The Kepler College faculty comprises some of the most creative leaders in the astrology community.

For more information, contact:

Kepler College of Astrological Arts and Sciences
Business Office
4630 200th St. SW
Suite L-1
Lynnwood, WA 98036
Phone: 435-673-4292
Fax: 425-673-4983
Internet: *www.kepler.edu*

Your Virgo Home Pages—
All About Your Life,
Friends, Family, Work,
and Style!

A practical earth sign ruled by Mercury, the planet of communication, Virgo is assigned the role of creating order, analyzing situations, finding flaws, and correcting them. It is your destiny to let us know what is wrong and how to fix it, how to improve ourselves. Used positively, this ability can make you one of the great teachers and healers of the zodiac.

You're the master of the details that make a difference, the one who holds us to high standards and encourages us to be the best we can be. But since you are naturally drawn to fault-finding, you can also be a harsh critic, so it is often necessary to tone down your perfectionism to accept the human flaws in others.

CHAPTER 11

Are You True to Type?

The Virgo Man—A Cool Customer

Contradicting the virgin symbol of your sign is one of the pleasures of being a Virgo man. Sean Connery and Hugh Grant epitomize the "sexiest man in the world" type of Virgo, who becomes even more attractive with age. Part of the Virgo man's appeal is his subtlety . . . you never come on strong. You are more likely to have a modest facade and to be as interested in a woman's mind as her body. In fact, Virgo usually lets the opposite sex do the chasing. Though you may be sexually skilled, you prefer to keep your feelings under wraps, leave grand passion to others, and remain tantalizingly out of reach. Perhaps that's the real secret of James Bond's appeal. Jeremy Irons, Harry Connick, Jr., Richard Gere, and Keanu Reeves are popular Virgo stars who epitomize the "thinking woman's" sex symbol aspect of their sun sign. Regis Philbin, star of the hit TV show *Who Wants to Be a Millionaire?* as well as a popular daytime TV talk show host, is the perfect example of a Virgo whose keen critical intelligence is disguised by a modest, low-key, "good guy" manner.

The Virgo man is not always as practical, health-conscious, and coolly aloof as he may appear. Underneath, you have a vivid fantasy life, full of adventure, like the world of James Bond, populated by perfect love partners (although the dream may get blurry at this point). You are never quite sure what the perfect partner is, but you know what she is *not*.

Virgo has extremely high standards in life and love. You reach your potential by seeing that everything is well run. Virgo usually chooses the functional over the flamboyant, mistrusting anything or anyone that seems uncontrollable. Your negative side is simply your good side carried to extreme—too-high standards make you overly critical of others, concern for health can become hypochondria, extreme neatness and organization can make you difficult to live with, and careful budgeting can become penny-pinching. The Virgo feels impelled to right whatever is not functioning or at least to point it out. Some Virgos, like Michael Jackson, actually create their own isolated perfect worlds, where the real world is excluded—one reason why the Virgo male is often called the bachelor of the zodiac. No one quite lives up to that fantasy image.

When you are forced to deal with the real world, Virgo either becomes the efficiency expert, the demanding perfectionist, or the teacher in some way. You are best when you are improving a situation or a person, either in body or mind—being the doctor or the teacher, and sometimes both at the same time.

In a Relationship

Virgo is a devoted partner when you find a mate who meets your high standards. Like everything else, you work hard at your relationships, but you may not express your tender romantic side easily. You like to have your house in order, and will expect your partner to stick to your agenda. You will tolerate her having a career, as long as she also maintains a well-ordered refuge from the outside world. However, a Virgo's woman is well advised to look beneath the surface of her man and encourage him to express his erotic, sensual side, those hidden "Agent 007" fantasies. Otherwise, as the Virgo man ages, he may decide to take a risk and live out some of his fantasies with a younger playmate. Many Virgos leave their sensible mates for a glamorous, far riskier partner who gives them a taste of adventure. As one aging Virgo entrepreneur described his glamorous second wife, "She spends all my money, but she's worth it!"

The Virgo Woman—
Sensible and Sensual

Like your male counterpart, the Virgo woman is a paradox. You're renowned for being a schoolmarm type, obsessed with neatness and tidiness. However, some of the world's most seductive women were born under the sign of the virgin—Raquel Welch and Sophia Loren, for example. Looking more deeply into the lives of these beauties, we find women who are extremely health-conscious, devoted to their families, and discriminating about relationships. They have cool business heads and often run multiple business ventures. These are not party girls by any means! Virgo is oriented toward work, not play (the Filofax must have been invented by a Virgo). You are the type who will turn down a glamorous spontaneous invitation, or an exciting man, if you have scheduled that time to do your laundry.

When you set a goal, you proceed in a very methodical and efficient way to attain it. Your analytical mind will take it apart, piece by piece, to discover where you can make improvements. You do this to people, too. (Caution: With Virgo's critical nature, you can win points, but lose your friends.)

Beneath the cool Virgo surface, there's a romantic in hiding, one who'll risk all for love, as did Ingrid Bergman, who scandalized the nation by leaving her family to run off with an Italian film director. Legendary Virgo beauty Greta Garbo specialized in portraying women who lived life romantically, like Mata Hari and Anna Karenina, the direct opposite of the Virgo image, and had a controversial ménage à trois in her personal life. Virgo Lauren Bacall blazed with Humphrey Bogart on and off screen, in spite of their considerable age difference. Many Virgos choose men who are contrary to the expectations of others—someone from an entirely different race or culture may tempt you to drop your careful plans and take a chance on love.

In a Relationship

The Virgo woman appeals to both mind and body, but even though you may appear supersensual, you are rarely promiscuous. You are more interested in commitment, in finding the perfect mate.

Virgo often has a high-strung temperament that zeroes in on your partner's weak points and doesn't rest until they are corrected. This constant nagging and fault finding can make you difficult to live with. A better approach is to use your talent and charm to provoke others to take action or to set a good example for others to follow.

Once committed, you're an excellent companion and one of the most helpful mates in the zodiac. Since you have been very careful about giving away your heart, you'll be an adoring wife. You are the perfect partner for a man who needs a helping hand and someone to take care of details. You will pull your weight in the relationship, stick by him in difficult times, and even support him financially if necessary. Needless to say, his life will get organized and his diet improved. Virgo is not sparing of a man's ego, however, and must be careful not to let criticism degenerate into nagging. When you let go and allow laughter and fun to enter your relationship, you may indeed achieve the perfect marriage.

Virgo in the Family

The Virgo Parent

Virgo, who enjoys providing useful service, makes a very effective parent. Your special strength is in practical matters that prepare your child for survival on his own, such as teaching him useful skills and providing the best health care and education possible. You'll also train your children well in the practical art of common sense.

Virgo's tendency to worry and be overly critical is better soft-pedaled with sensitive children, who need to develop inner confidence. You'll be more comfortable with the mental side of parenting than with the emotional demands of a needy child, and may have to compromise overly high standards to give affection and praise, as well as criticism. Though you naturally focus on perfecting details, realizing that making mistakes and taking risks are an important part of education will help you prepare your child for solo flights.

The Virgo Stepparent

You're the stepparent who keeps the home running smoothly and deals with your extended family with intelligence and objectivity. You'll allow time for the children to adjust before you make friendly moves, never forcing the relationship. But you may have to tone down your tendency to give advice for their own good. Build up their confidence first, by showing warmth, caring, and encouragement. In time, the children will respect your well-considered advice and come to you for constructive, analytical opinions.

The Virgo Grandparent

You're as lively and mentally sharp as ever! You know what's going on and have a well-considered opinion to offer, and surprise, more people are paying attention now. Maybe that's because you are more relaxed, open, and warm than ever, and your self-confidence is justified by years of experience. You're especially attractive to youngsters, who come to you for advice because you're the one who knows what works and what doesn't. They'll consult with you about all manner of problems or hash over the world situation (you're right up with the latest news). Though you're still a worrier, you realize now how many imaginary problems never came to pass, and you've become more philosophical with age. You'll happily offer advice and zero in with sharp criticism when necessary, but now it's tempered with psychological wisdom that truly <u>reflects</u> your deep concern for the welfare of others!

CHAPTER 12

"In Style" the Virgo Way

The key to looking and feeling your best is to go with the style that best suits your Virgo personality, which favors specific colors, surroundings, and attitudes. Follow these tips to maximize your own Virgo star quality.

The Virgo House Beautiful

Elegant, conservative decor, with clean lines and lots of efficient storage space, should suit you best. Many Virgos prefer modern decor, such as Bauhaus, or decor with a Japanese influence, because of the clean, uncluttered lines of these styles.

Virgos have a special genius for organization and can make even the tiniest space functional and efficient. Antique secretaries, oak file cabinets, printer's trays, and closet organizers get pressed into service. Because you're a reader, there should be plenty of bookshelves and safe storage for your prized record collection.

Virgos have an eye for the perfect detail, and nothing shares your environment unless it passes muster. Like Greta Garbo, who even designed her own rugs, you may prefer to craft your own furniture or cabinets. Your kitchen should be especially well planned, equipped with blenders, juicers, sprouters, and shelves for your vitamins.

Virgo Sounds

Virgo's discriminating taste in music runs to string quartets, Puccini operas, and all the classics. Virgo composers Dvořák, Bruckner, and John Cage appeal to the more intellectual types. You'll search out the definitive recordings of your favorites and state-of-the-art sound equipment to play them perfectly. Some Virgo musicians and composers who might add variety to your collection are Michael Jackson, Elvis Costello, Maria Muldaur, Dinah Washington, Mel Tormé, Paul Winter, Itzhak Perlman, Barry Gibbs, Bobby Short, and Michael Feinstein.

Virgo Travel Tips

Consider putting yourself in top condition at a health spa, either in the mountains here or in a fascinating foreign country. Switzerland or northern Italy have a variety of health resorts and hot springs to choose from. Choose one with a medical emphasis, as well as beauty and fitness.

With your interest in history, visits to the historical landmarks or houses of the period that interests you would make a stimulating and interesting vacation. Plan a tour of antebellum mansions or English country houses. You might take a vacation course in a subject that fascinates you, something completely divorced from your business, such as a gourmet cooking course in Paris, rock climbing in Colorado, or hiking through Wordsworth country, the lake district of England. Other Virgo places are Boston, Paris, Greece, and Washington D.C.

Your bags are probably well made and sturdy, as

well as good-looking. Save yourself some time identifying them at the baggage claim by labeling your bags with brightly colored stickers. You probably own a sturdy wheeled cart for easy baggage transport.

Save your meticulous and detailed packing lists. When you revisit the same destination or climate, your research will have been done—you'll know just what to take. Be sure to take along a good book or some stationery to make use of times when there are inevitable delays.

Virgo's Color Palette

Light, neutral earth tones are versatile, elegant Virgo colors. You also look chic in navy and white, or in gray tones. (You look especially sexy in a tailored suit!) All-white linen is another Virgo look—remember Ingrid Bergman's grand entrance in the film classic *Casablanca.* Bright colors are tricky with Virgo, because the wrong shade might jar your nerves. Use brights as accents to your basic neutral palette.

Virgo Fashion Styling

Simple, comfortable, elegant clothes suit Virgo best. Too many accessories or too much jewelry clutter up your style. Like Ingrid Bergman or Lauren Bacall (or Greta Garbo in private life), you'll look your best in beautifully cut, uncluttered, classic clothes. Even the most curvaceous Virgos like Salma Hayek, Raquel Welch and Sophia Loren keep their clothing styles simple, avoiding ruffles and flourishes. Your makeup should be subtle and carefully applied; you'll use earth tones rather than lavender eye shadow. Virgo's hair is perfectly cut and groomed. You'll probably find the ideal hairstyle and stick to it, like Claudette Colbert, who was known for her bangs, or Garbo, known for her pageboy.

Virgo fashion designers Tom Ford and Karl Lagerfeld are on your wavelength. Models Claudia Schiffer, Angie Everhart, and Kristy Hume strut the Virgo style on the runway.

The Virgo Diet

Finding the restaurant that pleases fussy Virgo is not easy. There should be a sound level that encourages conversation, attentive service, and food that is healthful as well as delicious. For a romantic evening, try a country inn or an elegant Japanese restaurant. Perhaps your town has a health food restaurant that's sure to be run by a Virgo. Since your sign rules wheat, a pasta restaurant would be an excellent choice. As Sophia Loren once said, "All I am, I owe to pasta!"

CHAPTER 13

The Healthy Virgo

Yours is a troubleshooting sign, one that is constantly checking (and worrying about) your progress, scheduling medical exams and diagnostic tests, and generally evaluating your health. You have probably learned that running your life efficiently does much to eliminate health-robbing stress, and it's a great comfort to know you've got a smooth health maintenance routine to back you up.

As your sign rules digestion, Virgos are naturally concerned about nutrition and can make quite an issue out of food quality and preparation. Many of you will follow a special diet to promote health, such as a macrobiotic diet. Potassium-rich vegetables are especially important to include in the Virgo diet. If you become overweight, it is usually because you are combating worries and frayed nerves with comfort foods. To counteract this tendency, be sure that there are activities in your life which promote peace of mind. Meditation, crafts, and detail work seem to be especially soothing to Virgo and could draw your attention away from overconsuming unhealthful food.

Mentally sharp Virgos especially benefit from exercises that stress the relationship of mind and body, such as yoga or tai chi. Sports that require a certain technical skill to master can also challenge Virgo. The key factor in Virgo-appealing exercises is to involve self-improvement on several levels simultaneously, not just a boring, routine, repetitive workout.

CHAPTER 14

Virgo at Work!

You need a business that needs you! Your best job is one where you can be constructive and use your critical talents. Glamour jobs that depend on a flashy presentation are not for you. Nor are you especially interested in public pizzazz. Your key word is "service," so your career should be involved with helping others improve themselves or provide a practical, useful product. You are the efficiency expert who saves the company money and time or monitors quality control. Your meticulous neatness and concern for health make you a natural in the fitness, health, medical, or nutrition fields. This is not to say that Virgo is not glamorous or creative. (Who could forget Bergman, Bacall, or Garbo?) But even in the arts, you are a flawless performer who takes a craftsmanlike approach.

Mercury-ruled Virgos have a talent for communicating their knowledge. You are the zodiac's most natural teacher, either in the educational system or in some facet of your job. Virgo's eye for detail is put to good use in editorial work, accounting, science, literary criticism (or any kind of criticism), and law. Avoid jobs where too much diplomacy, hand-holding, or flattery is required. Political power plays also irritate your delicate nerves.

The Virgo Leader

As a Virgo boss, you are a passionate perfectionist who expects others to meet your high standards. Your mind is systematic, and you are always aware of how smoothly an organization is run. When you spot an error or something out of order, you are quick to report the misdeed or flaw. But you also can be a wonderful teacher, who is known for developing your staff and eliciting peak performance. Though some may find your attention to detail irritating, others will benefit by your caring attention. You are always thinking of your subordinates' welfare, and will make sure they get the requisite benefits, sick leave, vacation time, etc. As a boss, however, you may place more emphasis on efficiency than creativity.

Virgo Teamwork

The Virgo worker is an employer's dream: punctual, efficient, detail-oriented, hardworking, and willing to put in long hours. You are modest and quiet (except when something's wrong!) and do meticulously neat and thorough work. You are the perfect "right-hand person" who troubleshoots for the boss. You are best when you can organize your job yourself, rather than cope with the inefficiency and slipups of others. On a team, your critical attitude may cause friction with less scrupulous types. You'll have to learn to phrase your criticisms diplomatically (usually you will not hesitate to deflate a fragile ego). You shine in a position where others appreciate your dedication and attention to quality.

To Get Ahead Fast

Pick a job where your services are vitally needed, then show what you can do. Play up these Virgo talents:

- Teaching ability
- Craftsmanship
- Organization
- Practicality
- Analysis
- Constructive criticism

Virgo Career Role Models

Study the careers of those Virgo millionaires for tips on how to exploit your Virgo talents to the fullest:

Regis Philbin
John Kluge
John Gutfreund
Alfred Knopf
Henry Ford II
Peter Ueberroth
Michael Jackson
Geoffrey Beene
Brian DePalma
William Friedkin
Duke Snider
Werner Erhard
Stephen King

CHAPTER 15

Virgo Rich and Famous!

We're fascinated by reading tabloids and gossip items about the rich, famous, and infamous in the post-Millennium, but astrology can tell you more about your heroes than most magazine articles. Like what really turns them on (check their Venus). Or what makes them rattled (scope their Saturn). Compare similarities and differences between the celebrities who embody the typical Aries sun sign traits and those who seem atypical. Then look up other planets in the horoscope of your favorites, using the charts in this book, to see how other planets influence the horoscope. It's a fun way to get your education in astrology.

Gene Kelly (8/23/13)
Shelley Long (8/23/49)
Vera Miles (8/23/30)
River Phoenix (8/23/70)
Patricia McBride (8/23/42)
Rick Springfield (8/23/49)
Steve Guttenberg (8/23/58)
Marlee Matlin (8/24/65)
Sean Connery (8/25/30)
Van Johnson (8/25/16)
Elvis Costello (8/35/54)
Walt Kelly (8/25/13)
Leonard Bernstein (8/25/18)

Mel Ferrer (8/25/17)
Anne Archer (8/25/50)
Macaulay Culkin (8/26/80)
Geraldine Ferraro (8/26/35)
Barbara Bach (8/27/49)
Lyndon Johnson (8/27/08)
Yasser Arafat (8/27/29)
Pee Wee Herman (8/27/52)
Martha Raye (8/27/16)
Tuesday Weld (8/27/43)
Scott Hamilton (8/28/58)
Ben Gazzara (9/28/30)
Donald O'Connor (9/28/25)
Emma Samms (8/28/61)
Charles Boyer (8/28/1899)
David Soul (8/28/43)
Shania Twain (8/28/65)
William Friedkin (8/29/39)
Michael Jackson (8/29/58)
Ingrid Bergman (8/29/15)
Richard Attenborough (8/29/23)
Dinah Washington (8/29/24)
Elliot Gould (8/29/38)
Robin Leach (8/29/41)
Rebecca DeMornay (8/29/61)
Cameron Diaz (8/30/72)
Shirley Booth (8/30/07)
Peggy Lipton (8/30/47)
Jean Claude Killy (8/30/43)
Richard Gere (8/31/49)
Van Morrison (8/31/45)
Paul Winter (8/31/39)
Itzhak Perlman (8/31/45)
Fredric March (8/31/1897)
James Coburn (8/31/28)
Lily Tomlin (9/1/39)
Vittoro Gassman (9/1/22)
Barry Gibb (9/1/46)
Yvonne DeCarlo (9/1/22)

George Maharis (9/1/33)
Gloria Estefan (9/1/57)
Jimmy Connors (9/2/52)
Keanu Reeves (9/2/64)
Christa McAuliffe (9/2/48)
Salma Hayek (9/2/68)
Mark Harmon (9/2/51)
Kitty Carlisle (9/3/15)
Irene Pappas (9/3/26)
Valerie Perrine (9/3/43)
Charlie Sheen (9/3/65)
Mitzi Gaynor (9/4/30)
Raquel Welch (9/5/40)
William Devane (9/5/37)
Joan Kennedy (9/3/35)
Bob Newhart (9/5/29)
Werner Erhard (9/5/35)
Jane Curtin (9/6/47)
Swoosie Kurtz (9/6/44)
Corbin Bernson (9/7/54)
Grandma Moses (9/7/1860)
Liz Tilberis (9/7/47)
Susan Blakely (9/7/48)
Buddy Holly (9/7/36)
Queen Elizabeth I (9/7/1533)
Elia Kazan (9/7/09)
Peter Lawford (9/7/25)
Michael Feinstein (9/7/56)
Peter Sellers (9/8/25)
Sid Caesar (9/8/22)
Hugh Grant (9/9/60)
Michael Keaton (9/9/51)
Cliff Robertson (9/9/25)
Otis Redding (9/9/41)
Billy Preston (9/9/46)
Kristy McNichol (9/9/62)
Amy Irving (9/10/53)
Charles Kuralt (9/10/34)
Jose Feliciano (9/10/45)

Margaret Trudeau (9/10/48)
Harry Connick, Jr. (9/11/67)
Brian DePalma (9/11/40)
Earl Holliman (9/11/28)
Linda Gray (9/12/40)
Barry White (9/12/44)
Maria Muldaur (9/12/42)
Mel Tormé (9/13/25)
Nell Carter (9/13/48)
Jacqueline Bisset (9/13/44)
Nicol Williamson (9/14/38)
Joey Heatherton (9/14/44)
Mary Frances Crosby (9/14/59)
Harve Presnell (9/14/33)
Zoe Caldwell (9/14/33)
Bobby Short (9/15/24)
Claudette Colbert (9/15/03)
Oliver Stone (9/15/46)
Tommy Lee Jones (9/15/46)
Agatha Christie (9/15/1890)
Jackie Cooper (9/15/22)
Peter Falk (9/16/27)
Lauren Bacall (9/16/24)
Ed Begley, Jr. (9/16/49)
David Copperfield (9/16/56)
B. B. King (9/16/25)
Susan Ruttan (9/16/50)
Greta Garbo (9/16/05)
John Ritter (9/17/48)
Roddy McDowall (9/17/28)
Dorothy Loudon (9/17/33)
Anne Bancroft (9/17/31)
Jack Warden (9/18/20)
Rossano Brazzi (9/18/16)
Frankie Avalon (9/18/40)
Jada Pinkett-Smith (9/18/71)
Joan Lunden (9/19/51)
Frances Farmer (9/19/10)
Jeremy Irons (9/19/48)

Duke Snider (9/19/26)
Twiggy (9/19/49)
David McCallum (9/19/32)
Sophia Loren (9/20/34)
Stephen King (9/21/47)
Larry Hagman (9/21/31)
Bill Murray (9/21/50)
Catherine Oxenburg (9/22/61)
Shari Belafonte Harper (9/22/54)
Paul Muni (9/22/1895)
Martha Scott (9/22/14)

CHAPTER 16

Virgo Pairs—How You Get Along with Every Other Sign

Before you commit or sign on the dotted line, check this tip list of pluses and minuses of every combination, so you'll know what to expect before you leap into love (or any other relationship).

Virgo/Aries

PLUSES:
Aries's sexual magnetism and positive energy warms up Virgo. You both share high ideals in pursuit of love. Aries puts lovers on a pedestal; Virgo sees them as perfect. Aries's honesty and directness earn your trust.

MINUSES:
Aries can be recklessly impatient, which you will find a serious weakness. Virgo's dedication to selfless service gets no credit from self-centered Aries, who wants recognition for services rendered. Virgo may get tired and feel abused or martyred by Aries's relentless demands. Unsympathetic Aries will see Virgo as a "downer."

Virgo/Taurus

PLUSES:
Taurus admires Virgo's analytical mind, while Virgo
admires Taurean concentration and goal orientation
and feels secure with predicable Taurus. You enjoy
taking care of each other. Relaxed, soothing Taurus
brings out Virgo's sensuality. Virgo brings the world
of ideas home to Taurus.

MINUSES:
Virgo's nagging can cause Taurus self-doubt, which
can show up in bullheaded stubbornness. Taurus's
slow pace and ideal of deep-rooted comfort could feel
like constraint to Virgo, who needs the stimulation of
diversity and lively communication.

Virgo/Gemini

PLUSES:
Both Mercury-ruled, your deepest bond will be mental
communication and appreciation of each other's intelligence. Virgo's Mercury is earthbound and analytical,
while Gemini's Mercury is a jack-of-all-trades. Gemini
shows Virgo the big picture; Virgo takes care of the
details. Your combined talents make a stimulating
partnership. Virgo becomes the administrator here,
Gemini the "idea" person.

MINUSES:
Your different priorities can be irritating to each
other. Virgo needs a sense of order. Gemini needs to
experiment and is forever the gadabout. An older
Gemini who has slowcd down somewhat makes the
best partner here.

Virgo/Cancer

PLUSES:
You two vulnerable signs protect and nurture each other. Moody Cancer needs your cool analytical nature to refine and focus emotions creatively. You give Cancer protective care and valuable insight. Cancer's charming romantic tenderness nurtures your shy side. Here is the caring lover of your dreams. You'll have good communication on a practical level, respecting each other's shrewd financial acumen.

MINUSES:
Cancer's extreme self-protection could arouse your suspicion. Why must they be so secretive? Virgo's protectiveness could become smothering, making Cancer overly dependent. You must learn to offer suggestions instead of criticism, to coddle Cancer's feelings at all times. (This is a sign that doesn't take criticism well, even if given with the best intentions.)

Virgo/Leo

PLUSES:
Leo confidence, sales power, and optimism, as well as aristocratic presence, is a big Virgo draw. Virgo will have a ready-made job efficiently running the mechanical parts of Leo's life, which Leo is only too happy to delegate. Leo's social poise brings Virgo into the public eye—and can help your shy sign bloom! Both are faithful and loyal signs who find much to admire in each other.

MINUSES:
You may not appreciate each other's point of view. Virgo is more likely to dole out well-meaning criticism and vitamins than the admiration and applause Leo

craves. Virgo will also protest Leonine high-handedness with the budget. Virgo makes the house rules, but Leo is above them, a rule unto itself. Leo always looks at the big picture, Virgo at the nitty-gritty. You could damp each other's spirits unless you find a way to work this out early in the relationship.

Virgo/Virgo

PLUSES:
There's a strong mental turn-on, since you both approach love in an analytical and rather clinical way. Two Virgo sign mates have a mutual respect and intuitive communication that is hard to beat. You'll evolve a carefully ordered way of being together, which works especially well if you share outside projects or similar careers.

MINUSES:
Be careful of constantly testing or criticizing each other. You need to focus on positive values, and not forever try to meet each other's standards or get bogged down in details. Bring a variety of friends into your life to add balance.

Virgo/Libra

PLUSES:
You are intelligent companions with refined tastes, perfectionists in different ways. Libra charm and elegant style works well with Virgo's clearheaded decision making.

MINUSES:
Libra responds to admiration and can turn off to criticism or too much negativity. Virgo will need to use

diplomacy to keep Libran scales in balance. Virgo values function as well as form, and sticks to a well-thought-out budget; extravagant Libra spends for beauty alone, regardless of the price tag.

Virgo/Scorpio

PLUSES:
With Scorpio, Virgo encounters intense feelings too powerful to intellectualize or analyze. This could be a grand passion, especially when Scorpio is challenged to uncover Virgo's earthy, sensual side. Your penetrating minds are sympatico and so is your dedication to meaningful work (here is a fellow healer), Virgo provides the stability and structure that keeps Scorpio on the right track.

MINUSES:
Virgo may cool off if Scorpio goes to extremes or plays manipulative games, while Scorpio could find Virgo's perfectionism irritating and approach to sex too limited.

Virgo/Sagittarius

PLUSES:
Sagittarius inspires Virgo to take risks and win, and brings fun, laughter, and mental stimulation to Virgo's life. Virgo supplies a much-needed support system, organizing and following through on Sagittarius ideas. These two signs fulfill important needs for each other.

MINUSES:
Virgo won't relate to Sagittarius's happy-go-lucky financial philosophy and reluctance to make firm commitments. Sagittarius would rather deal with the big

picture, and may resent Virgo's preoccupation with details. Sexual fidelity could be a key issue if this Sagittarius's casual approach to sex conflicts with Virgo's desire to have "everything perfect."

Virgo/Capricorn

PLUSES:
This looks like a sure thing between two signs who have so much in common. You're good providers, have a strong sense of duty and respect for order, similar conservative tastes, and a basically traditional approach to relationships. You could accomplish much together.

MINUSES:
You may be too similar! The strong initial chemistry could give way to boredom. Romance needs challenges to keep the sparks flying.

Virgo/Aquarius

PLUSES:
Aquarius inspires Virgo to get involved in problem solving on a large scale. You are both analytical, both inquisitive, and can both be detached emotionally. You'll appeal to each other's idealistic side and fuel interest with good mental communication.

MINUSES:
Virgo has a basically traditional, conservative outlook, while Aquarius likes to stay open to all possibilities and can swing into spur-of-the-moment action. Virgo's nerves could be jangled by Aquarian unpredictability and constant need for company. Aquarius could feel confined by Virgo's structured, ordered approach and focus on details.

Virgo/Pisces

PLUSES:
Virgo supplies what Pisces often needs most—clarity and order—while Pisces's creative imagination takes Virgo's life out of the ordinary. If you can reconcile your opposing points of view, you'll have much to gain from this relationship.

MINUSES:
There are many adjustments for both signs here. Virgo could feel "over your head" with Pisces's emotions and seeming lack of control—and frustrated when make-over attempts fail; while Pisces could feel bogged down with Virgo's worries and deflated by negative criticism. Try to support, not change, each other.

CHAPTER 17

Astrological Outlook for Virgo in 2002

You could be placed on the proverbial pedestal this year. People might compare you to historical figures. You could invent something that is unique and profitable.

Throughout the year, you are regarded as a "romantic figure." You'll be told by many, "You look different, you sound different, you could be an entirely different person!" That is part of the cycle for the year 2002—to be different and courageous, to take risks and exhibit much derring-do.

Leo and Aquarius persons will play important roles in your life this year. You can identify them this way: many will have these letters or initials in their names—A, S. J.

Lucky numbers: these numbers pop up more than by mere coincidence—1, 9, 8.

With Leo, you gain insights by looking back; you shed light on areas previously dark. The sun of Leo blends with your Mercury, and the result is mystery, intrigue, and the ability to go forth in areas where they say angels fear to tread.

With Aquarius, it is Uranus plus your Mercury. The result is once again the desire, the courage to pierce the unknown. With Aquarius, patience is necessary. Lessons you learn will be related to measurements, to potential, and to greater knowledge of statistical averages. You will do this for Aquarius, basing knowledge on factual data. In return, Aquarius will help you to be more adventurous and to live up to your great potential.

Your most memorable month this year is likely to be July. During January, there is much discussion of City Hall politics, cooperative efforts, partnership, and marriage. There could be a foot injury—get treatment as soon as possible.

You will meet unusual people this year; many will be at the top of the ladder and some could arouse controversy. Lend your writing talents without becoming involved in nefarious schemes. Almost like a bolt out of the blue, you could meet someone who proclaims "love at first sight."

In the following pages, you will find a day-to-day description of your year. Regard these pages as your "diary in advance."

It is time now to plunge into your future, doing so day-by-day. No more delays—start now by turning the page!

Eighteen Months of Day-by-Day Predictions: July 2001 to December 2002

JULY 2001

Sunday, July 1 (Moon in Scorpio to Sagittarius 11:13 p.m.)   On this Sunday, confer with a relative about the July 4th holiday. Aspects indicate you will be asked to be in charge of organizing. Cancer and Capricorn, who play outstanding roles, will have these letters in their names—H, Q, Z. Expect to have luck with the number 8.

Monday, July 2 (Moon in Sagittarius)   Stay close to home base if possible. You soon might be traveling, and there are loose ends. The current cycle reaches beyond the immediate. Communicate with someone in a foreign land. A reunion with a loved one will be exciting, dynamic, and even romantic. Aries figures prominently.

Tuesday, July 3 (Moon in Sagittarius)   A very exciting Tuesday! Money comes your way like a bolt out of the blue. You also locate a lost article, which has much sentimental value. Stress independence and originality and make a fresh start in a new direction. A love relationship might get too hot not to cool down. Leo plays the dominant role.

Wednesday, July 4 (Moon in Sagittarius to Capricorn 8:21 a.m.)   July Fourth—at last! The moon in Sagittarius relates to your fourth house. In turn that means home, property, being on familiar ground, and reuniting with relatives you've missed. Amid celebrating, kissing, hugging, and firecrackers, you have someone or a group reading Jefferson's Declaration of Independence.

Thursday, July 5 Lunar Eclipse (Moon in Capricorn) The full moon, lunar eclipse, falls in Capricorn, your fifth sector, relating to romance, children, and a variety of situations. It is cleanup time! The Jupiter keynote equates to travel, entertainment, and elements of timing and luck. You receive and deserve praise. Your lucky number is 3.

Friday, July 6 (Moon in Capricorn to Aquarius 7:32 p.m.)   For racing luck, try these selections at all tracks: post position special—number 4 p.p. in the fourth race. Pick six: 1, 4, 7, 4, 3, 8. Watch for these letters in the names of potential winning horses or jockeys: D, M, V. Hot daily doubles: 1 and 4, 3 and 6, 1 and 8. Horses that come in second and third could pay better than winners.

Saturday, July 7 (Moon in Aquarius)   Lucky lottery: 4, 5, 8, 16, 30, 51. Check details and correct mechanical defects. Get together for an off-the-record conference with a coworker. You might be humming, "Everything is going my way!" Gemini, Sagittarius, and another Virgo figure in this exciting scenario.

Sunday, July 8 (Moon in Aquarius)   It's an excellent time for a family get-together. The Aquarian moon relates to your health report, household pets, and a general feeling that you are doing all you can for your family.

Today's scenario also features flowers, candy, and gifts that may be practical. Libra plays a major role.

Monday, July 9 (Moon in Aquarius to Pisces 8:04 a.m.)   Within 24 hours, the moon will be in Pisces, your seventh house, relating to legal affairs, public relations, cooperative efforts, and your marital status. Be quiet within. Play the waiting game. Transform a tendency to brood into positive meditation. Pisces plays a top role.

Tuesday, July 10 (Moon in Pisces)   The key is results! A stamp of approval is received as your order is confirmed. The spotlight is on public perception of you and your product. Proposals are received that relate to your professional career, and marriage. You might be asking yourself, "What did I do to deserve this?" Capricorn plays a memorable role.

Wednesday, July 11 (Moon in Pisces to Aries 8:34 p.m.)   Expect to have luck with these numbers: 11, 22, 18. The Pisces moon is in your seventh house, which tells of activities in connection with publicity, advertising, speaking arrangements, and your marital status. Heed your inner voice!

Thursday, July 12 (Moon in Aries)   Let go of the past and take a cold plunge into the future. You know what you should do—so do it! Lack of confidence could cause a delay, therefore an opportunity could slip by. Review accounting procedures. A new love is on the horizon, so be prepared, both physically and emotionally. An Aquarian figures prominently.

Friday, July 13 (Moon in Aries)   Today is not unlucky for you! Focus on family, property, and the news of a possible inheritance. The emphasis is on direction, motivation, and family relationships. Get an expert opinion about mathematical procedures. Tonight you have company for dinner—relax and enjoy it. Capricorn is involved.

Saturday, July 14 (Moon in Aries to Taurus 7:12 a.m.)   Highlight versatility and diversity. Attend a social affair, during which you meet interesting people who can help you personally and in business. Gemini and Sagittarius, who play leading roles, have these letters in their names—C, L, U. Expect to have luck with the number 3.

Sunday, July 15 (Moon in Taurus)   Enjoy a slow pace. The Taurus moon relates to your ninth house, that section of your horoscope associated with communication, travel, publishing, and philosophical concepts. No matter what anyone else tells you, what was thought to be lost is going to turn up in a surprising way.

Monday, July 16 (Moon in Taurus to Gemini 2:23 p.m.)   There's light at the end of the tunnel—finally, you have located the right representative for your talent or product. A foreign language, or another nation could be involved. Focus on writing, teaching, and communicating with key people. Gemini, Sagittarius, and another Virgo are featured.

Tuesday, July 17 (Moon in Gemini)   Attention revolves around your home and family, and concerns decisions that loom large in connection with where you live or your marital status. What seemed out of reach becomes available. Look beyond the immediate in connection with beauty, luxury, romance, and love. Libra plays a role.

Wednesday, July 18 (Moon in Gemini to Cancer 5:55 p.m.)   Expect a variety of experiences, for Neptune and Mercury are involved, which means reflection as well as action. You'll get exclusive, behind-the-scenes information. People who fall victim to the green-eyed monster will criticize, complain, and cry that the world is not fair. Pisces is involved.

Thursday, July 19 (Moon in Cancer)   On this Thursday, with the moon in Cancer, your eleventh house, many of your hopes and wishes will be fulfilled. You will have good fortune in finance and romance. During this cycle, you win friends and influence people. Capricorn will play an exciting role.

Friday, July 20 (Moon in Cancer to Leo 6:42 p.m.)   The new moon in Cancer relates to your eleventh sector and your run of good luck continues. Play the number 9 and add these numbers: 3 and 6. Stress universality, studying the habits of people in other lands, including diet and ways of making love. Travel bargains are available.

Saturday, July 21 (Moon in Leo)   Clear away emotional debris! Keep resolutions about making a fresh start in a new direction. Don't allow pangs of conscience to stop you from moving ahead in a constructive, direct way. Leo and Aquarius persons will play dramatic roles. Lucky lottery: 1, 12, 15, 25, 26, 51.

Sunday, July 22 (Moon in Leo to Virgo 6:28 p.m.)   Within your family, find out who is doing what to whom. Your twelfth house is activated, which means secrets will be revealed in a fantastic way. Focus on showmanship, color coordination, and the possibility of a hospital visit. A friend who had been missing has actually been temporarily confined.

Monday, July 23 (Moon in Virgo)   Your cycle moves up; fun and frolic are featured. Be selective; choose only the best. The emphasis is on your personality, personal magnetism, and aura of sex appeal. Laugh and others will laugh, too. Gemini and Sagittarius, who will play pertinent roles, have these initials in their names—C, L. U.

Tuesday, July 24 (Moon in Virgo to Libra 7:07 p.m.)   Come down to Earth, put plans to practical use. Blueprints could be involved. The spotlight is on rentals, leases, and decisions relating to costs and prices. Taurus, Leo, and Scorpio play significant roles, and could have these letters in their names—D, M, V.

Wednesday, July 25 (Moon in Libra)   You could have an amazing amount of luck today. The number 6 will prove fortunate; but your keynote is the number 5. When you blend the two you come up with the mysterious number eleven. Interest in the mantic arts and sciences will increase, including palmistry, number mysticism, astrology.

Thursday, July 26 (Moon in Libra to Scorpio 10:17 p.m.)   On this Thursday, the emphasis is on money, payments, collections, and gifts that include art objects, luxury items, and cash. Grab hold of luck and don't let go! A question concerning marriage will loom large. Taurus, Libra, and Scorpio play astounding roles.

Friday, July 27 (Moon in Scorpio)   During this lucky period, you make at least two good friends. Define terms, be discreet, and don't tell all. People could now be regarding you as a mystery figure. Do not deny it! Pisces and another Virgo could dominate today's scenario.

Saturday, July 28 (Moon in Scorpio to Sagittarius 4:44 a.m.)   For racing luck, try these selections at all tracks: post position special—number 8 p.p. in the eighth race. Pick six: 1, 4, 4, 3, 2, 5. Look for these letters in the names of potential winning horses or jockeys: H, Q, Z. Hot daily doubles: 1 and 4, 6 and 8, 4 and 4. Big prices! Capricorn jockey brings in four horses.

Sunday, July 29 (Moon in Sagittarius) Complete a project, if possible. Communicate with friends and neighbors who have moved away. Life takes on an exciting hue—no matter what your chronological age, your vitality returns and your libido is activated. An Aries shares an interest in your product that will amaze and astound the orthodox.

Monday, July 30 (Moon in Sagittarius) Following the excitement of 24 hours ago, you are ready for a fresh start. Recognize the need to be independent in thought and action. New love is on the horizon. Before you know it, you will be dressing differently and wearing brighter colors. Your words will be lyrical and poetic. Leo is in the picture.

Tuesday, July 31 (Moon in Sagittarius to Capricorn 2:16 p.m.) On this last day of July, a family transaction will be completed. You will introduce a new love to people close to you, including your family. A unique dining experience caps this evening. Be wary about expressions of love, or things could get too hot not to cool down. A Cancer is involved.

AUGUST 2001

Wednesday, August 1 (Moon in Capricorn) The first day of August gets off to a romantic start. Your creative juices stir; life takes on a more vital meaning. People who claimed you had no romance in your heart will be eating those words. Aries and Libra, who play fascinating roles, have these letters in their names—I and R. Your lucky number is 9.

Thursday, August 2 (Moon in Capricorn) For racing luck, try these selections at all tracks: post position special—number 7 p.p. in the third race. Pick six: 1, 4, 7, 6, 2, 5. Watch for these letters in the names of potential winning horses or jockeys: A, S, J. Hot daily doubles: 1 and 4, 3 and 7, 6 and 6. Speed horses get out in front and win, Leo jockeys show exceptionally well.

Friday, August 3 (Moon in Capricorn to Aquarius 1:52 a.m.)   A health report received within 24 hours makes you happy. Questions continue to loom large about where you live and your marriage. Examine your own motivations—what is it you want to achieve? Cancer and Capricorn, who will play unusual roles, have these initials in their names—B, K, T.

Saturday, August 4 (Moon in Aquarius)   The Aquarian full moon relates to unusual developments at the workplace. A close associate announces plans to leave in an unusual way. Forces are scattered. If you don't know what to do, do nothing. Keep a close watch on your body image, and on how much you plan to weigh. Lucky lottery: 3, 33, 38, 46, 47, 51.

Sunday, August 5 (Moon in Aquarius to Pisces 2:29 p.m.)   Finish what you start, placing valuables under lock and key. A desperate friend wants something for nothing, and you could be the prime target. Taurus, Leo, and Scorpio could engage you in theological disputes. Correct mechanical defects in instruments at home and in your car.

Monday, August 6 (Moon in Pisces)   The moon in Pisces represents your house of partners, marriage, public relations, and legal affairs. Get your papers in order; organize plans to use special information in tax and license disputes. Take notes. It might be a good idea to start a diary. A dream tonight, properly interpreted, could prove prophetic.

Tuesday, August 7 (Moon in Pisces)   On this Tuesday, you will enjoy a clash of ideas. The Pisces moon in your seventh sector relates to verification of your views. The spotlight is on cooperative efforts and marriage. Taurus, Libra, and Scorpio, who figure prominently, have these letters in their names—F, O, X.

Wednesday, August 8 (Moon in Pisces to Aries 3:03 a.m.)   The moon is getting ready to leave Pisces and enter Aries. It's time to compare your winnings with your losses. Check bills; some deserve to be paid pronto. Take nothing for granted; avoid self-deception. Follow a hunch, seeing people, places, and relationships in a realistic way.

Thursday, August 9 (Moon in Aries)   On this Thursday, the key is organization. Someone did not do their job, and the responsibility for completion falls on your shoulders. Capricorn and Cancer, who figure prominently, will be known by these letters in their names—H, Q, Z. Your lucky number is 8.

Friday, August 10 (Moon in Aries to Taurus 2:21 p.m.)   For racing luck, try these selections at all tracks: post position special—number 8 p.p. in the ninth race. Pick six: 3, 6, 4, 7, 2, 1. Watch for these letters in the names of potential winning horses or jockeys: I and R. Hot daily doubles: 3 and 6, 1 and 8, 4 and 5. A horse from a foreign land surprises, winning and paying an excellent price. Aries jockeys shine.

Saturday, August 11 (Moon in Taurus)   Lucky lottery: 1, 12, 14, 18, 23, 24. Make a fresh start; evaluate your options in connection with marriage. Whatever you do today, do it with enthusiasm and passion. The Taurus moon relates to philosophy, publishing, promotion, and advertising. Leo will play a sensational role.

Sunday, August 12 (Moon in Taurus to Gemini 10:56 p.m.)   On this Sunday, refuse to be inviegled into a wild-goose chase. Stick close to home and family—those who plead "come with us" are speculating and have no place in particular to go. Save trouble by merely stating, "I thank you from the bottom of my heart, but I must get home."

Monday, August 13 (Moon in Gemini)   Within 24 hours, the spotlight will be on promotion and production, and you will be given more authority to do what you feel must be done. Gemini and Sagittarius, who play outstanding roles, have these letters in their names—C, L, U. A communication is received today from a foreign friend.

Tuesday, August 14 (Moon in Gemini)   The moon in Gemini relates to your tenth house, which holds sway over your career and business. You will have more responsibility and authority, and a financial reward will be satisfying. Taurus, Leo, and Scorpio figure prominently, and have these letters in their names—D, M, V.

Wednesday, August 15 (Moon in Gemini to Cancer 3:53 a.m.)   For racing luck, try these selections at all tracks: post position special—number 5 p.p. in the fifth race. Pick six: 1, 3, 4, 2, 5, 3. Watch for these letters in the names of potential winning horses or jockeys: E, N, W. Hot daily doubles: 1 and 3, 4 and 5, 5 and 5. A speed horse takes the lead but falls back to third. Leo jockeys will be in the winner's circle.

Thursday, August 16 (Moon in Cancer)   Attention revolves around music, home, and a domestic adjustment that could include an actual change of residence or marital status. The answer to your question: Diplomacy wins. If you attempt to force issues, you will lose. Turn down an offer of a third helping of a high-calorie dessert.

Friday, August 17 (Moon in Cancer to Leo 5:24 a.m.)   On this Friday, with the moon in Cancer, your eleventh house, there will be an abundance of friendship and romance. Be careful what you wish for; under these aspects, you get what you desire. So be sure you are in a position to handle all the material things desired. Pisces is involved.

Saturday, August 18 (Moon in Leo) Secrets are revealed. An investment offer is valid, but you might not be quite ready for it. Capricorn and Cancer play astounding roles, and could have these letters in their names—H, Q, Z. An older person takes you into her confidence. It's exciting, but don't go too far!

Sunday, August 19 (Moon in Leo to Virgo 4:52 a.m.) The new moon in Leo represents your ability to shed light on areas previously dark. Other aspects, including numerical, reveal that you are reaching far, and this could be the precursor to an overseas jaunt. Participate in humanitarian projects. People will be drawn to you with their questions, some quite intimate.

Monday, August 20 (Moon in Virgo) You will wake this Monday bright eyed and bushy tailed. Imprint your personal style. Lead the way; do not follow others. Wear bright colors; make personal appearances; get your strength up and be ready for a new, different kind of love. Avoid heavy lifting and don't break too many hearts!

Tuesday, August 21 (Moon in Virgo to Libra 4:18 a.m.) On this Tuesday, give much thought to questions about the sale or purchase of your property, or about the direction in which your life is going. The moon in your sign represents your high cycle. Designate where the action will be. Your judgment and intuitive intellect will hit the bull's-eye. Your lucky number is 2.

Wednesday, August 22 (Moon in Libra) Lucky lottery: 3, 7, 17, 26, 27, 50. Good news! Money that was coming to you for some time will be paid. A lost article is located. Your ideas click; you will be singled out for praise and you get credit long due. Gemini and Sagittarius will play sensational roles.

Thursday, August 23 (Moon in Libra to Scorpio 5:49 a.m.) Roadblocks, whether you realize it or not, were placed by you. It is up to you to transform those blocks into stepping-stones toward your ultimate goal. You accomplish this, despite the odds. Taurus, Leo, and Scorpio figure in today's dramatic scenario. Show the courage of your convictions.

Friday, August 24 (Moon in Scorpio) Keep your plans flexible. Today's scenario features a variety of feelings and sensations. Read and write; learn through the process of teaching others. You will exude an aura of personal magnetism, sensuality, and sex appeal. A flirtation is exciting, but know when to say, "Enough is enough!"

Saturday, August 25 (Moon in Scorpio to Sagittarius 10:59 a.m.) Lucky lottery: 4, 6, 12, 18, 19, 20. The focus is on your lifestyle, luxury items, art objects, and voice lessons. People comment today: "Your voice is so unusual, so nice to hear. I wish you would get training!" Taurus, Libra, and Scorpio are involved.

Sunday, August 26 (Moon in Sagittarius) Reflect on philosophical subjects; dig deep within to learn where you are going and why. Transform any tendency to brood into positive meditation. You learn that your intuition is on target and that you should follow your psychic impressions. Pisces and another Virgo figure prominently, and have these initials in their names—G, P, Y.

Monday, August 27 (Moon in Sagittarius to Capricorn 8:01 p.m.)   No blue Monday for you! Almost upon awakening, your mind revs up and lays out a complete program. On a personal level, a physical attraction is featured. Both you and your partner will be extremely temperamental—so be careful what you do and say. Capricorn plays a major role.

Tuesday, August 28 (Moon in Capricorn)   A project or a creative endeavor is completed. You will have something to celebrate this Tuesday! A Sagittarian provides subtle aid, helping put over a deal that many thought impossible. Highlight universal appeal, travel, and communication with those in another land.

Wednesday, August 29 (Moon in Capricorn)   The Capricorn moon relates to your psychic impressions, children, challenge, variety, and sex appeal. Your creative juices stir; many who find you appealing are drawn to you and become your allies. Leo and Aquarius, who figure prominently, have these initials in their names—A, S, J. Expect to have luck with the number 1.

Thursday, August 30 (Moon in Capricorn to Aquarius 7:47 a.m.)   On this Thursday, questions about marriage loom large. You will be invited to a seafood dinner by a Cancer. A long-distance call informs that an old-time friend will be coming to visit. No panic! Instead, enjoy your planning itinerary. By entertaining now, you will be entertained at a later date.

Friday, August 31 (Moon in Aquarius)   On this last day of August, with the moon in Aquarius, you get work done. Someone who was a professional associate will become your true friend. Avoid scattering your forces; finish what you start; discover ways of entertaining, challenging, and performing "magic." A Sagittarian is in the picture.

Saturday, September 1 (Moon in Aquarius to Pisces 8:31 p.m.)   Discover new ways of accomplishing minor, annoying tasks. Imprint your style, emphasizing independence and creativity. Leo and Aquarius play important roles in your life today. Your health report is encouraging—you are in better shape than you thought. Your lucky number is 1.

Sunday, September 2 (Moon in Pisces)   The full moon in Pisces represents your seventh house, which spotlights cooperative efforts, legal activities, and your marital status. Analyze a situation but don't analyze it to death! A theological discussion will involve Capricorn and Cancer.

Monday, September 3 (Moon in Pisces)   You'll be saying, "This is not like any other Monday that I remember!" Vim and vigor make a comeback, so stress versatility, humor, and optimism. Participate in a political or charitable campaign. You will be asked to take charge of the entertainment. A Sagittarian plays a role.

Tuesday, September 4 (Moon in Pisces to Aries 8:57 a.m.)   It will be announced to you, "This is your last chance, so make up your mind about marriage!" Obstacles are part of the scenario. However, you are capable of transforming roadblocks into positive stepping-stones. Taurus, Leo, and Scorpio, who play roles, have these letters, in their names—D, M, V.

Wednesday, September 5 (Moon in Aries)   For racing luck, try these selections at all tracks: post position special—number 3 p.p. in the second race. Pick six: 5, 3, 2, 1, 8, 8. Watch for these letters in the names of potential winning horses or jockeys: E, N, W. Hot daily doubles: 5 and 3, 2 and 2, 6 and 4. Speed horses win; Virgo jockeys give sensational rides and long-shot prices.

Thursday, September 6 (Moon in Aries to Taurus 8:16 p.m.)   Attention revolves around your home, as well as a domestic situation that could include a change of residence or marital status. Be diplomatic as you let it be known whom you love. Some will accuse you of being active in the playground of the occult. Libra presents original ideas.

Friday, September 7 (Moon in Taurus)   Good news! The moon enters Taurus, your ninth house, so you have been accepted for an assignment that relates to travel and special reports. Define your terms, accenting mystery, intrigue, and glamour. Play the waiting game, for time is on your side and you should refuse to be rushed. Pisces plays a role.

Saturday, September 8 (Moon in Taurus)   For racing luck, try these selections at all tracks: post position special—number 8 p.p. in the seventh race. Pick six: 3, 7, 4, 1, 8, 5. Watch for these letters in the names of potential winning horses or jockeys: H, Q, Z. Hot daily doubles: 3 and 7, 4 and 8, 5 and 3. Favorites run out of money; Capricorn jockeys must take care to avoid injuries.

Sunday, September 9 (Moon in Taurus to Gemini 5:40 a.m.)   Memories haunt. You'll be musing, "Long ago and far away!" A relationship is about to begin or end, and a new love is on the horizon. You will be thrilled to learn a technique you thought you already knew. In matters of speculation, stick with these numbers: 3, 6, 9. Aries is in the picture.

Monday, September 10 (Moon in Gemini)   You will be starting all over. You said, "If I could do it over, it would be so much better!" Today you get that chance—this time, do not overlook the obvious. Imprint your style, going straight for the mark and refusing to be interfered with by someone who says, "If you loved me, you would not go!"

Tuesday, September 11 (Moon in Gemini to Cancer 12:07 p.m.)   The moon in Gemini represents that area of your horoscope relating to career, business, and promotion. You will have to choose between two paths—one requires numerous short trips, the other permits you to remain close to home. Capricorn is involved.

Wednesday, September 12 (Moon in Cancer) Lucky lottery: 1, 12, 18, 22, 33, 50. Your social life accelerates. People confide problems, some of them intimate. Let it be known you are not capable of solving everything. Keep resolutions about exercise, diet, and nutrition. Keep your body in shape!

Thursday, September 13 (Moon in Cancer to Leo 3:14 p.m.)   The Cancer moon relates to your ability to fund a project. This could be an excellent day for you in finance and romance. Your wishes may be fulfilled in an unusual way. People embarrass you by expecting quick, accurate answers that hit the bull's-eye. Gemini will play a remarkable role.

Friday, September 14 (Moon in Leo)   Secrets catch up to you. As you think back to yesterday, you will wonder, "How did I do it?" The Leo moon in your twelfth house means that what was supposed to be secret could become public knowledge. Your lucky number is 5.

Saturday, September 15 (Moon in Leo to Virgo 3:38 p.m.)   For racing luck, try these selections at all tracks; post position special—number 2 p.p. in the fourth race. Pick six: 1, 3, 2, 2, 1, 7. Watch for these letters in the names of potential winning horses or jockeys: F, O, X. Hot daily doubles: 1 and 3, 6 and 6,

5 and 7. A record-breaking pace wins some races with Leo jockeys aboard.

Sunday, September 16 (Moon in Virgo)   On this Sunday, you will be elated as predictions come true. A Pisces pays a meaningful compliment and adds, "I really do love you!" Check a bruise on your hip—if neglected, it could create complications. Pay heed to your inner voice. Your intuitive intellect is on target.

Monday, September 17 (Moon in Virgo to Libra 2:59 p.m.)   The new moon in your sign represents a time when you will be at the right place and be part of the action. Take the initiative, letting it be known: "I am here and intend to stay!" Circumstances take a turn in your favor, so be selective and insist on quality. Capricorn plays a role. Your lucky number is 8.

Tuesday, September 18 (Moon in Libra)   Overcome distance and language problems. The Libra moon in your second house equates to increased earning power, mainly through music, entertainment, or participation in negotiations. Aries and Libra figure in today's scenario, which could also include travel for an exciting reunion.

Wednesday, September 19 (Moon in Libra to Scorpio 3:27 p.m.)   Everything goes your way if you display your pioneering spirit. Although it is not true, people feel that you have more money than you really do. Focus on home building, a vacation near water, and being attracted to or falling in love with an Aquarius. You will have luck with the number 1.

Thursday, September 20 (Moon in Scorpio)   A series of events seem to coincide and roll over each other, and you will be stating, "This must be déjà vu!" In fact, you will know what comes next and why and many people will feel you are psychic. Capricorn- and

Cancer-born persons will play astounding roles. Your lucky number is 2.

Friday, September 21 (Moon in Scorpio to Sagittarius 7:02 p.m.)   This could be the precursor to a weekend of fun and frolic. Be up to date on fashion; you will be in the spotlight and will want to look your best. Gemini and Sagittarius ask, "How do you always look fresh and appealing?" The key is to take such compliments with a grain of salt—don't let up on your efforts to be at your best, always.

Saturday, September 22 (Moon in Sagittarius) You could locate a shelter that would serve a purpose, whether for fun and games or to protect you from inclement weather. A roadblock will be transformed into a stepping-stone toward your ultimate goal. Once again, people will ask, "Do you have a magic wand? Otherwise how can you always be at the right place at the right time?"

Sunday, September 23 (Moon in Sagittarius)   Obtain a lease. Place valuables under lock and key. Some people will assert, "You cannot fool us: this is to be your love nest!" The more you deny, the more people believe you have set aside a place for clandestine meetings and romance. Gemini is in the picture.

Monday, September 24 (Moon in Sagittarius to Capricorn 2:48 a.m.)   Highlight diplomacy; say kind words to someone who is your main competition. Say to yourself: "I need all the allies I can get—why shouldn't I be kind?" Music will be part of this scenario, so obtain flowers to go with a romantic dinner at a fine restaurant. Libra is involved.

Tuesday, September 25 (Moon in Capricorn) Slow down! You could meet someone who takes you by emotional storm. A physical attraction plays the main role in this scenario. Pisces and another Virgo, who play astonishing roles, could have these letters in their names—G, P, Y. Separate fact from illusion.

Wednesday, September 26 (Moon in Capricorn to Aquarius 2:04 p.m.)   Whatever you do or say today, make it plain that you mean business. The Capricorn moon relates to your fifth house, that section of your horoscope equates to personal magnetism, sensuality, and sex appeal. You'll be busy today with challenge, change, and variety. Your lucky number is 8.

Thursday, September 27 (Moon in Aquarius)   Work associates express views, some of them startling. Do your best to understand, but don't break your back leaning over. Another Virgo plays a significant role, and could become your ally. Look beyond the immediate to formulate or finish plans for a journey overseas.

Friday, September 28 (Moon in Aquarius)   You did a very good job in putting the finishing touches on a delicate project. Now make a fresh start in a different direction, stressing independence, originality, and innovation. Make personal appearances; wear yellow and gold. Make sure people know you are here and will not be pushed aside. Leo is represented.

Saturday, September 29 (Moon in Aquarius to Pisces 2:49 a.m.)   Saturday night will be live for you. You'll be dealing with older people who express admiration for you. Focus on direction, motivation, and a desire to celebrate—you've earned it! Capricorn and Cancer will play sensational roles. Your lucky number is 2.

Sunday, September 30 (Moon in Pisces)   Since it will be next to impossible to keep secrets, let your itinerary be known. The question of marriage continues to loom large. You'll hear words of love and romance, but say this: "Would you mind please putting

206

those flowery words in writing?" Gemini and Sagittarius play vital roles.

OCTOBER 2001

Monday, October 1 (Moon in Pisces to Aries 3:06 p.m.) On this first day of October, you gain enlightenment. Stress originality, inventiveness, and independence, and remain willing to open yourself to romance. Cancer and Capricorn, who will play dominant roles, have these letters, in their names—B, K, T. Luck rides with you!

Tuesday, October 2 (Moon in Aries) The full moon in your eighth house represents arcane information and wisdom. It is football season. In matters of speculation, you will show amazing skill in picking winners. Gemini and Sagittarius figure prominently, and they will have these letters in their names—C, L, U.

Wednesday, October 3 (Moon in Aries) You will be approached by an enthusiastic Aries who declares, "You should exploit your skills!" That's a reference to your apparent ability to pick underdogs who upset favorites. Taking your show on the road at this time would prove negative. A Scorpio figures prominently.

Thursday, October 4 (Moon in Aries to Taurus 1:59 a.m.) Those who urge you to expand speculative ventures are thinking only of themselves. Read, write, and investigate various areas of life, including your own. What begins as a minor flirtation could be getting out of hand. It is imperative that you know when to say, "Enough is enough!"

Friday, October 5 (Moon in Taurus) The emphasis is on travel, imagination, publishing, and the promotion of your product. The spotlight is also on domestic issues and even a possible change of residence or marital status. Taurus, Libra, and Scorpio play roles, and they will have these letters in their names—F, O, X. Your lucky number is 6.

Saturday, October 6 (Moon in Taurus to Gemini 11:10 a.m.)   What a Saturday! You could become involved with someone from a foreign land. Activities will contain an aura of mystery and intrigue. You could be placing yourself in the middle of foreign intrigue. Protect yourself by seeing people as they are, not merely as you wish they could be.

Sunday, October 7 (Moon in Gemini)   What you began thinking about 24 years ago could become a "done deal" by tonight. This involves orpanization, funding, and communication with people in far-flung areas of life and interests. Listen, Virgo: You will be relied on to tie up loose ends, to become familiar with legal aspects and requirements.

Monday, October 8 (Moon in Gemini to Cancer 6:18 p.m.)   Some people urge you to take up residence in another city. Be sure it is your convenience they are thinking of, not merely making it more comfortable for themselves. Check accounting methods, and learn more about business license requirements. Aries plays the top role.

Tuesday, October 9 (Moon in Cancer)   It's a wonderful day! The moon in your eleventh house, plus the sun keynote, adds up to romance, style, creativity, and originality. You are going places and could be knocking on the doors of fame and fortune! Do it now; don't hesitate. Leo and Aquarius will clear a path; you're invited to join the "high and mighty."

Wednesday, October 10 (Moon in Cancer to Leo 10:52 p.m.)   Lucky lottery: 2, 4, 12, 18, 22, 51. The

Cancer moon favors appeals to the public. Timing and luck ride with you; you exude an aura of personal magnetism, sensuality, and sex appeal. A Capricorn, not necessarily your favorite, confesses, "I can hardly keep my hands off you!"

Thursday, October 11 (Moon in Leo)   Within 24 hours, secrets will be revealed, mostly of a favorable nature. The spotlight will be on drama, showmanship, color coordination, and up-to-date fashions. Your sense of perception will be heightened to extrasensory perception. Gemini and Sagittarius will act as your private cheering section.

Friday, October 12 (Moon in Leo)   Be willing to tear down in order to rebuild. It may try your patience, but proofreading is necessary. Light will be shed on areas previously dark. Leo brings good cheer, urging you to emerge from an emotional shell. A quixotic person challenges you to complete a puzzle.

Saturday, October 13 (Moon in Leo to Virgo 12:56 a.m.)   A written message brightens your day. Your skill as a communicator is verified. Some people, overcome by jealousy, will accuse you of writing racy material. Don't lose your temper; maintain your emotional equilibrium. Gemini, Virgo, and Sagittarius play memorable roles. Your lucky number is 5.

Sunday, October 14 (Moon in Virgo)   On this Sunday, a family gathering would be just fine. The moon in your sign, despite obstacles, represents your high cycle, and you will be at the right place at a unique moment. Wear fall colors as you engage in a speculative venture. You'll pick winners with amazing rapidity. Libra is in this picture.

Monday, October 15 (Moon in Virgo to Libra 1:25 a.m.)   See people, places, and relationships in a realistic way. Reject an offer to participate in a risky venture. The moon in Virgo represents your personality, adventure, intrigue, and sex appeal. Announce: "I have enough going for me right now—more than I can handle!" Another Virgo is involved.

Tuesday, October 16 (Moon in Libra)   When you look up today, you will note that the moon is new and in your money house, Libra. Your cycle continues high; you will know what to do and when to do it. Follow your intuition—and your conscience. Capricorn and Cancer will play memorable roles.

Wednesday, October 17 (Moon in Scorpio 2:02 a.m.)   Enlarge your horizon as the moon gradually becomes full. Look beyond the immediate, realizing that you are not limited by location or by ideas. Wear shades of blue and lime green. Libra and another Virgo will set the pace, but you will be highly regarded. Lucky lottery: 4, 6, 7, 12, 16, 19.

Thursday, October 18 (Moon in Scorpio)   Take the initiative. Take special care in traffic; deal gingerly with Scorpio. Highlight diversity, versatility, and intellectual curiosity. Leo and Aquarius will play dynamic, dramatic roles. A love relationship is intense, though not without complications. A new project will offer a major opportunity.

Friday, October 19 (Moon in Scorpio to Sagittarius 4:46 a.m.)   The Scorpio moon relates to relatives, trips, visits, and an opportunity to display humor. The emphasis is on where you live and whether or not to sell or purchase property. A Cancer extends a dinner invitation. Accept; relax and enjoy. You will decide it is best to remain on familiar ground.

Saturday, October 20 (Moon in Sagittarius)   A decision is reached involving a notary public. You learn it is best tonight to keep valuables under lock and key. Gemini and Sagittarius, who will play memorable roles, could have these letters, in their names—C, L, U. Let people know you are creative and talented and filled with intellectual integrity.

Sunday, October 21 (Moon in Sagittarius to Capricorn 11:12 a.m.) The moon in your fourth house equates to your ability to settle major issues with enthusiasm and aplomb. You will meet creative, determined, stubborn people, very likely born under Taurus, Leo, or Scorpio. Be willing to rewrite and rebuild, to learn more about structure and architecture.

Monday, October 22 (Moon in Capricorn) You'll be released from restrictions and exult in more freedom of thought and action. Past favors are repaid; you are becoming more important in the eyes of others and in your own consciousness. Take notes. For you, it all begins and ends with the written word. Gemini is represented.

Tuesday, October 23 (Moon in Capricorn to Aquarius 9:26 p.m.) Attention revolves around your home, relatives, visits, and the need to be careful in traffic. Today's scenario highlights art, music, literature, and the ability to dance to your own tune. Taurus, Libra, and Scorpio, who play memorable roles, have these letters in their names—F, O, X.

Wednesday, October 24 (Moon in Aquarius) For racing luck, try these selections at all tracks: post position special—number 1 p.p. in the sixth race. Pick six: 3, 4, 7, 8, 2, 1. Watch for these letters in the names of potential winning horses or jockeys: G, P, Y. Hot daily doubles: 3 and 4, 1 and 2, 8 and 8. Horses that run well on off-tracks will be in the money.

Thursday, October 25 (Moon in Aquarius) You obtain inside information that could apply to the stock market or horse racing. At a Thursday get-together with friends you shower affection on loved ones. Capricorn and Cancer play unusual roles, and could have these letters in their names—H, Q, Z. Expect to have luck with the number 8.

Friday, October 26 (Moon in Aquarius to Pisces 9:54 a.m.) You will entertain and be entertained by persons who speak foreign languages. You will be made to feel like king of the hill. Your self-esteem is on the rise. Make intelligent concessions about abandoning your basic principles. A long-standing project is completed.

Saturday, October 27 (Moon in Pisces) Lucky lottery: 1, 5, 11, 12, 18, 22. Avoid heavy lifting. Let others follow you, if they so desire. The emphasis is on unorthodox ideas, a clash of opinions, and your marital status. You'll be asked to follow through on ideas begun last week. Leo is involved.

Sunday, October 28—Daylight Saving Time Ends (Moon in Pisces to Aries 9:13 p.m.) A serious discussion involves the possibility of a new wardrobe. By pleasing a loved one, you'll also provide pleasure for yourself. Variations of the color green figure prominently. Partnership and marriage continue to hold sway—deal with it! A Cancer is involved.

Monday, October 29 (Moon in Aries) Expect an unusual affair for Monday—someone who seems ever ready to quarrel will be sent elsewhere. The element of luck rides with you. Your confidence builds in your personal and emotional life. Political issues arise. When your opinions are sought, give them straight from the shoulder!

Tuesday, October 30 (Moon in Aries) The moon in your eighth house represents the need to investigate further what happened to the money. Be ready to accept answers, pleasant or not. Financial problems will ease, and so will tension. Taurus, Leo, and Scorpio will play fascinating, dramatic roles.

Wednesday, October 31 (Moon in Aries to Taurus 7:46 a.m.) Two holidays are celebrated—National Magic Day and Halloween. If you own a black cat, keep it inside. Some unfeeling persons have the false notion it is all right to be cruel to black cats on Halloween. Check accounting procedures. Think about taking up magic as a creative hobby. Your lucky number is 5.

NOVEMBER 2001

Thursday, November 1 (Moon in Taurus) The full moon in Taurus represents your ninth house, which means romance could occur on the high seas or even on land. The Jupiter keynote indicates that, whatever you do, it turns out to be lucky. In matters of speculation this day, stick with the numbers 1, 2, and 3.

Friday, November 2 (Moon in Taurus to Gemini 4:11 p.m.) The emphasis is on theology, spiritual affairs, and the ability to reach beyond the immediate. Don't be discouraged by someone who knows the price of everything and the value of nothing. Check the fine print, read proofs, and transform roadblocks into stepping-stones toward your goal. Scorpio figures prominently.

Saturday, November 3 (Moon in Gemini) Be analytical; dig deep for information; be a muckraker. Determine to find what has been missing, possibly a bank book. Gemini, Sagittarius, and another Virgo figure in today's dynamic scenario. Write letters; start a diary; take notes on your dreams. Your lucky number is 5.

Sunday, November 4 (Moon in Gemini to Cancer 10:42 p.m.)   Attention revolves around sudden changes involving your home, family, and marriage. Emphasize sincerity and dedication, and be willing to fight if the cause is right. Music plays a role, so try singing outside of the shower! Taurus, Libra, and Scorpio will play instrumental roles, and may have these initials in their names—F, O, X.

Monday, November 5 (Moon in Cancer)   The moon is in your eleventh house, which represents fulfillment of your hopes, desires, and wishes. It's an excellent time to obtain funding, and to win friends and influence people. You have all of that to look forward to tomorrow! Tonight, another dream borders on the psychic.

Tuesday, November 6 (Moon in Cancer)   It's your power play day! You will have good luck in finance or romance. Fortunate for you, being invited to dine by a Cancer who is an excellent cook. You will receive critical acclaim for your written material, presentation, or format. Those who claim you were not ready will be red-faced.

Wednesday, November 7 (Moon in Cancer to Leo 3:32 a.m.)   Complete a project, looking beyond the immediate. Communicate with someone who will be performing a vital service. Focus on distance, language, and a better understanding of the personal habits of people in other lands. You could be playing an important role in international affairs. Your lucky number is 9.

Thursday, November 8 (Moon in Leo)   Make a fresh start, accenting showmanship and developing a different display for your product. With the moon in Leo, it is imperative that you use color coordination and display your individual touch. Leo and **Aquarius**, who will play dynamic, dramatic roles, will help you get the job done.

Friday, November 9 (Moon in Leo to Virgo 6:48 a.m.) Much happens backstage. A secret romance could be taking place, so don't be envious. A new love is awaiting you and will be in your arms before long. Organize priorities; purchase a gift for a family member whose feelings you recently hurt without meaning to. Drama!

Saturday, November 10 (Moon in Virgo) On this Saturday, your cycle moves up and circumstances turn in your favor. Emphasize your personality and initiative, as well as the courage of your convictions. The key is to be selective, insisting on quality. Highlight diversity and versatility. Let it be known: "I am not quitting!" Your lucky number is 3.

Sunday, November 11 (Moon in Virgo to Libra 8:52 a.m.) On this Sunday, review your past errors and determine to correct them. Deal with stubborn people who declare, "Why should I take orders from you!" Respond: "It is my way or the highway!" Taurus, Leo, and Scorpio, who play roles, have these initials in their names—D, M, V.

Monday, November 12 (Moon in Libra) The Libra moon relates to payments, collections, money, and earning power. People take a liking to you. Music, songs, and compositions figure prominently. Gemini, Sagittarius, and another Virgo, who play important roles, could have these letters in their names—E, N, W. You can have luck with the number 5.

Tuesday, November 13 (Moon in Libra to Scorpio 10:44 a.m.) What was neglected 24 hours ago will be taken care of today. Purchase an art object, beautify your surroundings, and obtain the biography of your favorite composer. Explain this to visitors without appearing to lecture them. Taurus and Libra will entertain with anecdotes that are "far out."

Wednesday, November 14 (Moon in Scorpio) For racing luck, try these selections at all tracks: post position special—number 1 p.p. in the sixth race. Pick six: 1, 6, 2, 7, 3, 1. Watch for these letters in the names of potential winning horses or jockeys: G, P, Y. Hot daily doubles: 1 and 6, 4 and 3, 7 and 7. Horses that run well on off-tracks will be in the money.

Thursday, November 15 (Moon in Scorpio to Sagittarius 1:51 p.m.) The new moon in Scorpio relates to trips, visits, and a passionate display of affection by someone whose motives are suspicious. What was lost is recovered in a mysterious way. You'll be asked to revise, review, rewrite, and rebuild. Funding will be obtained for a unique project. Capricorn plays a role.

Friday, November 16 (Moon in Sagittarius) A land transaction is featured, and you will feel good as a result. Let go of an unsavory situation. There is no need to carry a responsibility that belongs to another. Strive for universal appeal. Aries and Libra, who figure in this dynamic, fascinating scenario, have these letters in their names—I and R.

Saturday, November 17 (Moon in Sagittarius to Capricorn 7:39 p.m.) Lucky lottery: 1, 3, 9, 12, 30, 51. Make a fresh start, stressing originality, letting go of the past, and creating the future. Wear bright colors; make personal appearances; be ready, willing, and able to fall in love. Examine, explore, and decide vital issues involving romance and your marital status.

Sunday, November 18 (Moon in Capricorn) It's an excellent day for a family gathering, trading recipes, and displaying your sense of humor. A degree of perceptiveness borders on extrasensory perception. Highlight versatility, diversity, and your intellectual curiosity. Capricorn and Cancer, who will play dramatic roles, could have these initials in their names—B, K, T.

Monday, November 19 (Moon in Capricorn) The moon in your fifth house relates to creativity, children, challenge, change, variety, and sex appeal. People comment, "You don't act or look the same. I bet you are on to something we don't know about!" Respond: "You are correct—I do not tell everything all of the time!"

Tuesday, November 20 (Moon in Capricorn to Aquarius 4:54 a.m.) Don't trip over your own feet! Take care walking up and down stairs. Someone could be laying a trap for you. A young person, reckless and bored, decides to stir up excitement. Be on guard, protecting yourself in emotional clinches. Taurus, Leo, and Scorpio are in the picture.

Wednesday, November 21 (Moon in Aquarius) For racing luck, try these selections at all tracks: post position special—number 3 p.p. in the second race. Pick six: 8, 3, 2, 4, 5, 7. Be alert for these letters in the names of potential winning horses or jockeys: E, N, W. Hot daily doubles: 8 and 3, 4 and 5, 3 and 2. Long shots win and pay excellent prices, Sagittarius jockeys are in the winner's circle.

Thursday, November 22 (Moon in Aquarius to Pisces 4:51 p.m.) It's one of your best Thanksgiving dinners—harmony is restored and family relationships are mended. One gets hungry merely by interpreting your dinner and dialogue. Be pleasant and diplomatic, and keep an open mind without being naive. You will receive a very unusual gift.

Friday, November 23 (Moon in Pisces) There's much talk about turkey and the history of Thanksgiving. The Pisces moon relates to close relatives, recollections of past holidays, and a serious discussion of partnership, and cooperative efforts or marriage. Do plenty of listening! Pisces and another Virgo will figure prominently.

Saturday, November 24 (Moon in Pisces) Powerful forces are at work! Legal affairs dominate. Improve public relations; find out where you stand and what to do about it. The holiday spirit prevails despite complications and difficulties. With the moon in your seventh house, people who generally are uninterested in your problems will surprise you by being attentive or even affectionate.

Sunday, November 25 (Moon in Pisces to Aries 5:20 a.m.) Many areas of your life will reach a peak. Decisions need to be made about joining forces with relatives. A partnership or possible marriage remains a question that looms large. Aries and Libra figure prominently, and will have these initials in their names—I and R.

Monday, November 26 (Moon in Aries) The answer to your question: Affirmative. Show your independence, originality, and passion in lovemaking. Do not follow others, even at the risk of being dubbed stubborn. You have emerged from a pressure period; some will say you are a miracle of survival!

Tuesday, November 27 (Moon in Aries to Taurus 4:04 p.m.) The moon in Aries relates to your eighth house, which tells of the financial status of someone close to you, including your partner or mate. Become familiar with accounting procedures and delve deep into the motives of others. A Cancer will play an outstanding role.

Wednesday, November 28 (Moon in Taurus)   It's an excellent day to experiment, explore, and arrange a social affair to raise funds for politics or charity. The emphasis is also on travel, political policies, and determining what to embrace and what to leave strictly alone. Lucky lottery: 3, 6, 9, 18, 22, 36.

Thursday, November 29 (Moon in Taurus)   As this month draws to an end, you catch up on work previously pushed aside. Taurus, Leo, and Scorpio, who figure in today's scenario, will have these letters in their names— D, M, V. Be willing to revise, review, and tear down in order to rebuild on a more solid base.

Friday, November 30 (Moon in Taurus to Gemini 12:02 a.m.)   You will feel free, independent, creative, and in the mood to celebrate. You'll be invited to a party. By accepting, you could meet a new love or future soul mate. Be studious without appearing aloof. Gemini, Sagittarius, and another Virgo play sensational roles.

DECEMBER 2001

Saturday, December 1 (Moon in Gemini)   Today you will be planning way ahead. Believe it or not, some of those plans include Christmas and New Year's Eve. Leo and Aquarius will play dominant roles today and tonight. You will be happy to learn that proofreading is necessary, along with key revisions.

Sunday, December 2 (Moon in Gemini to Cancer 5:29 a.m.)   It's your kind of day! Lively discussions take place with relatives. The subjects include politics and religion. There is speculation about the effects of the millenium—philosophers and prognosticators have been having a field day. Because you are analytical and intelligent, your views will be sought.

Monday, December 3 (Moon in Cancer)   On this Monday, family affairs dominate. The moon will be in your eleventh house, revealing that many of your fondest hopes could be fulfilled. You will have good fortune in finance and romance, especially by sticking with the number 6. Libra will play a musical role.

Tuesday, December 4 (Moon in Cancer to Leo 9:14 a.m.)   An unusual menu will be prepared by a Cancer who proclaims, "I not only owe you a favor. I owe you so very much!" Define your terms; choose your words with care. You learn more about real estate, as well as the stock market. Pisces and another Virgo will dominate today's scenario.

Wednesday, December 5 (Moon in Leo)   What you worked for and hoped for will materialize. You might take an interest in spiritualism. As a result, you'll learn about Sir Arthur Conan Doyle and Houdini—and their fascinating friendship. Capricorn and Cancer appear to be jealous of your attention. Your lucky number is 8.

Thursday, December 6 (Moon in Leo to Virgo 12:10 p.m.)   For racing luck, try these selections at all tracks: post position special—number 8 p.p. in the first race. Pick six: 8, 5, 3, 1, 2, 2. Be alert for these letters in the names of potential winning horses or jockeys: I and R. Hot daily doubles: 8 and 5, 4 and 4, 2 and 7. Foreign jockeys and horses will be in the money.

Friday, December 7 (Moon in Virgo)   What appeared to be horrendous will turn out to be plain funny. Let go of preconceived notions. Instead of brooding about what might have been, take a cold plunge into the future. Imprint your own style; do not follow others. Plan ahead for the adventure of discovery. Leo is in this picture.

Saturday, December 8 (Moon in Virgo to Libra 2:56 p.m.) Lucky lottery: 1, 5, 6, 18, 32, 35. Focus on where you live, your relationships with relatives, and deciding which direction to take. You'll be dealing with a Cancer who talks about cooking, restaurants, and recipes, and who informs you about diet and nutrition.

Sunday, December 9 (Moon in Libra) On this Sunday, strive to sustain your emotional equilibrium. The moon in Libra represents your second house, which means money, payments, and collections, even though everything seems to be closed on Sunday. Gemini and Sagittarius play dominant roles.

Monday, December 10 (Moon in Libra to Scorpio 6:08 p.m.) A crossword puzzle demands your attention as you suddenly become interested in language and words. A lost article is located; investment information is valid. Be alert for opportunities; apply astrology to major decisions. Revise and review, and tear down in order to rebuild. Scorpio is involved.

Tuesday, December 11 (Moon in Scorpio) Interest in hidden affairs dominates. What appears lost, with no hope of finding, turns around, and you find the article among sheets, possibly in bed. A flirtation is exciting and stimulating, but know when the time comes to say, "Enough is enough!" Gemini plays a top role.

Wednesday, December 12 (Moon in Scorpio to Sagittarius 10:29 p.m.) Lucky lottery: 5, 6, 8, 12, 22, 33. Attention revolves around your home, an ability to beautify your surroundings, and your marital status. A gift is received with this note: "I love you!" Your reply should be along these lines: "I love you more!" Libra will play an exciting role.

Thursday, December 13 (Moon in Sagittarius) The focus is on land, real estate, and the conclusion of a significant transaction. You do not know what gives you this feeling of greater security—it could be love, money, or health. Whatever it happens to be, ride with the tide and enjoy it! Pisces and another Virgo are in the picture.

Friday, December 14—Solar Eclipse (Moon in Sagittarius) The moon, solar eclipse, falls in Sagittarius, indicating a shakeup in the pecking order. Land could be involved. Harder work is necessary, but will pay dividends. The family shouts, "You need us for your own safety!" You will remember this day as most important. Capricorn and Cancer will figure prominently.

Saturday, December 15 (Moon in Sagittarius to Capricorn 4:47 a.m.) Lucky lottery: 1, 3, 6, 9, 19, 45. Expand your horizons. People are drawn to you for opinions about international affairs and fashion. What appeared a loss at first will turn around and result in profit. Aries and Libra figure in this complicated scenario.

Sunday, December 16 (Moon in Capricorn) Memories come back—some to haunt, some to provide cheer. You emerge from the doldrums to make a fresh start in a new direction. In this last month of 2001, you will be vigorous, dynamic, and hungry for adventure. Leo and Aquarius, who will play outstanding roles, have these initials in names—A, S, J.

Monday, December 17 (Moon in Capricorn to Aquarius 1:43 p.m.) On this Monday, you are drawn closer to your family, especially your mother. A fabulous dining experience is promised for tonight. Your seafood dinner could include shrimp, oysters, and lobster. It will be commented that Sherlock Holmes and

Dr. Watson always celebrated the close of a successful case with buckets of oysters.

Tuesday, December 18 (Moon in Aquarius) The load is lifted. Work gets done and is accompanied by good cheer, excellent disposition, and confidence in the future. Gemini and Sagittarius, who play dramatic roles, have these letters in their names—C, L, U. Highlight versatility and diversity, while avoiding scattering your forces.

Wednesday, December 19 (Moon in Aquarius) Rebuild, rewrite, and review. Let people know, "I am keeping up with you—can you keep up with me?" As a Virgo, you often are accused of being overly critical. Your motive is to keep up a standard of excellence! Taurus, Leo, and Scorpio play meaningful roles. Your lucky number is 4.

Thursday, December 20 (Moon in Aquarius to Pisces 1:09 a.m.) Be analytical; don't believe everything you see in print (except if written by Omarr). Arrive at your own decisions; take more control of your destiny. Remember, the wise man controls his destiny, but astrology points the way! Another Virgo stands tall, insists on being counted.

Friday, December 21 (Moon in Pisces) You'll have more fun at home—be near water, if possible. Among your friends is an amateur magician who could provide much entertainment tonight. Be sure your Christmas shopping is done at a reasonable time. Create a calendar of events for Christmas Eve, Christmas and New Year's Eve.

Saturday, December 22 (Moon in Pisces to Aries 1:44 a.m.) Time is on your side. The Pisces moon relates to partnership, cooperative efforts, legal affairs, public relations, and marriage. Listen, Virgo: It is good

223

that you are so marvelous with details. Other people could not keep up with your schedule! Lucky lottery: 4, 7, 9, 18, 25, 33.

Sunday, December 23 (Moon in Aries)   On this Sunday, there will be serious talk about business, career, investments, and your marital status. A lively Gemini provides comedy material at exactly the right time. A Sagittarian declares, "I am with you, but please give me time to at least make a few phone calls on my own!"

Monday, December 24 (Moon in Aries)   This is Christmas Eve, and you receive a call or visit from someone who lives in a foreign land. You will be given a present that can be best described as exotic. This is one of your most unusual Christmas Eves—people with you all feel close to you, and you will feel the same toward them.

Tuesday, December 25 (Moon in Aries to Taurus 1:10 a.m.)   On this Tuesday, you wake up to realize it is Christmas Day! The world looks clean; the scenes original. You will muse, "I really am getting ready for a new year, and if it proves as nice as Christmas, then I will be pleased!" Merry Christmas!

Wednesday, December 26 (Moon in Taurus)   The Taurus moon relates to a long-distance communication, an exchange of greetings with someone that you know inwardly cares much for you. A fancy scarf captures your attention. Rare music of great artists will be played. You feel like you're walking on air! Capricorn plays top role.

Thursday, December 27 (Moon in Taurus to Gemini 9:37 a.m.)   What a Thursday! Social affairs accelerate. You might be musing, "I thought I was due for a rest, but the holiday spirit keeps jogging along!"

Gemini and Sagittarius, who figure prominently, will have these letters in their names—C, L, U. Enjoy a celebration, but go easy on the alcohol.

Friday, December 28 (Moon in Gemini) The Gemini moon relates to your career, promotion, and prestige, and to the realization you are loved, especially by a Gemini. Maintain your emotional equilibrium; rewrite, review, and rebuild. An annoying Scorpio will be put in place by guests who seem to have no schedule for going home.

Saturday, December 29 (Moon in Gemini to Cancer 1:38 p.m.) Make a list of New Year's Eve activities. Close dancing is featured, so don't wander too far from home, and definitely do not drive with someone who has been drinking heavily. It is two days before New Year's Eve—impress upon your memory what you want it to be like, and then make it come out that way. Your lucky number is 5.

Sunday, December 30 (Lunar Eclipse—Moon in Cancer) On the night before New Year's Eve, there's a full moon, lunar eclipse in Cancer. Focus on family, home, and a relationship with someone who at times haunts your memory. Your diet has undergone radical changes during this holiday season, so try to keep things on an even keel.

Monday, December 31 (Moon in Cancer to Leo 5:08 p.m.) New Year's Eve at last! There's plenty of romance, and sure enough, one guest will be inebriated. There will be proposals of marriage, along with grand gestures. Keep quiet within; make resolutions you really intend to keep. Pisces and another Virgo figure prominently and will help bring in the new year.

HAPPY NEW YEAR!

Tuesday, January 1 (Moon in Leo)   Happy New Year! You get in the spirit of the holiday. Focus on creativity, challenge, variety, and romance. Gemini and Sagittarius will play major roles on this first day of the year 2002. You are off to a grand start. Your popularity rating moves up and you are determined to enjoy life.

Wednesday, January 2 (Moon in Leo to Virgo 6:33 p.m.)   A vexing problem will be solved. It has to do with numbers, where you are going, and how far you are from ultimate goal. Taurus, Leo, and Scorpio figure in this scenario. Revise, rewrite, and tear down in order to rebuild. Have luck with number 4.

Thursday, January 3 (Moon in Virgo)   The moon in your sign represents your high cycle. Even as you read these words, circumstances are turning in your favor. The emphasis is on personal magnetism, an aura of sensuality and sex appeal. Some people, half smiling, say, "We didn't know you had it in you!"

Friday, January 4 (Moon in Virgo to Libra 8:23 p.m.)   Complications at home could keep you from maintaining the necessary pace. The key is to face the music directly without delay. What appears to be insurmountable could turn out to be quite simple. Know it and respond accordingly. Libra is involved.

Saturday, January 5 (Moon in Libra)   Within 24 hours, you will have a clear understanding of your financial position. Your cycle remains high, so be selective and choose quality. Recognize the purpose of flattery; it could be false. Define terms; get promises in writing. A Pisces figures prominently.

Sunday, January 6 (Moon in Libra to Scorpio 11:41 p.m.)   On this Sunday, organize priorities. Leaving things to chance could invite problems. A relative who has been "sheltered" might act in an eccentric way. Strive to understand and to be sympathetic without being weak. Capricorn is represented.

Monday, January 7 (Moon in Scorpio)   Suddenly, the financial picture brightens. Many people, among those you respect, make serious errors in judgment. However, you avoid that pitfall and that is why you have money coming to you. Aries and Libra will play astounding roles.

Tuesday, January 8 (Moon in Scorpio)   Review the past; base actions on lessons learned. A new kind of love is on the horizon. Make a fresh start in a new direction. Imprint your style; do not follow others. Wear bright colors; make personal appearances. Leo and Aquarius figure in this colorful scenario.

Wednesday, January 9 (Moon in Scorpio to Sagittarius 4:57 a.m.)   At the track: post position special—number 2 p.p. in the sixth race. A family member announces plans for a "short trip." Don't let a reasonable discussion deteriorate into a common scold. Use logic, but don't expect an immediate response.

Thursday, January 10 (Moon in Sagittarius)   Explore various avenues of expression. The lunar position highlights creativity, variety, and sensuality. A visitor from a distant city brings encouraging news, enough to make you say to yourself, "Life is worth living after all!" Gemini and Sagittarius will play dramatic roles.

Friday, January 11 (Moon in Sagittarius to Capricorn 12:18 p.m.)   You are in a position to mold your own future! There will be minor barriers. You'll overcome them, and thus gain admiration of those previously neutral. Taurus, Leo, and Scorpio figure in this dynamic scenario. Put together puzzle pieces and you will have the whole picture.

Saturday, January 12 (Moon in Capricorn) You exude sex appeal! Don't break too many hearts. At the very least offer tea and sympathy. People say you are not yourself; you are playing a a different role. This is you, but previously it was suppressed. Gemini and another Virgo will figure prominently.

Sunday, January 13 (Moon in Capricorn to Aquarius 9:41 p.m.) On this Sunday, you will have much to do with young persons who claim to "idolize you." Give full play to your creative resources; make necessary changes in your travel plans. Read and write, discover and report. Taurus, Libra, and Scorpio play fascinating roles.

Monday, January 14 (Moon in Aquarius) Hold off, wait and observe. All is not what appears on the surface. Remember that old saying: "All that glitters is not gold!" Be realistic in your appraisal of the current situation. Know this: You cannot force anyone to love you. You're doing the right thing!

Tuesday, January 15 (Moon in Aquarius) Patience pays off! A job gets done. You get credit for being wise and exercising restraint. A grievous error is corrected, and as a result, you could be knocking on the doors of fame and fortune. Capricorn and Cancer will play outstanding roles.

Wednesday, January 16 (Moon in Aquarius to Pisces) People have been working on your behalf, behind the scenes. Open lines of communication. Someone in another country wants to tell you something. There could be an applicant to represent your talent and product. Lucky lottery: 9, 12, 18, 36, 41, 50.

Thursday, January 17 (Moon in Pisces)   A new outlook concerns cooperative efforts, city hall politics, and your marital status. What you thought was "gospel" in the recent past could turn out to be old hat. Stress independence and the courage of your convictions. An Aquarian will play a spectacular role.

Friday, January 18 (Moon in Pisces to Aries 9:34 p.m.)   The focus continues on law, your reputation, and your ability to put ideas across. The emphasis also continues on your marital status. Do what you believe to be right, and you won't go too far wrong. A Cancer extends a dinner invitation. Accept, and expect a treat!

Saturday, January 19 (Moon in Aries)   On this Saturday, many subtle changes occur. Your forces tend to be scattered, and confusion results. However, the pressure is relieved in some quarters and this should help you financially. A relative you have been helping learns to stand on his own feet. Your lucky number is 3.

Sunday, January 20 (Moon in Aries)   On this Sunday, review accounting procedures. Also dig deep for information relating to the mantic arts and sciences. The solution to a dilemma is made by tonight. Incidentally, arcane literature practically describes your question to a T. Scorpio is involved.

Monday, January 21 (Moon in Aries to Taurus 9:45 a.m.)   Expend your creative energy. You are more attractive to some people than in the recent past. Someone of the opposite sex, half smiling, says to you, "I confess that at times I can hardly keep my hands off you!" Regard this as all in good fun.

Tuesday, January 22 (Moon in Taurus)   Much happens today in matters of career and family. Your role is to be an observer as well as an active participant in some areas. A family member seeks your approval in connection with a change of profession, moving away. Taurus will play a dynamic role.

Wednesday, January 23 (Moon in Taurus to Gemini 7:26 p.m.)   The focus is on romance, distant lands, and a sensual confrontation with Taurus. You might be saying to yourself, "I never thought Cupid's arrow would hit me and especially not on this day!" Pisces and another Virgo will figure in this active scenario.

Thursday, January 24 (Moon in Gemini)   You get results today without half-trying. Responsibilities add pressure, but you are up to them. Capricorn and Cancer play unusual roles and could become friends. A Gemini executive is also in picture. Treat him gingerly! Funding will be approved.

Friday, January 25 (Moon in Gemini)   A major decison will be made by a Gemini who has taken a liking to you. Show appreciation, without being obsequious. Travel to another land may be necessary to find a representative for your product and talent. Avoid being narrow-minded on any subject!

Saturday, January 26 (Moon in Gemini to Cancer 1:15 a.m.)   Your cycle comes around to you once again in a favorable way. This means you can pick and choose; you can make a fresh start in a different direction. A love relationship heats up, and could get too hot not to cool down. Bring forth your creative resources. Be open-minded, without being naive.

Sunday, January 27 (Moon in Cancer)   On this Sunday, stay on familiar ground with your family. The moon position is ultrafavorable. You can win friends and influence people. You also can obtain funding for a unique project. Questions loom large about politics, cooking, and your marital status.

Monday, January 28 (Moon in Cancer to Leo 3:29 a.m.) The full moon in Leo relates to your twelfth house. In turn, this means that you will be active in connection with theaters, hospitals, and institutions. Much that happens will be behind the scenes. You will be let in on secrets. A Sagittarius will be involved.

Tuesday, January 29 (Moon in Leo) Details unravel in connection with a project that had been "hush-hush." You will be fully informed; it will represent a more pleasant part of your life. Be receptive; display the courage of your convictions. Let others know you are a character who can be trusted.

Wednesday, January 30 (Moon in Leo to Virgo 3:39 a.m.) The moon is in your sign. You survived a "mysterious time." Circumstances are turning in your favor—emphasize your personality, talent, and creativity. People tend to fall in love with you today—don't break too many hearts! Your judgment and intuition are on target. Have luck with number 5.

Thursday, January 31 (Moon in Virgo) On this last day of January, you make peace with a family member who had been recalcitrant. Focus on diplomacy; make intelligent concessions. There is music in your life. You can dance to your own tune. A disturbing sound will be eliminated.

FEBRUARY 2002

Friday, February 1 (Moon in Virgo to Libra 3:44 a.m.) On this first day of February, you feel, correctly so, that you can handle success, money, and

231

happiness. Don't be turned off that feeling by envious people. Before the day is finished, you'll solve a mathematical problem. This elevates your prestige.

Saturday, February 2 (Moon in Libra) Loose money falls your way. Do plenty of reading, writing, and research. Efforts will be in demand. You'll be at the right place at a crucial moment. Gemini, Sagittarius, and another Virgo play special roles, and have these initials in their names: E, N, W. Your lucky number is 5.

Sunday, February 3 (Moon in Libra to Scorpio 5:34 a.m.) Your cycle is high where finances are concerned. Also, you locate a lost article and will be pleased with yourself. Wear shades of blue; make personal appearances. Questions will be asked and answered. Taurus acts as intermediary, and brings you together with Scorpio.

Monday, February 4 (Moon in Scorpio) Go slow; perceive potential. Don't be swept off your feet into any affair. Make your terms crystal clear. Check the plumbing at home. Something could be "leaking." Pisces and another Virgo figure in this scenario. Protect yourself in emotional clinches.

Tuesday, February 5 (Moon in Scorpio to Sagittarius 10:21 a.m.) You obtain the rights to present one of your favorites in literature or theater. Focus on taking responsibility. The pressure is on, but you are up to it. Someone you helped in the recent past will return the favor. A lively confrontation with Aries proves amazingly beneficial.

Wednesday, February 6 (Moon in Sagittarius) All indications point to travel, study, promotion, and an interest in international affairs. Look beyond the immediate. You are capable of predicting your own future. Don't hesitate; do it! Aries and Libra will play outstanding roles. Have luck with number 9.

Thursday, February 7 (Moon in Sagittarius to Capricorn 6:07 p.m.)   Look over a land or real estate deal. Know what you desire and make those wants and desires crystal clear. A fast-talking salesperson attempts to sway you, but hold fast to your original concept. Leo and Aquarius will play sensational roles. Have luck with number 1.

Friday, February 8 (Moon in Capricorn)   Check the plumbing. Be careful near or in water. Focus on your personal magnetism, creativity, children, change, travel, and variety. Cancer and Capricorn figure in this exciting scenario. Someone from your past will make a surprise appearance. Keep your emotions under control!

Saturday, February 9 (Moon in Capricorn)   A lively Saturday night! Your popularity rating is on the rise. Some people will tell you, "You are a natural entertainer!" That probably is so. You also would be good at writing "comedy acts." Gemini and Sagittarius play outstanding roles, and have these letters in their names: C, L, U.

Sunday, February 10 (Moon in Capricorn to Aquarius 4:14 a.m.)   On this Sunday, you should keep a steady pace, no matter what you do. Keeping your emotional equilibrium is of utmost importance. During this cycle, there are numerous details that tend to "pile up." Dig deep for information; do basic research.

Monday, February 11 (Moon in Aquarius)   Once you get rid of a "cloud of confusion," you will be on your way to knowledge and fulfillment. Read and write, give serious consideration to "science fiction."

A relationship with Gemini might be considered "hazardous." Start a diary!

Tuesday, February 12 (Moon in Aquarius to Pisces 3:52 p.m.)   The new moon is in Aquarius, your sixth house. This relates to work, service, and the ability to "fix things." Many will be surprised. Some will claim you must be "ambidextrous." You will excel at word games and solving mathematical puzzles. Libra figures in this scenario.

Wednesday, February 13 (Moon in Pisces)   Play the waiting game. Refuse to be cajoled into making snap decisions. See people and places in a realistic light. Pisces and another Virgo will play outstanding roles. Maintain an aura of mystery. Don't tell all. Don't confide or confess. Let others guess!

Thursday, February 14 (Moon in Pisces)   Much talk about your partnership and marital status. Don't make promises that cannot be kept. You'll receive many cards professing love on this Valentine's Day. Heed your own counsel and conscience. Capricorn and Cancer will play instrumental roles.

Friday, February 15 (Moon in Pisces to Aries 4:24 a.m.)   The moon leaves your seventh house. Legal pressure is off, and you can celebrate that fact. Look beyond the immediate, plan ahead, and actually predict your own future. A neighbor who dabbles in the occult wants a big favor—think about it, and offer tea and sympathy.

Saturday, February 16 (Moon in Aries)   This will be a lively Saturday—you'll be initiated into a "mystery organization." The number 1 numerical cycle promises adventure and a flirtation that could get hot and heavy. Imprint your style. Do not follow others. Make crystal clear that you are in control.

Sunday, February 17 (Moon in Aries to Taurus 4:57 p.m.) Spiritual values surface—you'll know once and for all that you are not alone. The realization that you can be lonely in a crowd hits home. Someone close to you, perhaps your partner or mate, tells of respect and love for you. A Cancer is involved.

Monday, February 18 (Moon in Taurus) The workweek begins on a social note. The focus is also on publishing, advertising, and communication with someone in a foreign land. Your critical skill will be called upon. Gemini and Sagittarius will play colorful roles. Questions of cost arise concerning a unique publication.

Tuesday, February 19 (Moon in Taurus) Someone attempts to thwart your efforts to communicate with a "special person." Keep trying! Taurus, Leo, and Scorpio figure in this dynamic scenario. These letters and initials are likely to appear in their names: D, M, V. You are going places!

Wednesday, February 20 (Moon in Taurus to Gemini 3:48 a.m.) Lucky lottery: 5, 8, 14, 22, 32, 40. A Gemini in an executive position extends the hand of friendship. Read and write; take note of your dreams; analyze character. You learn more about where you are going and why. A unique assignment promises thrills.

Thursday, February 21 (Moon in Gemini) Material once rejected could now be accepted. Stay close to home; create your own miracles. There will be music in your life; dance to your own tune. People comment on your voice—it is "nice" to hear. Libra plays an astonishing role.

Friday, February 22 (Moon in Gemini to Cancer 11:13 a.m.) You meet a "French person" and can learn a lot as a result. Don't tell all; don't confide or confess. Maintain an aura of mystery and intrigue—if you play the waiting game, you ultimately win. Pisces and another Virgo will figure in this scenario.

Saturday, February 23 (Moon in Cancer)   You get results, even though previous efforts failed. A Cancer-born individual lends experience, perhaps funding to give your project a jump start. Show appreciation, without being obsequious. Focus on production, promotion, added responsibility, and perhaps a "hot love affair."

Sunday, February 24 (Moon in Cancer to Leo 2:34 p.m.)   On this Sunday, you realize you are going in the right direction. The moon will be entering Leo, your twelfth house—that means you gain additional information through an unusual approach. Maintain a universal outlook, keep the faith, and realize that what goes around will come around.

Monday, February 25 (Moon in Leo)   Shed light on areas previously dark. People will be drawn to you for information and knowledge. Your bright light will attract moths. Don't be too patient with these people. Leo and Aquarius figure in dramatic activities—you could be engulfed in a spiritual adventure.

Tuesday, February 26 (Moon in Leo to Virgo 2:48 p.m.)   You're pulled in two directions—one direction could take you far from home. The other could bring you closer to your family, and perhaps to marriage. Almost effortlessly, you attract to yourself people who bestow privileged information. A Cancer is involved.

Wednesday, February 27 (Moon in Virgo)   The full moon in your sign indicates you will complete a project and could attract fame and fortune. Focus on mystery and romance. An embarrassing situation could find you turning down a married person. Gemini and Sagittarius play lively roles and help keep you aware and alert. Your lucky number is 3.

Thursday, February 28 (Moon in Virgo to Libra 1:46 p.m.) On this last day of February, with the moon in your sign, you will make a big splash. You'll not only make news, but be in the news. Many of your hopes and wishes will be fulfilled. You'll win friends and influence people and obtain funding for an unpopular project.

MARCH 2002

Friday, March 1 (Moon in Libra) On this first day of the month, consider yourself lucky where money is concerned. A valuable, lost recently, will be recovered. Read, write, teach, and share knowledge. A serious flirtation allows you time to continue a relationship. A dream tonight could prove prophetic.

Saturday, March 2 (Moon in Libra to Scorpio 1:52 p.m.) A family member interested in music and voice will seek your help. Be fair-minded, but don't lean over to avoid hurt feelings. By tonight, this message will be crystal clear. Much discussion revolves around where you live and your marital status. Have luck with number 6.

Sunday, March 3 (Moon in Scorpio) Spiritual values surface. You'll know many things without formal knowledge. Follow your instincts and your heart. In matters of speculation, stick with these numbers: 7, 3, 8. The Scorpio moon brings you closer to "occult subjects." Pisces plays a role.

Monday, March 4 (Moon in Scorpio to Sagittarius 4:54 p.m.)   Knowledge that had been hidden will be revealed—to your advantage. You exude an aura of personal magnetism and sex appeal. A bold member of the opposite sex confides, "I can hardly keep my hands off you!" Accept this as humorous flattery.

Tuesday, March 5 (Moon in Sagittarius)   Look beyond the immediate. Open lines of communication. Something in a foreign land will directly affect you. You will know the truth in the saying: "What goes around comes around!" A burden you should not have assumed in the first place will be lifted.

Wednesday, March 6 (Moon in Sagittarius to Capricorn 11:48 p.m.)   Lucky lottery: 6, 9, 12, 18, 22, 40. Make a fresh start in a new direction. Give some study to language and basic issues. You could win a major contest. You might be the talk of the town. Leo and Aquarius will play "fantastic" roles.

Thursday, March 7 (Moon in Capricorn)   At the track: post position special—number 2 p.p. in the sixth race. There's plenty of "movement" in your career and in business matters. Some people eye you suspiciously; others offer congratulations. A Cancer native extends a dinner invitation. Waste no time in accepting!

Friday, March 8 (Moon in Capricorn)   There are fun and games today. A flirtation is more serious than you originally anticipated. A relationship could get too hot not to cool down. Creative juices stir; others will know you have been around and will talk about you, mostly favorably. Your lucky number is 3.

Saturday, March 9 (Moon in Capricorn to Aquarius 9:56 a.m.)   The moon position relates to children, challenge, change, variety, and sex appeal. In plain words, you won't know what to do with yourself. Taurus, Leo, and Scorpio will play fascinating roles and have these initials in their names: D, M, V.

Sunday, March 10 (Moon in Aquarius)   There will be new experiences today. You make friends with a mysterious character who seems to be here, there, everywhere. An excellent day for writing and letting people know how well you express yourself. Another Virgo figures prominently. Draw and write—don't hold back!

Monday, March 11 (Moon in Aquarius to Pisces 9:56 p.m.)   Make intelligent concessions to your family, without abandoning your principles. What you regard as a broken promise may actually have been unavoidable. Be patient with others, but let them know: "Don't let it happen again!" Libra will play an instrumental role.

Tuesday, March 12 (Moon in Pisces)   Within 24 hours, you will give serious consideration to the current state of your marriage or partnership. Be lenient, but know when to say, "Enough is enough!" Domestic harmony could be restored, if you are willing to give others "wiggle room." A Pisces figures prominently.

Wednesday, March 13 (Moon in Pisces)   Lucky lottery: 7, 12, 13, 15, 20, 35. The lunar position highlights cooperative efforts, credibility, public relations, and marriage. You'll receive offers pertaining to your business, career, marital status. Don't sell yourself short!

Thursday, March 14 (Moon in Pisces to Aries 9:01 p.m.)   The new moon in your seventh house places emphasis on public appearances, debates, legal affairs, and your marital status. Someone who once dismissed you as a lover will make a dramatic reappearance.

Maintain your emotional equilibrium. Aries plays a top role.

Friday, March 15 (Moon in Aries)   What had been delayed gets moving tonight. In your high cycle, you face competition with grace and aplomb. Day and night, you win friends and influence people. Many are drawn to you for your expertise. Leo and Aquarius will play puzzling or dramatic roles.

Saturday, March 16 (Moon in Aries to Taurus 10:59 p.m.)   You are "let in on" mysteries and magic tricks. Show appreciation, without being obsequious. You could have luck today in the stock market. Someone who has been wanting to talk to you finally tracks you down. A Cancer is involved. Have luck with number 2.

Sunday, March 17 (Moon in Taurus)   Remember recent resolutions concerning moderation. Steer clear on this St. Patrick's night of one who is drinking heavily. An excellent day for social gatherings. Give full play to intellectual curiosity. Gemini and Sagittarius will figure in your scenario.

Monday, March 18 (Moon in Taurus)   On this Monday, your energy is recharged. A long-distance call verifies your views. Focus on philosophy, theology, and learning how the other half lives. Do some basic research. Learn more about accounting procedures. Be sure to get your money's worth. Scorpio is involved.

Tuesday, March 19 (Moon in Taurus to Gemini 10:18 a.m.)   Communication is received from someone vacationing in a foreign land. You are inspired to read, write, and teach. A member of the opposite sex, possibly a Gemini, states, "I can hardly keep my hands off you!" Another Virgo and a Sagittarian also play fascinating roles.

Wednesday, March 20 (Moon in Gemini) At the track: post position special—number 5 p.p. in the fourth race. An executive type follows you, and pours out a life story. Be patient, but find a way of diplomatically "escaping." Taurus, Libra, and Scorpio will play sensational roles.

Thursday, March 21 (Moon in Gemini to Cancer 9:05 p.m.) Define terms; don't be a victim of self-deception. See people and relationships as they are, not merely as you wish they could be. Higher-ups are considering you for a promotion and a raise in pay. Maintain your emotional equilibrium; emphasize self-esteem.

Friday, March 22 (Moon in Cancer) Elements of timing and luck ride with you. Fund-raising could be your forte. You win friends and influence people. Focus on promotion, production, and an intense relationship. Capricorn and Cancer will play outstanding roles. Your fortunate number is 8.

Saturday, March 23 (Moon in Cancer) On this Saturday, you will be discussing plans and ideas. Accent a universal outlook. Avoid anything that is narrow or narrow-minded. A long-distance communication verifies your views. Aries and Libra will have their say—on your side!

Sunday, March 24 (Moon in Cancer to Leo 12:10 a.m.) Stress originality and the courage of your convictions. What had been a secret will be revealed to your advantage. Leo and Aquarius will play outstanding roles. Wear bright colors; make personal appearances. Use your instinct for showmanship and color coordination.

Monday, March 25 (Moon in Leo) A family member "comes clean." This means what had been withheld will be freely discussed. You will be capable of shedding light on areas previously dark. Focus on cooperative efforts, a possible partnership, and your marital status. A Cancer is involved.

Tuesday, March 26 (Moon in Leo to Virgo 1:42 a.m.) Social activities accelerate. In your high cycle, you will be at the right place at a special moment—almost effortlessly. Make contacts, exude confidence, and let others know you are a winner. Gemini and Sagittarius play unique roles, and have these letters in their names—C, L, U.

Wednesday, March 27 (Moon in Virgo) A mathematical problem will be solved. You will get credit due. The moon in your sign means you exude an aura of sensuality and sex appeal. Taurus, Leo, and Scorpio figure in this scenario and could have these initials in their names: D, M, V. Have luck with number 4.

Thursday, March 28 (Moon in Virgo to Libra 1:03 a.m.) The full moon in your second house equates to money, payments, collections, and the ability to locate lost articles. A romantic interlude tonight should be kept in proper perspective. Focus on romance, creativity, and a poetic approach to questions and problems.

Friday, March 29 (Moon in Libra) Attention revolves around decorating, remodeling, and beautifying your home. There will be music in your life. Dance to your own tune. Your cycle is such that you can do almost anything, if you put your heart in it. Aries and Libra will play memorable roles.

Saturday, March 30 (Moon in Libra to Scorpio 12:21 a.m.) On this Saturday, be willing to find alternatives. Plans are subject to change. Keep your options open; show that you are not a "Johnny One-Note." Avoid self-deception. See people and relationships as they exist, not merely as you wish they could be.

Sunday, March 31 (Moon in Scorpio)   On this last day of March—although it is Sunday—your achievement record is reviewed and not found wanting. Capricorn and Cancer help fill in the missing blanks and ultimately will prove to be your valuable allies. Pressure increases, but you can handle it!

APRIL 2002

Monday, April 1 (Moon in Scorpio to Sagittarius 1:49 a.m.)   You won't be easy to fool, but you could fall victim to self-deception. This is not a day to completely trust others. Don't become an April Fool! Pisces and another Virgo may try to play tricks. Be alert—have fun but know when to say, "Enough is enough!"

Tuesday, April 2 (Moon in Sagittarius)   There's much success today! You are on solid ground. The way you behaved yesterday proves much to your advantage. Focus on family, the sale or purchase of property, and deciding on your marital status. Capricorn and Cancer will play fantastic roles.

Wednesday, April 3 (Moon in Sagittarius to Capricorn 6:68 a.m.)   Finish what you start. Look beyond the immediate. Help those who seek your aid in connection with "intimate problems." A Sagittarian says, "I have a deal for you!" Your response: "Put it in writing!" Aries and Libra will also play memorable roles.

Thursday, April 4 (Moon in Capricorn) On this Thursday, you will feel revived. You'll also be relieved of a burden that was not your own in the first place. Deal gingerly with Leo and Aquarius, who display a stubborn streak. Don't follow others. Imprint your own style. Your lucky number is 1.

Friday, April 5 (Moon in Capricorn to Aquarius 4:06 p.m.) At the track: post position special—number 6 p.p. in the fifth race. The emphasis is on family, music, entertainment, and a domestic adjustment that could relate to your marriage and residence. Taurus, Libra, and Cancer figure in this extraordinary scenario.

Saturday, April 6 (Moon in Aquarius) What at first seemed too complicated to succeed will boomerang in your favor. Stress versatility, humor, and a willingness to make intelligent concessions. Gemini and Sagittarius will play dramatic roles, and have these letters in their names; C, L, U. Have luck with number 3.

Sunday, April 7—Daylight Saving Time Begins (Moon in Aquarius) Be willing to dismantle a project in order to rebuild. In a way this is your "makeover day." Do some basic research, and plenty of proofreading. Taurus, Leo, and Scorpio figure in this mysterious scenario. Have luck with number 4!

Monday, April 8 (Moon in Aquarius to Pisces 4:57 a.m.) On this Monday, you'll awaken feeling "sexy." Members of the opposite sex will find you attractive, and you will feel sensual throughout the day. The spotlight is also on education, reading and writing, and sharing knowledge with others. Another Virgo is involved.

Tuesday, April 9 (Moon in Pisces)   Maintain a steady pace; make a friendly gesture to a family member who of late has been recalcitrant. Focus on music, flowers, and the ability to beautify your surroundings, especially at home. The moon position highlights legal affairs, public relations, and proposals of partnership and marriage.

Wednesday, April 10 (Moon in Pisces to Aries 5:39 p.m.)   Slow down! You accomplish much with a steady pace without accelerating. See people as they exist and not merely as you wish they could be. Be careful. Elements of deception are present. Ask yourself, "Is this relationship going anywhere?" Pisces is represented.

Thursday, April 11 (Moon in Aries)   All around you, strange happenings occur. Grapple with time; make time for yourself. Capricorn and Cancer figure in this unusual scenario. You might know them in this way—they could have these letters or initials in their names: H, Q, Z.

Friday, April 12 (Moon in Aries to Taurus 5:54 a.m.)   New accounting is required or at the very least a review of accounting procedures. Somewhere there appears to be an error. This could be a computer mistake. Focus on universal appeal. Open lines of communication. Locate a representative for your talent or product overseas.

Saturday, April 13 (Moon in Taurus)   Make way for the new. Discard preconceived notions. Within 24 hours, you could get the final word on a journey to take place in the near future. The emphasis is on advertising, promotion, publications, and a special talent for solving problems not your own. A Leo figures prominently.

Sunday, April 14 (Moon in Taurus)   The spotlight is on spirituality, special studies that include philosophy and theology, and the question of survival of the human personality after bodily death. The subject of Sir Arthur Conan Doyle's work might arise. Cancer and Capricorn will provide answers to professional dilemmas.

Monday, April 15 (Moon in Taurus to Gemini 4:55 p.m.)   The moon in Taurus is in your ninth house. That section of your solar horoscope is associated with "journeys of the mind." Excellent for the exploitation of a product, advertising, promotion, and publishing. Gemini and Sagittarius will play instrumental roles.

Tuesday, April 16 (Moon in Gemini)   Results! Your efforts pay dividends. You get the desired results. The moon at the top part of your chart in Gemini reveals that you have more than one chance to succeed. No need for you to go hat in hand. People sense that elements of timing and luck are riding with you.

Wednesday, April 17 (Moon in Gemini)   At the track: post position special—number 5 p.p. in the sixth race. Keep your plans flexible. You are due for a pleasant surprise tonight. Consider yourself very attractive, because you are—you'll be told so by a Gemini member of the opposite sex.

Thursday, April 18 (Moon in Gemini to Cancer) Within 24 hours, you will be able to call your own shots—this means your desires are fulfilled; you obtain what is requested. This could be the beginning of a winning streak. People approach you and say, "You must have some secret; let us in on it!"

Friday, April 19 (Moon in Cancer)   On this Friday, take it easy! Steer clear of someone who claims to know "all the answers." An element of deception exists. Protect yourself at close quarters. Pisces and another Virgo figure in today's dramatic scenario. Someone who sweet-talks is not to be trusted!

Saturday, April 20 (Moon in Cancer to Leo 8:19 a.m.) The moon in Cancer is in your eleventh house—that means you could have spectacular luck in matters of speculation. You win friends, and will be adept at obtaining funding for projects less than popular. You earn more money due to plans set in motion tonight. Your fortunate number is 8.

Sunday, April 21 (Moon in Leo) Look behind the scenes. Someone may be following you, with no mean intent. Emphasize your talent for showmanship and publicity. You are going places, but you don't want to go alone. Maintain a universal outlook. Avoid anything that even hints of narrow-mindedness.

Monday, April 22 (Moon in Leo to Virgo 11:33 a.m.) On this Monday, get ready for a fresh start in a different direction. The moon in Leo this morning provides enlightenment in the darker areas of your life. Admit to yourself what was wrong, then do something to correct mistakes. Wear bright colors; make personal appearances.

Tuesday, April 23 (Moon in Virgo) A family keepsake that had been missing will be recovered. The moon in your sign accents your personality and sex appeal. Wear fall colors, no matter what the weather. A Cancer insists on playing a featured role. Make a concession at this time.

Wednesday, April 24 (Moon in Virgo to Libra 12:20 p.m.) Lucky lottery: 3, 5, 6, 8, 12, 33. Diversify, and insist on quality. Circumstances are turning in your favor, even as you read these lines. Someone of the opposite sex confides, "I really do love and need you!" Don't believe everything you hear. Ask, "Would you please put that in writing?"

Thursday, April 25 (Moon in Libra) Check details, correct past errors, read and write, and share information. Taurus, Leo, and Scorpio will play outstanding roles, and could have these letters or initials in their names: D, M, V. A flirtation that began as a lark is getting too hot not to cool down.

Friday, April 26 (Moon in Libra to Scorpio 12:15 p.m.) Get ready for change, travel, and variety—Gemini and another Virgo will play top roles. Much that is significant will be in writing. Jot down your own impressions, too. Take note of your dreams—tonight's will be colorful and prophetic.

Saturday, April 27 (Moon in Scorpio) The full moon in your third house relates to trips, visits, and relatives. Someone close to you has problems and wants to share them with you. Wear sea green, speak at meetings, and emerge from your emotional shell. Libra plays a key role. Your lucky number is 6.

Sunday, April 28 (Moon in Scorpio to Sagittarius 1:13 p.m.) Lie low; play the waiting game. A relative is temperamental. Don't be too quick to answer. If you wait, the emotional storm will pass over. Pisces and another Virgo will figure in this scenario. Have luck with number 7.

Monday, April 29 (Moon in Sagittarius) A land or property transaction will be completed. Get sufficient rest; you'll need the extra energy. An older family member makes a conciliatory gesture. To save another's pride, say, "If you hadn't extended a hand of friendship, I would have. Thank you very much!"

Tuesday, April 30 (Moon in Sagittarius to Capricorn 5:02 p.m.) Finish what you start. Look beyond the immediate. You will finally be free to travel and to be "romantic." A burden you should not have assumed in the first place will be lifted, much to your relief. A relative who comes from a foreign land should be made welcome. This act of kindness will result in many dividends for you.

MAY 2002

Wednesday, May 1 (Moon in Capricorn) Protect yourself in emotional clinches. Someone is either romanticizing a situation or merely not telling the truth. Pisces and another Virgo will figure prominently. Define terms; see people as they are and not merely as you wish they could be.

Thursday, May 2 (Moon in Capricorn) On this Thursday, it is a "power play day" for you. The Capricorn moon is in your fifth house—this equates to children, challenge, change, and sensuality. People will ask for favors, not considering your personal needs. Capricorn and Cancer will play key roles.

Friday, May 3 (Moon in Capricorn to Aquarius 12:44 a.m.) On this day, you could be wishing someone well who is embarking on a journey. The separation hurts, but the reunion will be sweet. Finish a project that you started months ago. Funding will be made available for continuation. Aries and Libra will play dramatic roles.

Saturday, May 4 (Moon in Aquarius) You could make new acquaintances tonight—what begins on a polite level could be transformed into "intensity." Be aware of the details; obtain a background in basic research on specific subjects. Proofreading is necessary;

be familiar with motives and language. Your lucky number is 1.

Sunday, May 5 (Moon in Aquarius to Pisces 11:45 a.m.) Make a decision in connection with your direction and motivation. Work methods should be outlined and made crystal clear. Someone who takes you for granted should be told, "No more!" Capricorn and Cancer insert themselves in this current scenario.

Monday, May 6 (Moon in Pisces) On this Monday, with the moon in Pisces, most questions will concern credibility, legal rights, and marriage. The number 3 numerical cycle highlights versatility, your intellectual curiosity, and yearning to travel. Forces tend to be scattered. Finish one assignment before beginning or requesting another.

Tuesday, May 7 (Moon in Pisces) Focus on details associated with your home, property, real estate, and marital status. Be positive you are on the right track legally. One way of putting it: "Cover all the bases!" Taurus, Leo, and Scorpio figure prominently, and have these initials in their names—D, M, V.

Wednesday, May 8 (Moon in Pisces to Aries 12:21 a.m.) The pressure is lifted concerning legal rights and permissions. Get ready for change, travel, and a variety of experience. Read and write, teach and learn. Someone of the opposite sex claims you are "the most desirable." Be gracious in accepting a compliment.

Thursday, May 9 (Moon in Aries) Accounting procedures require review. Don't shortchange yourself. Keep your tax records up-to-date. Someone close to you, for one reason or another, wants you to trip and fall. Be on guard, financially and otherwise. A possible change of residence or marital status will figure prominently.

Friday, May 10 (Moon in Aries to Taurus 12:30 p.m.)   At the track: post position special—number 7 p.p. in the seventh race. Hot daily doubles: 7 and 7, 3 and 5, 2 and 1. A romance that starts off on the wrong foot will regain balance. Don't start anything you can't finish. Another Virgo figures prominently.

Saturday, May 11 (Moon in Taurus)   The emphasis is on production, manufacturing, and promotion to an executive position. You might be saying to yourself: "I never dreamed it would be this much work!" Deal gingerly with Capricorn and Cancer. The doors of fame and fortune are poised to open—when you are ready.

Sunday, May 12 (Moon in Taurus to Gemini 11:02 p.m.)   The new moon in Taurus relates to your ninth house. This places emphasis on philosophy, publishing, advertising, theology, and spiritual matters. Long-distance travel also fits into this equasion. A mission will be completed, and this will be reason to celebrate.

Monday, May 13 (Moon in Gemini)   On this Monday, you could be feeling bright and merry. Ideals are fulfilled. You know where you are going and why. Leo and Aquarius will play fascinating roles. Avoid heavy lifting, and protect yourself in emotional clinches. Your lucky number is 1.

Tuesday, May 14 (Moon in Gemini)   The question of marriage looms large. The Gemini moon relates to your career, leadership, and the ability to lay down rules about direction and motivation. Key people at the top have a falling out, thus leaving room for you. Don't be overly modest. Accept the challenge with enthusiasm.

***Wednesday, May 15 (Moon in Gemini to Cancer 7:32
a.m.)*** Lucky lottery: 3, 10, 13, 18, 30, 44. An excellent time for social gatherings and entertainment. Share recent good fortune with trusted friends. Some parts of your wardrobe need replacement—do something about it. Gemini and Sagittarius figure prominently in this scenario.

Thursday, May 16 (Moon in Cancer) The moon position is excellent for winning friends and influencing people. You'll have luck in matters of speculation, especially by sticking with number 4. A dinner party is being planned for you, and could have been a surprise had you not read about it here.

***Friday, May 17 (Moon in Cancer to Leo 1:50
p.m.)*** The answer to your question: Yes, make the change but don't burn bridges behind you. Maintain an aura of good will. Keep a level of pleasantness. There will be hints of "calling you back." Gemini, Sagittarius, and another Virgo will play featured roles.

Saturday, May 18 (Moon in Leo) On this Saturday, attention revolves around your home, security, children, and romance. As much as you might tell yourself this is not serious, the facts indicate it *is* serious, much more than you anticipated. Taurus, Libra, and Scorpio figure in this scenario.

Sunday, May 19 (Moon in Leo to Virgo 6:00 p.m.)
Imagination is wonderful, but be ultrapractical in connection with financial transactions. An aura of romance mingles with real estate and property matters. Obtain full value, count your change, and don't be shy about seeking a bargain prices. Avoid self-deception.

Monday, May 20 (Moon in Virgo) Your cycle is such that you can push ahead, make contacts, and let people know you are the best that they ever hoped to obtain. In some ways you feel you have been through this before—déjà vu. The spotlight is on love, money, and health. Capricorn is involved.

Tuesday, May 21 (Moon in Virgo to Libra 8:17 p.m.)   Your cycle continues high. You will be at the right place at a crucial moment. Focus on personal magnetism, sensuality, and sex appeal. People welcome you into their hearts. They know, somehow, that you will not disappoint them. Aries and Libra help fight for your rights.

Wednesday, May 22 (Moon in Libra)   Lucky lottery: 1, 6, 7, 10, 12, 14. Take the initiative in closing a financial transaction. You exude personal magnetism and an aura of sensuality, and sex appeal. You get almost anything you ask for—so ask for some things that you actually need. Leo is in the picture.

Thursday, May 23 (Moon in Libra to Scorpio 9:37 p.m.)   One more approval is required before a big money deal gets under way. Turn on your charm, and use creative criticism. Take special care in connection with water. Check the plumbing in your home. A Cancer declares, "You think more of others than you do of yourself!"

Friday, May 24 (Moon in Scorpio)   Be discreet; you will be tempted to "tell a secret." Short trips could involve relatives and legal matters. Acquiesce, but be sure you are not getting involved in a wild-goose chase. Gemini and Sagittarius will play in moving dramas. Have luck with number 3.

Saturday, May 25 (Moon in Scorpio to Sagittarius 11:21 p.m.)   Be aware of cycles, economic and otherwise. Solve a mathematical problem and do it with aplomb. You will be surprised at a good reception from those you thought were "against you." Stress versatility, choose the best, and stick to your convictions. Scorpio is involved.

Sunday, May 26 (Moon in Sagittarius)   The full moon in Sagittarius on this Sunday relates to home, security, and details which previously were ignored. Some procedures require changing; others need review. Very good for reading and writing, teaching and learning. A Sagittarian enters this scenario with a bang!

Monday, May 27 (Moon in Sagittarius)   Attention revolves around your home, familiar ground, and a family dispute over who owns what. It will pay you to be diplomatic, so don't force issues. Music plays some sour notes, so dance to your own tune. Taurus, Libra, and Scorpio will play dominant roles.

Tuesday, May 28 (Moon in Sagittarius to Capricorn 2:54 a.m.)   Within 24 hours, the lunar position will feature change, travel, variety, and romance. Pisces and another Virgo play the top roles. Define terms, outline boundaries, and be positive you are getting a "fair shake." A favor you did in the past will be returned—you'll say, "The Golden Rule certainly does work!"

Wednesday, May 29 (Moon in Capricorn)   This is your kind of day! You get results. Your personal life is fortified by good will and romance. Your professional life sees you in a higher position and having more money. This is one day you will not forget. Take advantage of this cycle. Buy and sell; let others know you are serious and here to stay.

Thursday, May 30 (Moon in Capricorn to Aquarius 9:35 a.m.)   You have universal appeal. People who speak another language will also speak "your language." You gain added recognition. You will know once and for all that your love is not unrequited. You will be happier and you deserve happiness! Aries plays a role.

Friday, May 31 (Moon in Aquarius) Make a fresh start in a new direction. Your work methods take on an unusual twist—Aquarius will be involved. Imprint your style; don't follow others. Avoid heavy lifting, if possible. Someone who promises love is sincere, but there remain problems to overcome. Leo figures prominently.

JUNE 2002

Saturday, June 1 (Moon in Aquarius to Pisces 7:36 p.m.) On this Saturday, show your muscle. This means concentrate on power, authority, and responsibility. On a personal level, a relationship is intense, and might be considered too hot not to cool down. Capricorn plays a fantastic role. Lucky lottery: 9, 12, 15, 18, 22, 33.

Sunday, June 2 (Moon in Pisces) Accent universal appeal. Permit spiritual values to surface. Focus on credibility, legal affairs, and marriage. Those who claim you will fail will have red faces. Look beyond the immediate, and examine the particulars in connection with travel to another country.

Monday, June 3 (Moon in Pisces) Make a fresh start. Discuss seriously questions about cooperative efforts, partnership, and your marital status. Steer clear of those who take you for granted. You have much to offer that is valuable. Know it, and respond accordingly. Leo will play a dramatic role.

Tuesday, June 4 (Moon in Pisces to Aries 7:50 a.m.) Within 24 hours, you check on accounting procedures and learn whether any cheating was involved. Focus on a two-way street, joining forces with another, and marriage. Your marital status is reaffirmed or broken up—decide which you want and your wishes will be obeyed.

Wednesday, June 5 (Moon in Aries)   At the track: post position special—number 3 p.p. in the eighth race. Hot daily double: 3 and 6. Use this day to experiment, to socialize, to make crystal clear what you want and expect. Gemini and Sagittarius will figure in this dynamic scenario.

Thursday, June 6 (Moon in Aries to Taurus 8:05 p.m.)   On this Thursday, you attend to essentials, including details relating to accounting methods. You could be earning more or less money than you anticipated. Find out. Don't leave it to a guessing game. Taurus, Libra, and Scorpio play major roles. Number 4 is lucky!

Friday, June 7 (Moon in Taurus)   Many changes occur, some favorable or otherwise. Be realistic in assessing who is important to you and whom you should "let go." Avoid self-deception. Pisces and another Virgo play important roles, and could have these initials in their names: E, N, W.

Saturday, June 8 (Moon in Taurus)   Attention revolves around money, payments, and decorating and remodeling your home. Strive to restore domestic harmony. Emphasize design, color coordination, and architecture. On this Saturday, a Libra approaches and offers his or her services. Don't be shy about asking costs.

Sunday, June 9 (Moon in Taurus to Gemini 6:28 a.m.)   Your creative juices stir; vitality returns. Don't expect something of value for nothing. Pisces and another Virgo play meaningful roles, and could have these letters or initials in their names—G, P, Y. A lost love is back in the picture with certain demands, including marriage.

Monday, June 10 (Moon in Gemini)   Questions arise concerning promotion, production, added responsibility, and an increase in salary. Some people challenge, "This will settle once and for all whether you are worth what you say." Capricorn and Cancer will play instrumental roles.

Tuesday, June 11 (Moon in Gemini to Cancer 2:13 p.m.)   Someone in a position of authority calls on you for help and suggestions. Leave your options open; put forth unorthodox concepts. You will be commended for your honesty. You will also have made a very valuable contact. Communicate with someone in another nation.

Wednesday, June 12 (Moon in Cancer)   On this Wednesday, you have good fortune in matters of speculation, including the lottery. Try these numbers: 6, 7, 12, 13, 22, 51. Imprint your style; don't follow others. Some will accuse you of being domineering. Leo will be definitely on your side.

Thursday, June 13 (Moon in Cancer to Leo 7:38 p.m.)   With the moon still in your eleventh house, you are persuasive enough to win friends and influence people. You obtain funding with apparent ease. A less than popular subject will benefit from your efforts. Tonight, a Cancer prepares a superb dinner.

Friday, June 14 (Moon in Leo)   Diversify; add touches of glamour and showmanship. People vie to be with you, to wine and dine you. Be grateful for your talents; show them off. A Sagittarian is by your side and helps overcome "memory difficulties." Gemini refuses to be left out of this picture.

Saturday, June 15 (Moon in Leo to Virgo 11:22 p.m.) On this Saturday, look behind the scenes. A surprise awaits. Leo and Aquarius are very much involved and have good intentions, but could display "clumsiness." Take special care with packaging and wrapping. Yes, you are being watched. Scorpio is involved.

Sunday, June 16 (Moon in Virgo) Express admiration for the poor, simple life. Point up religious analogies, expect a debate, and be knowledgeable. Let people know where you stand, but be diplomatic about it. Read and write; emphasize drama. People will be interested in what you say.

Monday, June 17 (Moon in Virgo) Every day cannot be a circus with balloons, buffoons, and clowns. Yet you manage to make this day interesting. You compel attention. You fight for what is right and you *will* fight, if the cause is right. Your cycle is high, so you will be at the right place at a special moment, almost effortlessly.

Tuesday, June 18 (Moon in Virgo to Libra 2:10 a.m.) On this Tuesday, confusion could dominate. Hold fast to realism. Let people know when they are deceiving themselves. Focus on land, real estate, and illusion. Pisces and another Virgo figure in this dramatic scenario. A gift is received. You're caught off guard!

Wednesday, June 19 (Moon in Libra) The moon in Libra represents your second house, that section of your horoscope dealing with money and the ability to locate lost valuables. Your cycle is such that you need not go anywhere hat in hand. Exude confidence, personal magnetism, and sex appeal. Have luck with number 8.

Thursday, June 20 (Moon in Libra to Scorpio 4:41 a.m.) Some people comment, "This is not like you!" Your response: "You're looking at the new me—get used to it!" Focus on travel, a universal outlook, and being close to someone who speaks a foreign language. Aries and Libra will play meaningful roles.

Friday, June 21 (Moon in Scorpio) On this Friday display the "new you." Wear bright colors; make personal appearances. Try something new, including new cuisine and love. Don't follow others; let them follow you, if they so desire. Leo and Aquarius will play dramatic roles, and have these initials in their names: A, S, J.

Saturday, June 22 (Moon in Scorpio to Sagittarius 7:41 a.m.) A relative issues a challenge, berating you for often being late for appointments. Be patient, and deal gingerly with a Scorpio. No use explaining about traffic or other circumstances—just sit there and take it for what it's worth. Capricorn is represented.

Sunday, June 23 (Moon in Sagittarius) You'll meet people of interest, especially at church. Diversify; accent versatility and intellectual curiosity. Remember recent resolutions about exercise, diet, and nutrition— then do something about it. A Sagittarian plays a fascinating role.

Monday, June 24 (Moon in Sagittarius to Capricorn 12:01 p.m.) The full moon in Sagittarius represents your fourth house, emphasizing land, real estate, security, and the sale or purchase of a home. Don't be caught off guard by someone who "sweet-talks" you. Taurus, Leo, and Scorpio play dynamic roles, have these letters in their names—D, M, V.

Tuesday, June 25 (Moon in Capricorn) On this 25th day of June, you find ways to earn more money.

People joke about it, calling you "Solomon." "How do you find money?" they ask. Your answer: "I smell it!" Gemini, Sagittarius, and another Virgo play fascinating roles, and have these initials in their names: E, N, W.

Wednesday, June 26 (Moon in Capricorn to Aquarius 6:35 p.m.)   Your creative juices are activated—you will excel at creative endeavors. Focus on children, challenge, change, and a variety of sensations. Your fifth house emphasis spotlights your ability to finish what you failed to complete in the recent past. Your lucky number is 6.

Thursday, June 27 (Moon in Aquarius)   It seems far away, that moon in Aquarius, your sixth house. Work that had been abandoned can now be completed in an almost "supernatural" way. Pisces and another Virgo figure prominently, and will have these letters or initials in their names—G, P, Y.

Friday, June 28 (Moon in Aquarius)   On this Friday, you have "good feelings." Work is accomplished; a goal is practically achieved. There may be added pressure and responsibility, but you will be up to it. Someone from a sun-drenched country visits and invites you to be his guest, too. Capricorn is involved.

Saturday, June 29 (Moon in Aquarius to Pisces 4:02 a.m.)   A romantic Saturday night! Married or single, you rediscover the sexual side of your nature. Within 24 hours the subjects of partnership, cooperative efforts, marriage will loom large. Aries and Libra pay homage— quite surprising! Your lucky number is 9.

Sunday, June 30 (Moon in Pisces)   A new approach is necessary in connection with politics, charity, and your marital status. Some people comment, "You're very merry and bright this Sunday." Your response: "Thank you. I needed that!" Leo and Aquarius will play fantastic roles; you'll be happy about it.

JULY 2002

Monday, July 1 (Moon in Pisces to Aries 3:48 p.m.) There will be emotional fireworks this month. Place your cards on the table face up. Music blares. Dance to your own tune. A relationship is at the beginning or end—avoid self-deception. Libra and Aries play key roles. Don't be afraid to ask for help, if you need it.

Tuesday, July 2 (Moon in Aries) Stick to your original concept. Following others would be an error. Focus on your marital status, partnership, and publicity, as contrasted to notoriety. Don't surprise others with radical plans. People will look to you for stability—don't disappoint them.

Wednesday, July 3 (Moon in Aries) Take special care around water, including plumbing. The spotlight is on where you live and with whom. Capricorn and Cancer will play "stunning" roles. You will be pulled in two directions simultaneously. Stick to familiar ground; be near your family. Have luck with number 2.

Thursday, July 4 (Moon in Aries to Taurus 4:15 a.m.) Catch up on history during this holiday. A good idea would be to have someone read aloud Thomas Jefferson's Declaration of Independence. You will find yourself "getting along" with people who previously were cool toward you. Sagittarius is involved.

Friday, July 5 (Moon in Taurus) Strive for emotional equilibrium. The moon in Taurus, your ninth house, depicts "hunger for knowledge." Find out what it's all about and where you fit in. A Scorpio who can be stubborn will turn on the charm. Everybody benefits as a result.

Saturday, July 6 (Moon in Taurus to Gemini 2:59 p.m.) Today features flirtation, experimentation, and the fulfillment of your emotional "hunger." Look beyond the immediate. Open lines of communication. Someone, perhaps in a foreign land, wants very much to "tell you something." Lucky lottery: 5, 9, 12, 19, 37, 38.

Sunday, July 7 (Moon in Gemini) Spiritual values become part of this scenario, much to your ultimate advantage. For answers to perplexing questions, consult arcane literature. People look to you for solutions to dilemmas—make it clear you are only human, but will do your best.

Monday, July 8 (Moon in Gemini to Cancer 10:34 p.m.) You might be saying, "Although this is Monday, it is beginning to feel like Sunday!" See people and places as they exist, not merely as you might imagine them to be. Pisces and another Virgo will play dynamic, dramatic roles. Hide and seek!

Tuesday, July 9 (Moon in Cancer) Don't run away! Face the music early. Consult a Gemini executive. Avoid running away; don't change horses in midstream. You are "marked" as a winner. Capricorn and Cancer will find ways to help your cause. Be serious about using your writing talent.

Wednesday, July 10 (Moon in Cancer to Leo 3:06 a.m.) At the track: hot daily doubles: 2 and 2, 4 and 1, 3 and 2. Post position special—number 2 p.p. in the second race. Finish what you start. Let go of someone who takes you for granted. Aries and Libra figure in this scenario.

Thursday, July 11 (Moon in Leo)   Your intuitive intellect works overtime. You will know without knowing. Trust your hunch and your heart. Make a new start; highlight original material. Wear bright colors; exude confidence and sex appeal. Leo and Aquarius will play quixotic roles.

Friday, July 12 (Moon in Leo)   A family member confesses to being "a day late and a dollar short." Be sympathetic, without being weak. Let it be known that you have your problems, too. Cancer and Capricorn will survey the situation, and could come up with solutions. Your lucky number is 2.

Saturday, July 13 (Moon in Leo to Virgo 5:39 a.m.)   You'll be told, "You are so much more fun to be with, now that you have lightened up!" Be gracious; show your sense of humor and the courage of your convictions. Remember recent resolutions about exercise, diet, and nutrition. Have luck with number 3.

Sunday, July 14 (Moon in Virgo)   On this Sunday, there are numerous problems, some of them puzzles or mathematical challenges. You might get more credit than actually deserved. Take a bow anyway! Your cycle is high, so you emit personal magnetism, an aura of sensuality, and sex appeal.

Monday, July 15 (Moon in Virgo to Libra 7:38 a.m.)   Circumstances take a sudden turn in your favor. Be selective; choose the best—written material will fill in the blanks. Be perceptive and analytical. You will say to yourself: "After all, I seem to be a natural writer and character analyst!" Sagittarius is in this picture.

Tuesday, July 16 (Moon in Libra)   Focus on art, literature, music, and your ability to appreciate them and to put your feelings on paper. Taurus, Libra, and

Scorpio will play major roles, and could have these letters or initials in their names: F, O, X. A family member surprises you by displaying psychic ability.

Wednesday, July 17 (Moon in Libra to Scorpio 10:12 a.m.) Look beyond the immediate. Don't deny your "inner feelings." Money comes your way; you say to yourself, "I wish I could remember how I did it!" Some people feel you are your own severest critic. Pisces and another Virgo insist on playing featured roles.

Thursday, July 18 (Moon in Scorpio) A short trip may be necessary in connection with a Scorpio relative. Make it crystal clear that you do not intend to get involved in a wild-goose chase. Give full rein to your intellectual curiosity. Make inquiries. Don't be satisfied with evasions. Ask direct questions and expect honest answers.

Friday, July 19 (Moon in Scorpio to Sagittarius 2:01 p.m.) You'll be saying "goodbye," but this is only temporary. Before you know it, you will be saying "hello." Be cheerful, merry, and bright. You cannot be defeated, unless you acquiesce to it. You will be checking the terrain, meeting new people, and perhaps "falling in love."

Saturday, July 20 (Moon in Sagittarius) A new approach to publishing or psychology would prove beneficial. Don't follow others; let them follow you if they so desire. Wear bright colors, including shades of yellow and gold. You'll be told more than once, "You are an inspiration to be near!" Have luck with number 1.

Sunday, July 21 (Moon in Sagittarius to Capricorn 7:27 p.m.) If single, you could meet your future mate. Attend an auction if possible. You possess a knack today for obtaining bargains. Cancer and Capricorn are attracted to you and will help promote your cause. A person who lives near water could invite you to "spend the day with us."

Monday, July 22 (Moon in Capricorn) Your creative juices stir. People want to be near you. A special member of the opposite sex whispers, "I can hardly keep my hands off you!" Take this in the spirit in which it is given, a spirit of fun and adventure. Gemini and Sagittarius will play "amazing" roles today.

Tuesday, July 23 (Moon in Capricorn) Allot enough time to read proofs and to check mathematical equations. If thorough, you win. Otherwise, who knows what could happen. Read between the lines; detect subtle meanings. A Scorpio confides plans for a "financial killing." Thanks but no thanks!

Wednesday, July 24 (Moon in Capricorn to Aquarius 2:39 a.m.) At the track: hot daily doubles—2 and 2, 8 and 9, 3 and 5. Post position special—number 3 p.p. in the fifth race. Today, you learn more about who you are and why you are here. You discover the purpose of your life. Read, write, and teach.

Thursday, July 25 (Moon in Aquarius) Attention revolves around your hopes and wishes—especially in connection with living quarters. Make intelligent concessions, without abandoning your principles. You are a perceptive, generally unselfish person—if others don't know it, make sure they are aware of it today.

Friday, July 26 (Moon in Aquarius to Pisces 12:04 p.m.) As you prepare for the weekend, double-check invitations. directions, and obligations. There is a job that must be done—do not push it aside. Define terms; show interest in real estate or a land sale or purchase. Pisces and another Virgo will play instrumental roles.

Saturday, July 27 (Moon in Pisces)   This could be your power play day! The focus is on cooperative efforts, a clash of ideas, legalities, and your marital status. The spotlight is on production, added responsibility, and the need to recognize priorities. Capricorn will play an assertive role. Your lucky number is 8.

Sunday, July 28 (Moon in Pisces to Aries 11:38 p.m.)   You can solve a mystery—refuse to be afraid of the "unknown." Some of the finest minds in the history of science have dedicated themselves to prove that the human personality survives bodily death. Aries and Libra will display enthusiasm and become your allies.

Monday, July 29 (Moon in Aries)   The moon leaves Pisces, your seventh house. A decision relating to marriage continues to loom large. The number 1 numerical cycle equates to the sun, which blends with your Mercury. This should be your lucky day, and could be the start of a winning streak.

Tuesday, July 30 (Moon in Aries)   The moon in Aries relates to mystery, intrigue, accounting procedures, and the necessity for "counting your change." If you open yourself to "tomfoolery," there will be plenty of it. Imprint your own style; stress independence and originality. Leo insists on playing a dramatic role.

Wednesday, July 31 (Moon in Aries to Taurus 12:15 p.m.)   Experiment, make discoveries, write and publish, advertise and exploit. Laugh at your own foibles. Help others to see that to make mistakes is not the end of the world. On this, the last day of July, entertain and be entertained. Lucky lottery: 8, 10, 12, 19, 31, 51.

Thursday, August 1 (Moon in Taurus)   You hear of or receive a mail order proposition. One that makes you laugh on the outside, while you may be crying on the inside, has to do with "libido." Whether or not you require this medical aid does not matter. It is graphic enough to cause you to say, "My God, how things have changed!"

Friday, August 2 (Moon in Taurus to Gemini 11:44 p.m.)   The moon in Taurus in your ninth house equates to distance, travel, philosophy, and theology. There will be much discussion among friends and associates concerning the times, present and future. Questions also arise concerning cooperative efforts and your marital status.

Saturday, August 3 (Moon in Gemini)   Social activities accelerate. This promises to be a "lively Saturday night." Gemini and Sagittarius will figure prominently. You'll receive an invitation to attend a prestigious affair. Don't accept unless you really feel you can make it. Have luck with number 3.

Sunday, August 4 (Moon in Gemini)   You seem to be on familiar ground. This causes you to ask yourself, "Is this déjà vu?" There are familiar places and faces. Get enough rest; do not ignore "spiritual signals." Taurus, Leo, and Scorpio play extraordinary roles. A puzzle is solved tonight!

Monday, August 5 (Moon in Gemini to Cancer 8:00 a.m.)   A dream could prove prophetic—resolve to take notes about a dream upon awakening. Jung, the Leo Swiss psychologist, said that dreams represent our guideposts to the future. Gemini, Sagittarius, and another Virgo play leading roles. Watch for these letters in their names: E, N, W.

267

Tuesday, August 6 (Moon in Cancer)   You will be reviewing recent lessons. A puzzle is solved. You will know the way to get around bureaucrats. Taurus, Libra, and Scorpio figure in this intriguing scenario. Focus on domestic issues, your income potential, and obtaining an item which can serve as a beauty mark in your home or as a working project.

Wednesday, August 7 (Moon in Cancer to Leo 12:25 p.m.)   At the track: hot daily doubles—7 and 4, 3 and 2, 5 and 2. Take your time in defining terms and outlining boundaries. Those who attempt to rush you mean no good for you. The moon is in your eleventh house; therefore, the element of luck rides with you. This could be the start of a winning streak.

Thursday, August 8 (Moon in Leo)   The world will seem brighter. What you feared as possible "devastation" will now be the subject of humor. Line up your priorities. Focus on production, distribution, and added responsibility. Capricorn and Cancer play dynamic roles. Have luck with number 8.

Friday, August 9 (Moon in Leo to Virgo 2:02 p.m.) You get so much recognition that you might be flirting with fame and fortune. It's important to communicate with or visit a friend confined to home or hospital. You could be on the brink of a major discovery—know it, and don't go hat in hand. Aries plays a role.

Saturday, August 10 (Moon in Virgo)   Show off your talents. Be in charge of entertainment. The moon in your sign represents your high cycle. Circumstances are turning in your favor. Be selective; choose quality. The emphasis is on your personality, sensuality, and sex appeal. Have luck with number 1.

Sunday, August 11 (Moon in Virgo to Libra 2:37 p.m.)   You get almost anything you want. Be sure you also request things you need. A Cancer fulfills a promise, which makes a bright day for you. The spotlight is on stepping forward, and an ability to review past lessons. Focus on direction, motivation, and meditation.

Monday, August 12 (Moon in Libra)   Although it is Monday, social activities begin early. You'll be saying, "This is one of the most unusual Mondays I've experienced." Focus on diversity, versatility, and humor. Someone you laugh with could also be one you love with. Sagittarius plays a role.

Tuesday, August 13 (Moon in Libra to Scorpio 4:00 p.m.)   The money picture is brighter than originally anticipated. A valuable lost article can be located. Stick to a tried-and-true routine. Basic research and proofreading will bring the desired results. Taurus and Scorpio will play an extraordinary roles.

Wednesday, August 14 (Moon in Scorpio)   A relative shows up in the nick of time and pitches in to get a project on its way. Gemini, Sagittarius, and another Virgo play major roles, and could have these letters or initials in their names—E, N, W. Those who think you have been backed into a corner will have another think coming. Your fortunate number is 5.

Thursday, August 15 (Moon in Scorpio to Sagittarius 7:25 p.m.)   At the track: post position special—number 2 p.p. in the fifth race. Hot daily doubles: 4 and 6, 6 and 6, 3 and 3. Attention also revolves around a family member who is experiencing problems with his voice. Taurus, Libra, and Scorpio will play helpful roles.

Friday, August 16 (Moon in Sagittarius)   You could be brooding, "I haven't really been anywhere so that I could say I have seen the world!" This theory is emphasized today. You'll deal with it through a romantic haze. Just when you are in the dumps, Aries and Libra tell of possibilities for travel overseas.

Saturday, August 17 (Moon in Sagittarius)   On this day, your number 8 numerical cycle, you get things done and earn respect and money for doing so. Focus on priorities—which came first and how to deal with them. People "at the top" want very much to give you a boost up. Capricorn plays role.

Sunday, August 18 (Moon in Sagittarius to Capricorn 1:15 a.m.)   On this Sunday, spiritual values will be much in evidence. Look beyond the immediate, and realize you can predict your own future and make it come true. As a Virgo, you naturally are cynical—but today you will be convinced. Aries plays a key role.

Monday, August 19 (Moon in Capricorn)   There's spice in your life! A "different" kind of romance is featured. You are puzzled by the question you ask yourself: "Is it love or lust?" If you are lucky, it will be a combination of both. Leo and Aquarius will be witness to a certain phenomenon.

Tuesday, August 20 (Moon in Capricorn to Aquarius 9:16 a.m.)   You will be pulled in two directions simultaneously. This marks a continuation of a tug-of-war. Either remain close to familiar ground and family—or you can step out into the world and make your way. Plan ahead for a holiday which could bring you close to water.

Wednesday, August 21 (Moon in Aquarius)   On this Wednesday, you will be popular and lucky. Let's try it—lucky lottery: 4, 5, 12, 14, 18, 22. Diversify, experiment, investigate, and report. Keep recent resolutions about exercise, diet, and nutrition. Don't let others talk you into a "social outing" when you know you should be "lifting weights."

Thursday, August 22 (Moon in Aquarius to Pisces 7:10 p.m.)   A change of routine—work methods will differ, which will be to your advantage. An unorthodox Aquarian could become your loyal friend—listen and learn. The full moon in Aquarius today represents your house of health and work. Don't neglect either!

Friday, August 23 (Moon in Pisces)   You receive proposals regarding career, business, or marriage. It's important to take note of dreams, to write impressions of places and people. Your creative juices stir—don't ignore them! Brush up on mathematics and spelling. Be prepared to "go places."

Saturday, August 24 (Moon in Pisces)   On this Saturday, be wary about finding yourself in an enclosed building. This means steer clear of theaters or hospitals or similar places. You need not be neurotic about this; just use ordinary care in locating the exit. Taurus is involved.

Sunday, August 25 (Moon in Pisces to Aries 6:47 a.m.)   It is fine to use your imagination, but don't let it run away with you. Genuine spiritual experiences are available—be open to them. Maintain an aura of glamour and intrigue—don't confide, confess, or tell all. "Discretion is the better part of valor!"

Monday, August 26 (Moon in Aries)   This will not be a Blue Monday. You will be engaged in an exciting project. You could get more responsibility and additional funds. The "fund keeper" will cast narrow glances, but will make no aspersions. You will get what you request.

Tuesday, August 27 (Moon in Aries to Taurus 7:30 p.m.) A project will be completed. You'll get credit long overdue. You could be closer to fame and fortune than might be imagined. Stop worrying about the problems of others, until you solve your own. "Physician, heal thyself" is an excellent motto. Finish it tonight!

Wednesday, August 28 (Moon in Taurus) Taurus helps with distribution, and encourages you to finish what you started. The moon in your ninth house coincides with publishing, advertising, and letting the world know that you are here and intend to see the job completed. Lucky lottery: 2, 7, 12, 17, 20, 50.

Thursday, August 29 (Moon in Taurus) This could be your kind of day—you do two jobs at once and you do them well. Focus also on the spice in your life, romance, and creativity. The lunar position also accents money, and as for money, you will get what you need.

Friday, August 30 (Moon in Taurus to Gemini 7:44 a.m.) Within 24 hours, you will get more authority, as you requested. An excellent day for experimenting, investigating, publishing, and showing your ability to laugh at your own foibles. Gemini and Sagittarius are part of this scenario. You will like them and let theme know it.

Saturday, August 31 (Moon in Gemini) On this Saturday don't be shy about contacting associates and coworkers by telephone. Also dispatch notes about your policies; make them crystal clear. Don't feel guilty about being "up there"—you earned a promotion and a raise in pay. Taurus plays a sympathetic role.

SEPTEMBER 2002

Sunday, September 1 (Moon in Gemini to Cancer 5:13 p.m.) On this day, be quiet within. The answers to many questions will be forthcoming. You may have told yourself you were honorable, even if withholding information. Being honorable is doing the right thing when nobody is looking. Questions arise concerning marriage.

Monday, September 2 (Moon in Cancer) Events transpire to place you on top of your game. You will have a leadership role, and can call the shots as you see them. Many hopes and desires are fulfilled. Don't ask for more than you can handle. Social obligations loom. Deal gingerly with Gemini and Sagittarius.

Tuesday, September 3 (Moon in Cancer to Leo 10:34 p.m.) You get established! People know who you are—they will not oppose you. Elements of timing and luck are with you—this could be your lucky day. This also could be the start of a winning streak. Taurus, Leo, and Scorpio will play fascinating roles.

Wednesday, September 4 (Moon in Leo) You will be asked to survey your situation, including your home condition. Be open-minded, without being naive. Read and write your reports. A dancing engagement enters into the picture. Keep your plans flexible. A flirtation could be considered "delicious." Practice restraint!

Thursday, September 5 (Moon in Leo) You will be in a position to provide enlightenment in areas previously dark. Family relationships surge forward. Face the music and do something about it. Visit someone confined to home or hospital. Use showmanship to create an audience for a unique project.

Friday, September 6 (Moon in Leo to Virgo 12:14 a.m.) As you get ready for this weekend, ask yourself what you are looking for and why. Be sure to compare horoscopes, and be creatively selfish. No matter if people laugh; you do know what you are doing. You wonder why America has taken dogs to heart. The answers tonight!

Saturday, September 7 (Moon in Virgo to Libra 11:56 p.m.) Circumstances turn in your favor. You will be at the right place at a special moment. The moon in your sign highlights your personality, sensuality, and sex appeal. Some individuals confide their fierce attraction. Maintain your emotional equilibrium. Have luck with number 8.

Sunday, September 8 (Moon in Libra) On this Sunday, you learn where you stand and what to do about it. A relationship is intense, likely to involve a Capricorn. Look beyond the immediate, "peer into the future." What seemed a mishap will turn out in your favor. Refuse to be taken for granted. Aries is involved.

Monday, September 9 (Moon in Libra to Scorpio 9:48 p.m.) The answer to your question: yes, do start something new. Be careful that a relationship isn't more about lust than about love. People gather around you, and seek your advice on all types of subjects, including marriage. In different projects, you find that Leo and Aquarius prove to be most cooperative.

Tuesday, September 10 (Moon in Scorpio) What seemed impossible to overcome will prove to be pliable and friendly. You ask yourself, "What took me so long?" People who made threats turn out to be weak, cannot back up statements. Focus also on cooperative efforts, political involvement, partnership, and marriage.

Wednesday, September 11 (Moon in Scorpio)   A relative "with a temper" makes a startling accusation. Let things cool for a while. Later, have your say. Before nightfall, you reach an understanding and are friends once again. The spotlight is on entertaining and being entertained. Lucky lottery: 3, 5, 8, 10, 12, 33.

Thursday, September 12 (Moon in Scorpio to Sagittarius 1:44 a.m.)   A change of pace today will be welcome. Be aware of details. Do proofreading and basic research. Some envious people will claim you are "in league with the devil." Don't attempt to answer. Smile awhile. Taurus, Leo, and Scorpio play major roles.

Friday, September 13 (Moon in Sagittarius)   You have freedom of choice. You will be lucky on this Friday the 13th. Lost valuables will be recovered, but don't ask too many questions. Someone who took a liking to you claims now it is more than a "liking." Watch your step; protect yourself at close quarters.

Saturday, September 14 (Moon in Sagittarius to Capricorn 6:47 a.m.)   Repair work on your knee may be essential—don't take chances on injuring it further. Gemini, Sagittarius, and another Virgo play outstanding roles, and could have these letters or initials in their names: F, O, X. On this Saturday night, there will be music. Tread lightly; dance to your own tune.

Sunday, September 15 (Moon in Capricorn)   Relax; lie low. Heed your innermost thoughts. Focus on investigating, reporting, and meditation. You are able to "see things" that no one else sees. The Capricorn moon relates to a "stirring of creative juices." A young person confides a problem—don't laugh!

Monday, September 16 (Moon in Capricorn to Aquarius 2:54 p.m.)   Congratulate yourself! You survived the weekend. Unannounced changes took place, which might have directly involved you. Somehow, a misunderstanding with a person you admire was avoided, although it was a close call. Capricorn and Cancer will play memorable roles.

Tuesday, September 17 (Moon in Aquarius)   Look beyond the immediate. Take a peek into the future. Restore confidence in yourself. What you drew close to might be taken away. Hurdle obstacles. Realize that what is taking place is ultimately for your own good. Aries plays a top role.

Wednesday, September 18 (Moon in Aquarius)   At the track: hot daily doubles—3 and 1, 3 and 6, 4 and 5. Post position special—number 3 p.p. in the fourth race. Make a fresh start in a new direction and do take a chance on romance. A change of pace works wonders. Leo and Aquarius display derring-do and come up with original ideas.

Thursday, September 19 (Moon in Aquarius to Pisces 1:17 a.m.)   Within 24 hours, the lunar position will coincide with your partnership and marital status. Repair the damage made to your reputation in a recent contretemps. Be aware of legal rights and permissions. A Cancer makes a proposal which is constructive and potentially profitable.

Friday, September 20 (Moon in Pisces)   Questions loom large about public relations, your credibility, reputation, and marriage. Avoid confrontations, if possible. Time is on your side, so play the waiting game. Diversify and give full play to your intellectual curiosity. A Sagittarian knows what you want and will try to make your dreams come true.

Saturday, September 21 (Moon in Pisces to Aries 1:10 p.m.) The full moon in your marriage house indicates romance, partnership, and legal agreements that ultimately will prove beneficial. Don't step on the toes of others; make sure people understand you will not tolerate *your* toes being stepped on either. Taurus, Leo, and Scorpio will play important roles, and have these letters in their names—D, M, V.

Sunday, September 22 (Moon in Aries) On this Sunday, people are drawn to you, will confide and confess, and seek your opinion on creative projects. The truth really is not that they want your opinion; they seek your approval. Be aware of this, and you will know how to deal with it.

Monday, September 23 (Moon in Aries) This is Monday, September 23rd, 2002. You will remember this date, because of a possible change of residence or marital status. Walk a fine line. Be diplomatic, without abandoning your principles. One you formerly loved will make a surprise appearance. Maintain your emotional equilibrium.

Tuesday, September 24 (Moon in Aries to Taurus 1:53 a.m.) On this Tuesday, check computers, and be closely aware of your bank balance. It will not be easy for others to fool you, but you could become the victim of "self-deception." To avoid this, see people, places, and relationships as they are, not merely as you wish they could be.

Wednesday, September 25 (Moon in Taurus) Don't neglect your travel plans. Do not equate delay with defeat. Powerful forces are on your side, whether or not you are aware of it. Cancer and Capricorn have faith, and will express it. You are on the precipice of fame and fortune. Respond accordingly.

Thursday, September 26 (Moon in Taurus to Gemini 2:25 p.m.) This cycle is favorable for creative activities and travel. A financial burden is lifted. You'll be saying to yourself, "What took me so long?" You're moving now in the right direction. Look beyond the immediate; find someone to represent you and your product overseas.

Friday, September 27 (Moon in Gemini) With the moon in Gemini, your tenth house, you will be given more responsibility and money. Accept a leadership role. Enjoy "new power." Romance is fun, but could eventually be troublesome. Know when to say, "Enough!" Leo sets the stage for a dramatic performance.

Saturday, September 28 (Moon in Gemini) You are asked to judge the performance of two associates. Choose quality and loyalty. Focus on staying power, and the ability to let your feelings be known without appearing arrogant. Capricorn and Cancer play astounding roles. Have luck with number 2.

Sunday, September 29 (Moon in Gemini to Cancer 12:59 a.m.) Your spiritual values surface. Most of the day will be filled with writing, advertising, and laughing. Be conscious of your weight and the necessity for exercising, diet, and nutrition. Gemini and Sagittarius play rollicking roles, and could have these letters or initials in their names—C, L, U.

Monday, September 30 (Moon in Cancer) On this last day of September, with the moon in your eleventh house, many of your hopes, wishes, and desires will be fulfilled. Necessary papers will be filled out. You'll be told in so many words, "You are very good!" This

278

is your lucky day and could be the start of a winning streak.

OCTOBER 2002

Tuesday, October 1 (Moon in Cancer to Leo 7:56 a.m.) On this Tuesday, you "learn" how to have fun at home. Humorous memories surge forward and are shared with your family. Gemini and Sagittarius will play featured roles and could have these letters or initials in their names—C, L, U. Have luck with number 3.

Wednesday, October 2 (Moon in Leo) At the track: hot daily doubles—4 and 4, 2 and 5, 1 and 1. Post position special— number 4 p.p. in the first race. During this day, you attend to details, read proofs, and do basic research. Look behind the scenes for answers; light replaces darkness in areas previously dim.

Thursday, October 3 (Moon in Leo to Virgo 10:50 a.m.) On this day, you find out that someone has been holding back information. Leo will help obtain the complete story. It's important to look backward in order to regain your emotional balance. Yes, someone has been eluding you. Discover the hiding place and do something about it.

Friday, October 4 (Moon in Virgo) On this day, attention will revolve around the protection of your home, property, and family. Be diplomatic in negotiations, not weak. Give opponents "wiggle room." Do not insist on surrender without honor. Taurus, Libra, and Scorpio will play fascinating roles.

Saturday, October 5 (Moon in Virgo to Libra 10:50 a.m.) A lively Saturday! The moon is in your sign, so circumstances turn in your favor. You will exude personal magnetism and sex appeal. Pisces and another Virgo will play outstanding roles. People comment, "I would not have recognized you; you seem to be a different person!"

Sunday, October 6 (Moon in Libra)   The new moon in your money house symbolizes different, creative ways to increase your earnings. Furthermore, take a chance on romance. This "new you" commands recognition, affection, and the ability to meditate. Capricorn and Cancer figure in today's exciting scenario.

Monday, October 7 (Moon in Libra to Scorpio 9:57 a.m.)   Seeds planted will bear fruit—what you have practically given up on as a paying proposition will come back to life to your advantage. Look beyond what appears to be the finish line. Plan ahead for travel, perhaps overseas. Aries is involved.

Tuesday, October 8 (Moon in Scorpio)   Take special care in traffic. Avoid riding with someone who has been drinking. The moon in Scorpio in your third house represents travel, traffic, and vulnerability to accidents. Leo and Aquarius play sensational roles. Have luck with number 1.

Wednesday, October 9 (Moon in Scorpio to Sagittarius 10:21 a.m.)   Focus on cooperative efforts, partnership, and your marital status. Many will attempt to tell you what to do. You reply: "Thanks, but no, thanks!" Cancer and Capricorn will play "interesting" roles. Someone you felt was cool toward you will change your mind by displaying affection.

Thursday, October 10 (Moon in Sagittarius)   The focus is on fourth house activities, including the sale or purchase of property. A family member needs reassurance of your love. Gemini and Sagittarius play outstanding roles, and could have these letters or initials in their names—C, L, U. Your lucky number is 3.

Friday, October 11 (Moon in Sagittarius to Capricorn 1:45 p.m.) Do plenty of proofreading and basic research. A Sagittarian will help with details, but your main effort must come from *you*. A romantic episode should not overwhelm you—maintain your dignity and emotional equilibrium. Don't give up something of value for nothing in return.

Saturday, October 12 (Moon in Capricorn) Read, write, teach, and allow yourself to love and be loved. It's quite a Saturday night! Your shell is removed, and the "real you" is brought forward, which will work much to your advantage. Gemini, Sagittarius, and another Virgo figure prominently. Your lucky number is 5.

Sunday, October 13 (Moon in Capricorn to Aquarius 8:51 p.m.) A young person delights with questions revealing intellectual curiosity. Patiently answer, and encourage this person to go further and to ask more meaningful questions. The focus is also on your home, decorating and remodeling, and music. Soon you will be receiving important visitors—be ready!

Monday, October 14 (Moon in Aquarius) Within 24 hours your work schedule will change. Ride with the tide; don't object merely for the sake of objecting. avoid self-deception. See relationships as they are, not merely as you wish they could be. Take special care near water. This applies especially when it comes to diving.

Tuesday, October 15 (Moon in Aquarius) At the track: hot daily doubles—4 and 8, 3 and 6. Post position special—number 5 p.p. in the third race. A relationship that cooled will regain "heat." Focus on a business arrangement or your marital status. Cancer and Capricorn will play dynamic roles.

Wednesday, October 16 (Moon in Aquarius to Pisces 8:51 p.m.)   At the track: hot daily doubles: 3 and 6, 4 and 5, 1 and 8. Post position special—number 1 p.p. in the eighth race. Plan ahead for travel. A dramatic reunion occurs tonight. Aries and Libra will play major roles. Maintain a universal outlook; avoid narrow-mindedness.

Thursday, October 17 (Moon in Pisces)   Make a fresh start. Show independence of thought and action. Make personal appearances; wear bright colors. Someone who once "claimed" your love will make a surprise appearance. Emphasize emotional equilibrium. This means do not fall apart!

Friday, October 18 (Moon in Pisces to Aries 7:12 p.m.)   Focus on familiar ground. Don't wander too far afield. During this cycle, if single, you could meet your future soul mate. Focus on partnership, cooperative efforts, and your marital status. Cancer and Capricorn play outstanding roles, and have these letters in their names: B, K, T.

Saturday, October 19 (Moon in Aries)   Highlight versatility and diversity, and be in a position to "pick and choose." Focus also on humor, and the ability to laugh at your own foibles. Your popularity rating soars. People who previously were cool toward you will now confide, "I can hardly keep my hands off you!" Your lucky number is 3.

Sunday, October 20 (Moon in Aries)   On this Sunday, you'll be asked to solve many problems. These will be either material or spiritual—you will do very well, especially if numbers enter picture. In word games, you'll find that the "right word" comes to mind instantaneously.

Monday, October 21 (Moon in Aries to Taurus 7:55 a.m.)　　This will be a lively Monday! The full moon in your eighth house relates to accounting procedures, mystery, intrigue, and the occult. Get ready for dealings with Gemini, Sagittarius, and another Virgo. Here's how you might know them: they are apt to have these letters in their names—E, N, W.

Tuesday, October 22 (Moon in Taurus)　　Attention revolves around your home, family, creativity, and romance. Long-distance communication verifies your views, and could be responsible for uplifting your morale. Taurus, Libra, and Scorpio play instrumental roles, and could have these letters or initials in their names: F, O, X. Have luck with number 6.

Wednesday, October 23 (Moon in Taurus to Gemini 8:16 p.m.)　　Lucky lottery: 7, 12, 15, 18, 20, 33. Define terms. See people and relationships as they are, not merely as you wish they could be. Deception is involved; be sure you ask that promises be put in writing. Avoid self-deception; maintain an aura of mystery and intrigue.

Thursday, October 24 (Moon in Gemini)　　A power play day! Within 24 hours, your "conditions" will be met. The moon will be transiting your tenth house. That section of your horoscope relates to leadership. Don't resign this position; emphasize it, and push forcefully ahead. Capricorn and Cancer will play meaningful roles.

Friday, October 25 (Moon in Gemini)　　The moon is at the top part of your chart. People will follow your example and actually "wait for orders." Fulfill the role with dignity, grace, and confidence. You could be paving the way for happiness and prosperity. Complete a project; finish what you start. Aries plays a major role.

Saturday, October 26 (Moon in Gemini to Cancer 7:09 a.m.)   You might be saying, "What goes around, comes around." You encounter familiar places and faces. It could be déjà vu, or it could mean it is time for you to make a fresh start in a different direction. Imprint your own style; don't follow others. Leo and Aquarius figure prominently. Your lucky number is 1.

Sunday, October 27—Daylight Saving Time Ends (Moon in Cancer)   Moneymaking plans and propositions are featured. Your cycle is such that you win friends and influence people. You'll also obtain funding for a project that is not necessarily popular. People you thought did not care will show that they do care and will be on your side.

Monday, October 28 (Moon in Cancer to Leo 2:18 p.m.)   This is one Monday during which you will celebrate. You put over a deal that is both creative and profitable. Elements of timing and luck ride with you. This could be the start of a winning streak. Don't go anywhere with your hat in hand—instead, exude an air of confidence and personal magnetism.

Tuesday, October 29 (Moon in Leo)   Look behind the scenes for the answers. Your answers will come from within. Check hidden source material. Visit someone confined to home or hospital. Agree on a transaction that seems foolproof. Taurus, Leo, and Scorpio will play "sensational" roles.

Wednesday, October 30 (Moon in Leo to Virgo 6:58 p.m.)   Be analytical. Take nothing for granted. Do take a chance on romance. You exude personal magnetism, and an aura of sensuality and sex appeal. Gemini, Sagittarius, and another Virgo figure prominently. Today's scenario highlights change, travel, and a variety of sensations, experiences. Your lucky number is 5.

Thursday, October 31 (Moon in Virgo) You will wake up smelling the coffee and flowers. Romance is in the air! During this cycle, you could change your residence or marital status. Be gentle and diplomatic— that way, you get your way. Enjoy Halloween. Don't force issues. Make intelligent concessions.

NOVEMBER 2002

Friday, November 1 (Moon in Virgo to Libra 8:27 p.m.) On this first day of November, your cycle is high, and you will be at the right place at a special moment almost effortlessly. Follow your instincts and your heart. Taurus, Leo, and Scorpio figure in this scenario. In matters of speculation, stick with number 4.

Saturday, November 2 (Moon in Libra) You will be "on the money." Elements of timing and luck ride with you. This could be the start of a winning streak. On a personal level, you'll know that your love is not unrequited. Read, write, and teach. Gemini, Sagittarius, and another Virgo play dramatic roles.

Sunday, November 3 (Moon in Libra to Scorpio 8:09 p.m.) Make this a peaceful Sunday—if you can! There appears to be a dispute concerning property, who owns what, and how to decorate and remodel. Money is involved, but so is faith, experience, and the need to mollify "hurt feelings." Libra will play an outstanding role.

Monday, November 4 (Moon in Scorpio)   On this Monday, you receive a call from a relative that could result in a debate or a short trip. Be alert and sensitive to trends. Refuse to be cajoled into abandoning your principles. You are correct; know it and act accordingly. Pisces is represented.

Tuesday, November 5 (Moon in Scorpio to Sagittarius 8:01 p.m.)   Get down to business! The "business" could represent not only your career but a personal relationship which dominates your moods. Find out where you stand and why. Someone attempts to toss a "hot potato" to you. Don't reject it, but let others know you did not recently fall off a turnip truck.

Wednesday, November 6 (Moon in Sagittarius) Obtain a futuristic look—this means do what you are capable of, and peek into the future. You'll be offered a "trade" which involves land, real estate, and finances. Aries and Libra that will play instrumental roles. Don't fight the inevitable. Bob and weave; find ways to avoid the onrushing train.

Thursday, November 7 (Moon in Sagittarius to Capricorn 10:00 p.m.)   You've been waiting for this day! A long-distance call verifies your views. You are vindicated. Don't go anywhere hat in hand—exude confidence; make a fresh start in a different direction. Wear bright colors; make personal appearances. Have luck with number 1.

Friday, November 8 (Moon in Capricorn)   Family members argue and eventually ask that you be an arbiter. Playing umpire is no fun. See if you can get out of it in a graceful way. Capricorn and Cancer figure in this dynamic scenario. In matters of speculation, stick with number 2.

Saturday, November 9 (Moon in Capricorn) On this Saturday, entertain and be entertained. The moon in your fifth house "stirs your creative juices." Focus on children, challenge, change, variety, and sexuality. This will be a live Saturday night for you. Take note of your dreams. Write impressions of places and people. Your lucky number is 3.

Sunday, November 10 (Moon in Capricorn to Aquarius 3:27 a.m.) On this Sunday, take time to reflect: "Am I doing the right thing at the correct time?" The answers will be forthcoming; puzzle pieces will fit. Be willing to tear down in order to rebuild. Material will be acceptable, but rewriting may be necessary. A Scorpio means business!

Monday, November 11 (Moon in Aquarius) Make necessary changes, then go forth with a positive attitude. Gemini flirts, but the motives are not exactly pure. Have fun, but protect yourself in clinches. With Gemini, you enter new terrain and could be at the mercy or judgment of others. Be careful!

Tuesday, November 12 (Moon in Aquarius to Pisces 12:41 p.m.) Within 24 hours, the answers to questions about partnership and marriage will be made available. The focus tonight will be on a discussion concerning beauty, remodeling, decorating, and whether or not to change your residence. Questions also arise concerning money and marriage.

Wednesday, November 13 (Moon in Pisces) Lucky lottery: 3, 7, 12, 17, 30, 50. The spotlight is on going your own way or hooking up with one who promises "everything." Promises are exciting, but get them in writing. Pisces and another Virgo figure prominently, and could have these letters or initials in their names—G, P, Y.

Thursday, November 14 (Moon in Pisces to Aries 12:37 a.m.) Combine imagination with materialism. Envision what is desired, then make it come true. It is a blend for you of Saturn and Neptune—if you work it right, you'll come out on top with considerable profit. Capricorn and Cancer will play dramatic, leading roles.

Friday, November 15 (Moon in Aries) This is one Friday you won't soon forget! The lunar position and numerical aspects point to a day of creative achievements. Aries and Libra will be part of this scenario, whether or not you approve. Money will be dealt with fairly. Let others know you are not asleep.

Saturday, November 16 (Moon in Aries) Have a quiet talk with someone in charge of your accounting. Request, don't demand, a new and different way of arriving at conclusions. This could be the start of something big. Leo and Aquarius figure in this dramatic scenario. Have luck with number 1.

Sunday, November 17 (Moon in Aries to Taurus 1:22 p.m.) Reestablish contact with a family member who of late has displayed an unruly temperament. Show affection; make an intelligent concession. This individual, likely a Cancer, has been lonely and needs you. Within 24 hours, you receive exciting news about a possible journey overseas.

Monday, November 18 (Moon in Taurus) A Sagittarian outlines the possibility of blending business with pleasure during travel. A Gemini is also in the picture and is realistic about "getting you a deal." Highlight versatility, diversity, and intellectual curiosity. No doubt, you are being "courted."

Tuesday, November 19 (Moon in Taurus) A romantic Tuesday! You will be "in touch" with your creative force. Tear down in order to rebuild. Make this your "makeover" day. People comment favorably. "You look different—much better!" Maintain your emotional equilibrium. Get promises in writing. Have luck with number 4!

Wednesday, November 20 (Moon in Taurus to Gemini 1:23 a.m.)   The full moon, lunar eclipse is in Taurus, your ninth house. Much activity and talk are indicated in connection with religion, spirituality, and learning more about people in other nations, their language, and their ways of living and loving. Plans could change abruptly. Sagittarius is involved.

Thursday, November 21 (Moon in Gemini)   On this Thursday, stick close to your home and family, if possible. Remember: Pride goeth before a fall. Make intelligent concessions. Let it be known: "I'm in the mood for love!" Focus on style, music, and the ability to beautify your surroundings. A Libran will create harmony.

Friday, November 22 (Moon in Gemini to Cancer 11:46 a.m.)   An offer received is valid, but not quite ready to be fulfilled. Someone at the top, possibly a Gemini, is ready to take a great fall. Do not offer unsolicited advice. Strive for balance and emotional equilibrium. Pisces and another Virgo figure prominently.

Saturday, November 23 (Moon in Cancer)   Wake up! The moon in your eleventh house means you win friends and influence people. Your popularity rating zooms. Use your powers of persuasion to obtain funding for a project you believe in, but which is not popular. Capricorn and Cancer reach understanding levels with you.

Sunday, November 24 (Moon in Cancer to Leo 8:01 p.m.)   You can make this a memorable Sunday! A burden is lifted; you'll be free to write, talk, travel, and engage in a romantic episode. Stress universal appeal; avoid narrow-mindedness. You will receive "personal information" about air-sea travel. Aries is represented.

Monday, November 25 (Moon in Leo)   Throw aside preconceived notions—emphasize your pioneering spirit; enjoy the adventure of learning. Stress independence, originality, and a willingness to make way for a new, different kind of love. If married, strive to appreciate the arrangement. If single, you could meet your future soul mate.

Tuesday, November 26 (Moon in Leo)   At the track: hot daily doubles—3 and 2, 4 and 6, 5 and 5. Post position special—number 6 p.p. in the fifth race. Focus on cooperative efforts, and a willingness to see both sides of questions without abandoning your principles. A family member expresses "hunger" for your latest recipe.

Wednesday, November 27 (Moon in Leo to Virgo 1:40 a.m.)   Lucky lottery: 4, 9, 12, 18, 36, 40. Diversify and experiment. In your high cycle, you will be at the right place at a special moment. Don't fight the feeling! Follow your inner voice and your heart. Be kind to one who wants to "make love." At the very least, offer tea and sympathy!

Thursday, November 28 (Moon in Virgo)   Your cycle remains high on this Thanksgiving Day. Take the initiative. Reveal some fascinating information about the background of the holiday and how it relates to "modern times." Emphasize bright colors; maintain an optimistic attitude; realize you can inspire people to succeed.

Friday, November 29 (Moon in Virgo to Libra 4:53 a.m.) On this day after Thanksgiving you realize once and for all there is more to the holiday than just food. Take time to write your impressions. Your creative juices are activated—allow them to have expression, your self-expression. Gemini plays a dynamic role.

Saturday, November 30 (Moon in Libra) On this last day of November, the emphasis will be on where you live, beautifying your home, and learning more about sound and the subtle nuances of musical compositions. A domestic adjustment will be successful, and opens the way to romance and love. Taurus, Libra, and Scorpio will play fantastic roles. Your lucky number is 6.

DECEMBER 2002

Sunday, December 1 (Moon in Libra to Scorpio 6:14 a.m.) This day should be lucky for you—possibly the beginning of a winning streak. Reading material provides many answers, even if not exactly on target. Someone of the opposite sex will play a major role, especially Gemini. Have luck with number 5.

Monday, December 2 (Moon in Scorpio) A family dispute is settled, and should not have been taken too seriously in the first place. A special purchase helps beautify your home—do what you know is right, without unnecessarily offending others. Taurus, Libra, and Scorpio will play exciting roles.

Tuesday, December 3 (Moon in Scorpio to Sagittarius 6:57 a.m.) Many myths will be exploded. You might be saying to yourself, "I knew it all the time!" It is a matter of emotional beliefs up against each other—the stuff of religious wars. Don't run away!

Important people can be impressed by your logic and foresight.

Wednesday, December 4 (Moon in Sagittarius) The new moon, solar eclipse is in Sagittarius, your fourth house. Translated, this means that many things associated with real estate and land that seemed out of reach will become available. Avoid fire hazards; don't tempt fate where safety is concerned. Your lucky number is 8.

Thursday, December 5 (Moon in Sagittarius to Capricorn 8:38 a.m.) Look beyond the immediate; "buy for the future." Be aware of the potential. Examine transportation bargains. Aries and Libra will play outstanding roles, and could have these letters or initials in their names: I and R. A long-distance communication reveals you are on the right track.

Friday, December 6 (Moon in Capricorn) Your creative juices stir. Your personality is highlighted. You exude sex appeal. One individual, an attractive Capricorn, confides to you: "At times, I can hardly keep my hands off you!" You'll be hobnobbing with the high and mighty—enjoy yourself. You are not inferior.

Saturday, December 7 (Moon in Capricorn to Aquarius 12:54 p.m.) Memories flood consciousness. Focus on vitality, youth, and the ability to put special programs across. The numerical cycle accents proposals that include a business partnership or marriage. A Cancer plays a majestic role. Lucky lottery: 4, 6, 7, 12, 13, 50.

Sunday, December 8 (Moon in Aquarius) An unusual "religious experience" take place. A Sagittarian attempts a "scientific explanation." A clash of ideas proves stimulating. Praise your opponent; let it be known you are open-minded, but not so open-minded that your brains fall out.

Monday, December 9 (Moon in Aquarius to Pisces 8:46 p.m.)   A young relative proudly announces new ways of making money. Be receptive; don't be stingy with praise. Taurus, Leo, and Scorpio will play fantastic roles. You receive orders that are akin to stop-and-go. In matters of speculation, stick with number 4.

Tuesday, December 10 (Moon in Pisces)   Keep your plans flexible. Present an innovative program. Focus on flirtation and variety. An unusual experience that will include Gemini, Sagittarius, and another Virgo. Use your natural ability as a character analyst. Your creative juices stir. Read and write; learn by teaching.

Wednesday, December 11 (Moon in Pisces)   At the track: hot daily doubles—3 and 3, 4 and 6, 1 and 5. Post position special: number 2 p.p. in the sixth race. A reunion with a family member is featured; there will be music in your life tonight—dance to your own tune. Libra is in the picture.

Thursday, December 12 (Moon in Pisces to Aries 7:57 a.m.)   An element of deception exists—know it, and protect yourself accordingly. Get promises in writing. Use your natural psychic ability. What seemed out of reach will become available. Define terms, outline boundaries, and be aware of real estate opportunities.

Friday, December 13 (Moon in Aries)   This will be a lucky day, despite the date. Focus on priorities, production, and the ability to handle more responsibility. Someone "at the top" expresses confidence in you. You can say thanks, without being obsequious. Cancer and Capricorn play leading roles.

Saturday, December 14 (Moon in Aries to Taurus 8:42 p.m.) The moon is in that section of your chart having to do with numbers, accounting, and balance sheets. Hold tight to your possessions; you could be surrounded by people who want something of value for nothing. Capricorn and Cancer continue to exert influence, along with Libra and Aries.

Sunday, December 15 (Moon in Taurus) You wake up refreshed, despite a rather hectic Saturday night. Plan ahead for a fresh start in a new direction. Be ready for love of a "different" kind. If you are daring and innovative, this could be a turning point. Leo and Aquarius play dramatic roles.

Monday, December 16 (Moon in Taurus to Gemini 8:41 a.m.) Be a good listener. Find out more about ethnic cuisines. Cancer and Capricorn exert influence, and could be instrumental in bringing you closer to your family. In matters of speculation, stick with these numbers: 2, 4, and 8. You could be lucky!

Tuesday, December 17 (Moon in Gemini) You have reason to celebrate. Back royalties will be paid, and you get more for your money and more money than you originally anticipated. Taurus will be involved. Keep plans flexible. Highlight versatility. Give full play to your intellectual curiosity.

Wednesday, December 18 (Moon in Gemini) Lucky lottery: 4, 7, 16, 18, 19, 22. Take special care in traffic. Avoid being in an automobile with someone who has been drinking. Check legal documents. You may be in need of some of them. Taurus, Libra, and Scorpio will play "serious" roles.

Thursday, December 19 (Moon in Gemini to Cancer 6:29 p.m.) The full moon is in Gemini, your tenth house. Translated, your career gets a boost. A fast-talking individual will talk on your side and for your benefit. Show gratitude, without being obsequious. What had been evasive will become available. Pounce on the opportunity!

Friday, December 20 (Moon in Cancer)   Attention revolves around your home, repairs, and plumbing facilities. The spotlight is also on domestic harmony, sound, music, and the ability to make intelligent concessions without abandoning your principles. Taurus, Libra, and Scorpio play roles. People compliment you on the sound of your voice.

Saturday, December 21 (Moon in Cancer)   Emotions dominate. Know it, and strive for equilibrium. You are subject to falling madly in love. Give logic equal time. Someone could be playing tricks on you. Pisces and another Virgo figure in this dramatic scenario. Have luck with number 7.

Sunday, December 22 (Moon in Cancer to Leo 1:47 a.m.)   Your vitality makes a dramatic comeback. It is Sunday, so spiritual values are revised. You'll be dealing with people who belong in the class of the high-and-mighty. Focus on promotion, production, advertising, and showmanship—even though it is Sunday. Capricorn is involved.

Monday, December 23 (Moon in Leo)   Your intuitive intellect can cover many areas. Refuse to be limited by those who are themselves "limited." You gain recognition. Fame and fortune will no longer be strangers. Aries and Libra will play fascinating roles. A project can be completed.

Tuesday, December 24 (Moon in Leo to Virgo 7:04 a.m.)   It's Christmas Eve—you will hear numerous innovative interpretations of what the holiday means. The numerical cycle number 1 indicates that people will be giving and receiving gifts that are original and entertaining. Leo will play a fascinating role.

Wednesday, December 25 (Moon in Virgo)   Be close to your family, if possible. The moon in your sign promises to make this Christmas one to remember. People ask questions, some on the sarcastic side. Give the answers straight, from the way you see it. Electrical disruptions could last for approximately five minutes. A knowledgeable Aquarian comes to the rescue.

Thursday, December 26 (Moon in Virgo to Libra 10:52 a.m.)   Christmas memories—all in all, you tell yourself, "This was one of the best Christmas holidays I've ever enjoyed." You are vulnerable to love and could fall madly in love. Get ready for New Year's Eve; have invitations and plans in order.

Friday, December 27 (Moon in Libra)   Check details and repairs. The moon position highlights money, payments, and collections. Television and music are involved. You are being tested, and you come through with flying colors. Be willing to tear down in order to rebuild—strive for a "new look." Scorpio plays a role.

Saturday, December 28 (Moon in Libra to Scorpio 1:40 p.m.)   As the year comes to a close, your creativity is activated. Read and write; teach and learn; enjoy in a flirtation that can do no real harm and could bring joy. A valuable lost article will be recovered. That in itself is worth celebrating! Have luck with number 5.

Sunday, December 29 (Moon in Scorpio)   A relative has valid suggestions for the holiday. Listen and learn. Music could and should be involved. Wear shades of blue; make intelligent concessions; stand tall for your principles. Taurus and Libra display enthusiasm, and want to be of service.

Monday, December 30 (Moon in Scorpio to Sagittarius 4:00 p.m.) Some changes are required. A heavy drinker should be warned, "We will not tolerate your making a fool of yourself!" Pisces and another Virgo play dynamic roles. Intentions are good. Don't stray too far from home. Your psychic faculties surge to the forefront.

Tuesday, December 31 (Moon in Sagittarius) Have plans in order. Go easy on adult beverages. If you do, you'll feel much better tomorrow, the first day of the new year. People tonight tend to make wild promises. Be selective and discriminating. You'll hear good news concerning promotion, production, and money.

HAPPY NEW YEAR!

ABOUT THE AUTHOR

Born on August 5, 1926, in Philadelphia, Sydney Omarr was the only person ever given full-time duty in the U.S. army as an astrologer. He also is regarded as the most erudite astrologer of our time and the best known, through his syndicated column (300 newspapers) and his radio and television programs (he was Merv Griffin's "resident astrologer"). Omarr has been called the most "knowledgeable astrologer since Evangeline Adams." His forecasts of Nixon's downfall, the end of World War II in mid-August of 1945, the assassination of John F. Kennedy, Roosevelt's election to the fourth term and his death in office . . . these and many others are on the record and quoted enough to be considered "legendary."

ABOUT THIS SERIES

This is one of a series of twelve
Day-to-Day Astrological Guides
for the signs of 2002
by Sydney Omarr.